T0360812

SWEDISH ECONOMIC THOUGHT

Explorations and advances

The impact of Swedish economists on the development of modern economic analysis has been profound. This volume contains twelve essays dealing with various aspects of the development of economics and economic thought from the mid-eighteenth century to the middle of the twentieth century. Most of the essays cover the golden age of Swedish economics, the early decades of the twentieth century, and deal with such figures as Knut Wicksell, Gustav Cassel, Eli Heckscher, Bertil Ohlin, Erik Lindahl and Erik Lundberg.

It illustrates the constant involvement of Swedish economists in current affairs. Economists have taken an active part in practically every debate of importance in Sweden since the turn of the century. Those discussed here include the 8-hour workday, the New Economics of the 1930s and forestry economics. Economists in Sweden have had a significant impact on public affairs and public debate – perhaps stronger than in any other country. The book accounts for this in terms of the consistency of their attempts to make public contributions.

The book also includes a chapter on an unpublished manuscript of Knut Wicksell's, which is reproduced in English for the first time.

Lars Jonung is Professor of Economics at the Stockholm School of Economics. He has published several books in Swedish and English, including *The Long Run Behavior of Velocity* (with M.D. Bordo, 1987), *The Political Economy of Price Controls* (1990) and *The Stockholm School of Economics Revisited* (editor, 1991). He is presently serving as Chief Economic Adviser to the Prime Minister of Sweden.

SWEDISH ECONOMIC THOUGHT

Explorations and advances

Edited by Lars Jonung

Routledge
Taylor & Francis Group

LONDON AND NEW YORK

First published 1993
by Routledge
2 Park Square, Milton Park, Abingdon, Oxfordshire OX14 4RN

Simultaneously published in the USA and Canada
by Routledge
711 Third Avenue, New York, NY 10017

Transferred to Digital Printing 2007

First issued in paperback 2014

Routledge is an imprint of the Taylor & Francis Group, an informa business

© 1993 Lars Jonung

Typeset in Baskerville by Leaper & Gard Ltd, Bristol

British Library Cataloguing in Publication Data
A catalogue record for this book is available from the British
Library.

ISBN 978-0-415-75559-7 (pbk)

Library of Congress Cataloging in Publication Data
Swedish economic thought : explorations and advances /
edited by Lars Jonung.
p. cm.
Includes bibliographical references and index.
ISBN 978-0-415-05413-3 (hbk)
ISBN 978-0-415-75559-7 (pbk)
1. Economics–Sweden–History. I. Jonung, Lars.
HB116.5.A2S94 1992
330′.09485–dc20 92–19680
CIP

Publisher's Note
The publisher has gone to great lengths to ensure the quality
of this reprint but points out that some imperfections in the
original may be apparent

CONTENTS

CONTENTS

FIGURES AND TABLES

FIGURES

TABLES

ACKNOWLEDGEMENTS

The idea for this book was born when I was preparing a conference to celebrate the fiftieth anniversary of the Stockholm School of Economics that took place in the autumn of 1987. I came into contact with several Swedish economists interested in the development of economic thought, in particular in the history of Swedish economics. I concluded that there were sufficient contributions, actual or potential, to form the nucleus of a book. I therefore started to gather submissions. This book is the final product of this process; it has taken several years to come to fruition.

The Swedish Council for Research in the Humanities and Social Sciences has made this publication possible by means of a generous grant. Alan Harkess has skilfully improved the 'Swenglish' of most of the authors. Axel Leijonhufvud has given valuable guidance. My greatest debt is to the authors, who have endured a long gestation period with an editor prone to suggest alterations before they could finally see their work in print.

Lars Jonung
Stockholm and Lund
March 1992

INTRODUCTION AND SUMMARY

Lars Jonung

Swedish economists have as a rule not paid much attention to the history of their subject. It has been more fashionable to study other issues, in particular policy-oriented ones. This interest in economic policy has inevitably involved Swedish academic economists in current affairs and events, rather than in studies of the past. Economists have taken an active part in practically every public debate of importance in Sweden since the turn of the century.[1]

In recent years there have been signs of a growing interest in the development of Swedish economics. This volume is a witness to this trend. Here Swedish economists and economic historians, representing all the major universities in Sweden, explore various aspects of Swedish economic thought.[2] The essays are organized in chronological order. Like a smörgåsbord, they offer considerable variety. The emphasis, however, is on the golden age of Swedish economics, that is on the period from the end of the nineteenth century to the outbreak of the Second World War, covering two brilliant generations of economists. The first one consisted of David Davidson, Knut Wicksell, Gustav Cassel and Eli Heckscher, the founding fathers of modern economics in Sweden; the second one, later to be known as the Stockholm School of Economics, included Erik Lindahl, Gunnar Myrdal, Bertil Ohlin and Erik Lundberg.

Göran Ahlström examines the economic doctrines that prevailed in Sweden during the eighteenth century. The mercantilist influence on Swedish economic thought during this period represented a continuation of the economic policy of earlier centuries. Although mercantilism tended to hold sway over the actual policies pursued, liberal economic ideas were introduced into Swedish corn policy from the 1770s. Ahlström shows that the influence of English economic thought was gradually replaced by French doctrines from the middle of the eighteenth century.

Three Swedish thinkers and theorists are of significant interest. In the socio-political field we find the radical liberal Anders Chydenius – well ahead of Adam Smith – and in the area of liberal economic theory, Pehr Niclas Christiernin. If the latter's work from the early 1760s had been available in English, it would most probably have been considered a significant contribution in an international context. As Ahlström points out, Christiernin's theory of the exchange rate anticipated the work of later economists. The work of the third major thinker of the time, Anders Wappengren, was not marked by the same theoretical rigour as Christiernin. Nevertheless, his early argument in the 1790s in support of a permanent paper standard should not be overlooked.

The mercantilist economic policy was generally not abolished until the middle of the nineteenth century. The academic textbook on political economy from the 1740s by Berch – the first professor in economics in Sweden and probably the fourth in the subject in Europe – was not replaced until about 1830. However, liberal economic ideas were gradually introduced. According to Ahlström, the importance of Adam Smith in that process was likely to have been fairly limited.

Mats Persson and **Claes-Henric Siven** describe the life and work of Pehr Niclas Christiernin, focusing on his contribution to the quantity theory of money as displayed in his treatise of 1761. This was Christiernin's only major work in economics; in it he analysed recent Swedish monetary events.

The background was as follows: Sweden took part in the Seven Years War between 1756 and 1763, financing the war effort with the help of the printing press. The volume of Riksbank notes increased threefold. The general price level followed suit and the Swedish currency depreciated in relation to foreign currencies. The party responsible for inflation lost power in 1765–6. The new government adopted a deflationary policy, resulting in falling production and employment, and rapidly lost popularity.

These developments gave rise to a lively debate on the causes of movements in prices and exchange rates. According to Persson and Siven, only Christiernin was able to present a correct analysis of the monetary events of his day. He was familiar with the work of David Hume, Richard Cantillon and John Locke and capable of extending monetary theory independently. His policy recommendation was that the price level should be stabilized, rejecting both inflation and deflation as sustainable alternatives. After this impressive work in the early 1760s, Christiernin did not produce anything of lasting value, either in economics or philosophy, the new field in which he became engaged. The latter part of his life was littered by scandals, academic infighting and misfortunes.

Björn Hansson examines the following Wicksellian enigma: is it possible that capital, under stationary conditions and neutral time preferences, can be a permanent source of income, i.e. can a positive rate of interest exist in a stationary state? Knut Wicksell did not present an explicit solution to this problem in his writings. However, he provided parts of an answer. Hanson pulls these fragments together to construct a formal solution to Wicksell's proposition that the rate of interest, based solely on the physical productivity of capital, can be positive in a stationary state.

Hansson's approach leans heavily on certain strategic assumptions which all clearly belong within a Wicksellian framework: capital is treated as saved-up labour; the production function is homogenous of degree one with falling marginal productivities of current labour and machines; the process of capital accumulation is characterized by less current labour being used to produce the output and the 'younger' machines.

Torun Hedlund-Nyström et al. comment on a previously unpublished manuscript by Knut Wicksell. The manuscript has no title and is incomplete. It is undated, but the treatment of interest, the average period of investment, capital and the production function suggests that it was written no earlier than 1898, and no later than 1902. It can be regarded as a link between Wicksell's approach to capital theory in his nineteenth-century books and his approach from the second edition of *Lectures* onwards. From the former emerges the basic structure: a model of flow-input–point output type. The latter develops the use of compound rather than simple interest (which Wicksell had used earlier). The concept of capital is also similar to that in *Lectures*.

Wicksell adopts forestry on valuable land as his example. He presents the correct optimum solution for the rotation period, a solution which is equivalent to the Faustmann solution, upon which many prominent economists have stumbled. See also the final contribution in this volume by Karl-Gustaf Löfgren who considers the Swedish tradition in forest economics.

Marianne Sundström describes how the demand by the labour movement for the 8-hour workday was examined by Swedish economists during the period 1889–1935. She also discusses how economists influenced the labour movement's views on the issue of working hours. The year 1889 is her starting-point since it was in that year that the 8-hour workday became the chief demand of the Swedish labour movement. Sundström demonstrates how Knut Wicksell, who held a highly pessimistic view on future productivity increases and population growth, repeatedly criticized this demand, and thereby alienated himself from the labour movement.

It was not until 1920 and the social unrest at the end of the First World War that the 48-hour working week was introduced by law in Sweden. A few years after the reform, several official investigations were carried out, providing data for an economic analysis of the effects of the reduction in working hours during the 1920s.

Sundström stresses the difference in emphasis between the Swedish economic debate which focused on the effects on productivity, production and national income, and the European discussion which dealt mainly with the effects on unemployment. European unions viewed reduced hours as an efficient cure for mass unemployment. Consequently, the ILO in 1935 adopted this approach in a resolution demanding the 40-hour working week to combat unemployment. In Sweden, however, this view did not gain much support from unions. Sundström points out three main reasons for this lack of support. First, Wicksell along with his successors had carefully explained why reduced hours would not be an efficient means of combating unemployment. Second, as early as the late 1920s Swedish economists held an 'advanced' view on the causes and remedies of unemployment. Third, the analyses carried out by economists were popularized and disseminated to the labour movement by Alf Johansson and others. The Committee on Unemployment played an important role here as a forum for intellectual exchange between economists and labour leaders.

Lars Magnusson starts from Brinley Thomas's statement that economists in Sweden probably had 'a better public reputation than elsewhere' and demonstrates that this esteem was largely due to the groundwork carried out by an earlier generation of Swedish economists and popularizers of academic economics. He first describes how the image of the economist as a neutral expert speaking the language of reason and rationality was conveyed to the Swedish public up until the 1930s. According to this message, the academic economist, equipped with a 'value-free' box of tools, was useful as a designer of practical solutions to economic political problems.

Magnusson illustrates the popularization efforts of the early generation of Swedish economists by studying three cases: Gustav Cassel, Eli Heckscher and Sven Brisman. Cassel in particular is well known – perhaps even notoriously so – for his campaigns and his efforts to present a value-free economics. Less is known about Heckscher and Brisman in this context. Along with other economists such as Knut Wicksell and more obscure popularizers such as Gunnar Silverstolpe, they also played an important role in launching economics as a 'useful' social science in Sweden before the 1930s. The Stockholm School generation of the 1930s – Gunnar Myrdal, Bertil Ohlin, Erik Lindahl among others – was able to profit from the groundwork laid by these early economists. This tradition of participation in public debate and discussion has survived among Swedish economists until today.

Eskil Wadensjö examines the life of Gösta Bagge. Bagge was one of the best known economists in Sweden during the inter-war period, taking part in public debate as well as initiating much of the research in economics during that period. Bagge defended his PhD dissertation *Arbetslönens reglering genom sammanslutningar* (*The Regulation of Wages by Organizations*) in 1917 at the age of 35. It dealt with the effects of unions on wages and employment. It was widely acclaimed and Bagge received a professorship at the *Stockholms Högskola* in 1921. The professorship was combined with the directorship of the new School of Social Work and Public Administration. He also became head of the Social Science Institute at the *Stockholms Högskola*.

In 1925, Bagge arranged for the Social Institute to receive a grant from the Rockefeller Foundation – a grant that was followed by several others. These grants enabled him to start a project based on his dissertation. In 1927, Bagge became one of the members of the Committee on Unemployment – a governmental committee that provided work for many of the younger generation of economists. All of the members of the subsequently famous Stockholm School of Economics were engaged on one or both of 'Bagge's projects'. He thus contributed to the advent of the Stockholm School although he was not held in high regard by the younger members of this school.

Bagge became a Member of Parliament in 1932 and was appointed leader of the Conservative Party in 1935. In practice, he left research for good although he spent a few years at *Stockholms Högskola* after he had resigned as party leader in December 1944.

Klas Fregert provides a critical review of Erik Lindahl's programme for monetary policy as laid down in his two-part treatise *The Aims and Means of Monetary Policy*, published in 1924 and 1930. Lindahl is surprisingly modern in his arguments in favour of rules instead of discretion. He stresses the importance of establishing credibility for the monetary regime by official announcements and enforcement by an independent central bank. The analysis is based on a discussion of the role of expectations which puts him close to the present-day rational expectations school. In a pamphlet from 1957 at the end of his life, *Spelet om penningvärdet* (*The Game over the Value of Money*), Lindahl makes the prediction that discretion leads to high inflation without the benefit of higher production, which is the basic case for rules over discretion in present-day game-theoretic treatments.

According to Lindahl's preferred rule, prices should move in inverse proportion to productivity. (He was not alone in this choice, in Sweden or elsewhere.) The preferred rule should minimize uncertainty and variability due to unanticipated shocks which may cause and aggravate business cycles. His primary analysis is devoted to the effect of three different rules – stable prices, inverse productivity norm or stable exchange rates – on debt contracts between entrepreneurs/borrowers and capitalists/lenders when unforeseen shocks hit the economy. Allowing prices to increase when productivity declines, protects entrepreneurs because they are compensated by the increase in prices in direct proportion to the fall in productivity.

Conversely, the benefits of increases in productivity are enjoyed by debtholders. In this way entrepreneurs' incomes are stabilized, which Lindahl believes will stabilize the business cycle through the avoidance of bankruptcies in downturns and excessive speculation in upturns. The inverse productivity rule effectively transforms debts into contingent claims, i.e. equity, through its feedback from productivity to prices. Fregart argues that Lindahl's stress on debt contracts implicitly assumes the lack of an adequate equity market. Strangely, Lindahl does not discuss the equity market or why it may be too small.

The effects of the three rules are also analysed for other types of markets and contracts. In most cases, the inverse productivity norm is the preferred one. Lindahl explicitly states that the inverse productivity norm tends to stabilize both nominal wages and nominal incomes – rules that have been suggested today. Fregert ends with an account of the adoption in 1944 in Sweden of the Lindahl rule.

Harry Flam examines the roots of Bertil Ohlin's contributions to international economics. Ohlin was influenced by Knut Wicksell, Gustav Cassel and Eli Heckscher. They are commonly viewed as the founding fathers of Swedish economics. They inspired a new generation of outstanding economists. Bertil Ohlin was one of the members of this generation which eventually reached world-wide recognition as the Stockholm School of Economics. In the 1920s, this generation was preoccupied with the development of standard price theory. As a result of the depression of the 1930s and the rise of unemployment as the major social issue, macroeconomics became the prime field of research for this second generation.

An article by Heckscher published in Swedish in *Ekonomisk Tidskrift* in 1919 was the major source of inspiration for the young Ohlin. The main elements of the Heckscher–Ohlin theory, i.e. the Heckscher–Ohlin theorem and the factor price equalization theorem, was already there in Heckscher's account. Ohlin combined Heckscher's original insights with Cassel's general equilibrium approach – as borrowed by Cassel from Walras without due reference – and generalized Heckscher's approach in a number of ways, as well as challenging factor–price equalization. According to Flam, Ohlin's 'most original contribution to international economics' was 'his integration of real and monetary capital flows' – not the Heckscher–Ohlin theory. When Keynes discussed the German reparations at the end of the 1920s, Ohlin was thus well prepared to challenge Keynes's views.

Flam ends with a twist. Ohlin always regretted that his macro-economic work of the 1930s was not available in English before the *General Theory* appeared. Had Heckscher's 1919 article been published in English, the Heckscher–Ohlin theory might simply have been known today as the Heckscher theory.

Benny Carlson describes how Eli Heckscher and Gustav Cassel responded to the new ideas that challenged their position as prominent spokesmen for orthodox liberal–conservative views. When the harbingers of the 'New Economics' began to appear during the late 1920s and early 1930s, Cassel and Heckscher at first denied, on theoretical grounds, the possibility of the government being able to increase demand and create job opportunities without pulling resources away from other fields and creating unemployment there.

Heckscher made a theoretical retreat in the autumn of 1931 and shifted his resistance to the arena of practical political arguments. For example, he argued that unless public works were not restricted by constitutional guarantees or were paid at wage rates lower than those of the free market, they would in the long run tend to expand unduly. Cassel continued to offer resistance at the theoretical level. However, he also resorted increasingly to practical objections such as the risk that public works at market wages might become permanent, that the state could not manage the 'timing' factor in counter-cyclical policy, and that budget deficits might run out of control. Cassel grappled with these problems year in and year out until his death in 1945.

Claes Berg discusses the origin and development of inflationary gap analysis in Sweden. He demonstrates that the inflationary gap was first formalized by Erik Lundberg in his dissertation in 1937, not as is generally asserted by Keynes in his *How to Pay for the War* of 1940. The Swedish discussion was able to benefit from the terminology introduced by the Stockholm School, which drew attention to the differences between planned (*ex ante*) and actual (*ex post*) quantities on the demand side and the supply side. These concepts were used by Bent Hansen, Erik Lundberg and Ralph Turvey to demonstrate the limitations of the Keynesian equilibrium approach to inflationary gap analysis. Among the difficulties that attracted attention were the problem of timing in measurement of the factor gap and the instability of the consumption, savings and investment functions in an inflationary situation.

Karl-Gustaf Löfgren surveys the development of forest economics in Sweden – an important field considering the role of forestry in the Swedish economy. The correct solution to the classical problem regarding when to cut down a forest stand, formulated by the Germans Faustmann and Pressler, was known to Swedish foresters as early as the 1870s. However, it is fair to say that few people had a firm grip of the analytical fundamentals.

Some of Sweden's most prominent economists contributed to the discussion. Eli Heckscher participated in the so-called profitability war with a slightly incorrect harvesting criterion, borrowed possibly from Jevon's and Wicksell's insights into the economics of wine ageing. Bertil Ohlin then solved the rotation problem correctly as a young student in a successful attempt to join Heckscher's seminar.

Gunnar Myrdal contributed indirectly through his thesis, which influenced one of Sweden's leading forest economists, Thorsten

Streyffert in his classic work *Den skogsekonomiska teorin* (*The Theory of Forest Economics*) from 1938. Finally, Gustav Cassel made early contributions to the principles of forest taxation. It has been recently discovered that Knut Wicksell in a previously unpublished paper, given his 'indirect' approach to both forestry and wine ageing, came up with the correct first-order condition for the optimal rotation period. (See his contribution presented in this volume.) Nevertheless, it is true that in Sweden contemporary forest economics was very slow in assimilating relevant modern economic theory. Roundabout techniques have long been used to solve problems that the contemporary Hicks–Samuelson comparative static methods would take care of in a couple of pages.

No contribution in this volume covers the post-Second World War period, a period when Swedish economics became integrated into the mainstream Anglo-American tradition, losing much of its unique character. The past forty years are presumably too close to generate much historically-oriented work. However, in the coming years, we will see studies on the development of Swedish economic thought during the second half of the twentieth century. The relationship between the economics profession and the rise of the Swedish model, the growth of the welfare state and the design of economic policies will most likely attract a great deal of attention.

NOTES

1 For a description of the national style in Swedish academic economics, see L. Jonung, 'Economics the Swedish way 1889–1989', chapter 2 in L. Engwall (ed.), *Economics in Sweden. An Evaluation of Swedish Research in Economics*, Routledge, 1992.
2 This book should be regarded as a companion volume to Bo Sandelin (ed.), *The History of Swedish Economic Thought*, Routledge, 1991.

1

SWEDISH ECONOMIC THOUGHT IN THE EIGHTEENTH CENTURY*

Göran Ahlström

The foundation of the economic policy conducted in Sweden during the eighteenth century, and even at the beginning of the nineteenth, was a mercantilistic conception of society such as had prevailed for a couple of hundred years.

It is true that no clear-cut definition of the term mercantilism has ever existed but only a series of mercantilistic principles which, at different periods and with varying intensity, were manifested in the way economic policy and economic legislation were conducted. But for that very reason, the practical policy of the eighteenth century can be seen as a continuation of the policy implemented in the sixteenth and seventeenth centuries.

In the debate about specific issues, it is already possible by the middle of the eighteenth century to find in Sweden advocates of more liberal views of society. However, it was only in respect of the internal trade in corn that these liberal and/or 'reformed mercantilist' elements were implemented as practical policies during the eighteenth century. It was not until the nineteenth century that the liberal economic elements were reflected in economic legislation. Nor did mercantilist ideas lose their influence in academic teaching until the middle of the nineteenth century.

Despite the fairly slow progress in the economic policy field, there was, however, some interesting discussion of economic theory in eighteenth-century Sweden. Furthermore, there were individuals who held ideas that were original for their time. This applies both to the socio-political field generally and to that of economic theory. Behind names such as Chydenius, Christiernin and Wappengren there are thinkers who, with a greater or lesser degree of cogency, presented and elaborated ideas which in an international perspective must be regarded as early and original.

The great interest taken in economic questions during the eighteenth century, especially as revealed by a comprehensive body of contemporary literature, must be viewed largely against the background of Sweden's expanding manufacturing and 'industrial' sector of that time. The latter was a result of the state's mercantilist policy, which involved *inter alia* a balancing of the distribution of resources between different sectors of society and therefore also wide-ranging economic legislation.

Because of the government's role in managing and controlling society and in 'adjusting' the economy – i.e. its efforts to achieve harmony between the nation's production and consumption of different utilities – there was little room for individual freedom of economic action. The right of the individual to enter or leave a given occupation in accordance with his own judgement was restricted.

Regardless of whether this mercantilist policy is viewed from the consumer's or the producer's standpoint, it implied a policy of constraint and tutelage over the various categories of the population. Nevertheless, it was designed at the same time to afford them a degree of support and prosperity. For the producer–entrepreneur (e.g. the factory owner, master craftsman and landowner) and his business operations, the aim was to furnish a smooth and buoyant market. Among the instruments for achieving this aim, we may cite tariffs and rates of various kinds, tolls, bounties and corn stores. Because of the state's role as regulator and controller of production, however, the producer's freedom was circumscribed by detailed rules governing what was to be produced and its quality. In this way, the consumer's interests were provided for as well.

For the producer–worker (e.g. the factory worker, journeyman–craftsman or apprentice, and farm servant) the aim was to provide permanent employment and in that way a meagre livelihood. The means to this end included the fixing of tariffs of food prices and of servants' wages.

However, when it came to the principle of wage-fixing, this meant in practice that a low-wage policy was pursued. The wage-earner was assumed to be satisfied when he was able, by his own hand, to meet his most elementary needs from his labour–income. It was also assumed that the individual worker did not understand how to use a higher wage sensibly.

This support-and-prosperity policy, which today appears somewhat dubious, did however have a theoretical justification. The overriding aim of the policy practised was to stimulate 'national production'. It was believed that this was best achieved by holding down production costs, which consisted essentially of wages. These should be determined solely by the prices of the necessities of life, whose prices were thus regulated by means of tariffs laid down or controlled by the state. If costs were not regulated in this way, then first domestic consumption would suffer through high prices for all kinds of goods, while second, foreign trade would feel the effects of deteriorating sales opportunities on the international market.

Mercantilist writers attached special importance to the balance of trade and the means of achieving one that was favourable. Efforts were made to overcome what Swedish writers called the 'under-weight' – i.e. import surplus – in the trade balance and to bring about an export surplus, which signified an inflow of foreign exchange. National prosperity was sometimes regarded as synonymous with the possession of precious metals such as gold and silver, but this was not a prominent concern of Swedish eighteenth-century mercantilists.

The division of labour which was advocated between different occupations and categories of population inside a country's boundaries was not regarded as appropriate between countries. Since the volume of international trade was presumed to be of a certain fixed magnitude, the profit of one country must necessarily mean a loss for another. Account was not always taken of the consequences of a heavy influx of foreign currency on the internal price level and thus on a country's international competitiveness (see above).

To what extent eighteenth-century Swedish mercantilist literature was merely a result of direct foreign influence or was the product of conditions specific to Sweden is somewhat unclear, and opinions on this question in recent Swedish literature vary. Petander, for example, considered that 'mercantilism in the Age of Freedom ... on the whole developed gradually from special indigenous conditions and ripened on Swedish soil'.[1] The resemblances to the foreign variety were viewed as a consequence of the international character of mercantilism at this time. Heckscher, on the other hand, contended that the economic writers of the Age of Freedom were unaware of their native forerunners, and his general assessment of eighteenth-century Swedish economic literature was that the ideological content, with one or two exceptions, lacked originality and lagged far behind that of the more important foreign literature.[2]

However, two foreign writers who probably did have a great influence on Swedish economic literature and development were the Englishmen Thomas Mun and Sir Josiah Child, through their works from the latter part of the seventeenth century. The former's 'England's Treasure by Forraign Trade, or the Balance of our Forraign Trade is the Rule of our Treasure' (1664) was also translated into Swedish both in 1732 and 1745, and it is cited frequently in the Swedish literature of the Age of Freedom.[3] It is true that Child's works never appeared in Swedish translation, but they were often cited or reviewed.

Of the Swedish authors who advocated a mercantilist policy, Anders Berch may be singled out, although this is not because his economic thinking was distinguished by any originality. As Heckscher pointed out, Berch's principal work, *Inledning til Allmänna Hushållningen* (*Introduction to General Housekeeping*) (1747), contained no economic theory in the true sense of analysis of the causal connections of the economy.[4] The work consisted merely of a series of general rules for the study of housekeeping (signifying 'national housekeeping', i.e. economics). It therefore amounted to a form of economic advice in harmony with the official conceptions of the time, in which the interests of the individual, promoted via strong state regulation, had the central place.[5]

Nevertheless Berch and his work are of interest and significance, chiefly from two other aspects. The first is that Berch occupied the first professorial chair in economics in Sweden (Uppsala, 1741). It was probably the fourth professorship in the subject in Europe. Secondly, his work, published in 1747, remained for eighty years the only Swedish textbook on the subject and, if translations from foreign languages are included it was, for fifty years, the only one in Swedish. It is obvious that *Inledning til Allmänna Hushållningen* thus contributed greatly to the long-lasting dominance of mercantilist ideas, especially in the field of academic teaching.

Despite the dominance of mercantilism in practical politics during the period under consideration here, advocates of a more liberal conception of society are to be found in Swedish literature as early as the middle of the eighteenth century. This circumstance may be best explained and interpreted first as a reaction against mercantilism's relative indifference towards agriculture and second as a reflection of a general feeling that the principles of mercantilism had been carried much too far. At bottom, the point at issue was how to achieve the greatest national prosperity – through strong central direction of the economy or through decentralization.

In practical political terms, this reaction against indifference to agriculture was already showing itself at the beginning of the Age of Freedom, but not until the 1740s, e.g. during the 'controversy over the precedence of occupations' (i.e. to which occupations the state ought to devote its primary interest), do we find Swedish economic literature taking an increased interest in the agricultural sector. It is difficult to decide to what extent foreign influence was of significance in this respect.

What is clear, however, is that the previous direct influence, principally English, on Swedish economic literature at mid-century was replaced by French. In the late 1750s and especially during the 1760s, when the role of agriculture was under vigorous discussion, we find a clear influence emanating from French so-called reform mercantilism.

This economic position can be best described as an 'agriculture-friendly' form of mercantilism which, under English influence, developed in France during the first half of the eighteenth century and found expression in French economic literature during the 1730s and 1740s. One figure here who was of special importance to Swedish developments was J.F. Melon, whose *Essai politique sur le Commerce* (1734) was published in Swedish translation in 1751 under the title *Et politisk Försök om Handel* (*A Political Essay on Trade*).[6]

Melon held that a country's strength lay in its agriculture, which supplies the population with its most indispensable necessities. The state and its laws ought therefore to be concerned primarily with the home market and the trade in corn, not with production for markets abroad. A well-ordered trade, in which freedom and protection ought to be the paramount guiding principles, should be the instrument by which to achieve a steady corn price for the encouragement of agriculture.

These economic principles were put into practical effect during the 1770s through the corn policy followed by J. Liljencrantz, finance minister under King Gustav III.[7]

C. Leuhusen may be cited as representative of the upholders of the reform–mercantilist conception in Swedish economic literature, *inter alia* because of his *Tankar om de rätta och sannskyldiga medel till Sveriges välmåga* (*Thoughts on the correct and true means to Sweden's well-being*) (1761, 1763).

It is possible to find elements of physiocracy in the corn policy implemented by Liljencrantz. However, if physiocracy is considered to represent a fully elaborated system of political economy based upon fixed economic principles, i.e. a theoretically consistent doctrine, then there is only one representative of this doctrine in Swedish economic literature, namely C.F. Scheffer. But this is a physiocracy 'bottled in Sweden', as Herlitz would say.[8] Scheffer's conception found expression chiefly in *Bref til Herrar Riksens Råd* (*Letter to the Gentlemen of the State Council*) (1770). For the most part, however, this work was merely an abridged translation of François Quesnay's *Maximes générales du gouvernement économique d'un royaume agricole et notes sur ces maximes.*

Nevertheless, the fact that Scheffer omitted certain parts of Quesnay's work, such as his call for large leasehold farms, and his passing over of all mentioning of 'sterile' expenditures or wealth – which Quesnay held to apply to everything outside the sphere of agriculture – indicates that he did not lack opinions of his own. Furthermore, the Swedish work adopts a position which is less than conclusively negative with regard to government borrowing, which Quesnay believed to draw wealth away from the countryside and create 'sterile' fortunes. Scheffer distinguished between borrowing at home and borrowing abroad, and he considered the latter did not lead to a nation's impoverishment, since a loan 'could create a new annual National Revenue, which would exceed what had to be paid in Interest'.[9]

But as Heckscher and Herlitz pointed out, in the main the doctrine of physiocracy lacked champions in Sweden.[10] It therefore appears more plausible to denote the generally 'agriculture-friendly' attitude of many eighteenth-century Swedish writers, along with the frequently repeated calls for greater freedom, as characteristic of reform mercantilism.

Although a long series of books and other contributions appeared from the middle of the eighteenth century onwards, arguing against the principles of mercantilism, there was only one representative of eighteenth-century Swedish socio-economic literature who advocated a thoroughgoing liberal national economy. This was Anders Chydenius (1729–1803), who, beginning in 1765, published a series of works in what was from the standpoint of the age a highly radical vein. These writings provoked much written controversy. We may cite here Chydenius's *Källan till Rikets Wan-Magt* (*The Source of the Kingdom's Impuissance*) (1765), in which he attacked the *produktplakat* (the Commodity Act of 1724, which resembled the English Navigation Acts in barring foreign ships from Swedish trade except when carrying cargoes of the ships' own nationality), and *Den Nationnale Winsten* (*The National Profit*) (1765), which contains a principled summing-up of the author's anti-mercantilism stance. In *Tankar om Husbönders och Tienstehions Naturliga Rätt* (*Reflections on the Natural Rights of Masters and Servants*) (1778), which was a contribution to the debate on the servant question, Chydenius argued against the inhuman vagrancy laws of the day.

In Chydenius's view, the complete absence of regulation of any kind, and of all production and export bounties, would be to the advantage both of the nation and of the individual. In his comprehensive work of 1765, Chydenius started off by defining the national profit, which corresponded to the difference between a country's export and import values: 'That by which the value of outgoing wares exceeds that of the incoming, is rightly called the Nation's profit, and that by which the incoming surpasses the Value of those carried outward, is always its loss....'[11] Thus Chydenius shared the mercantilist conception of the balance of trade, which ought to be as favourable as possible from the standpoint of the individual country. But at that point all resemblance to the mercantilists ceased, save in one particular case (see below).

Chydenius held that in order to achieve the biggest possible profit, a nation ought to work at those occupations which paid best, i.e. in which the smallest number of individuals produced goods to the highest value or, to put it another way, in which production per worker was greatest. A country ought not to aim primarily at having the largest possible number of occupations.

A people's wealth thus consisted of the value of the country's production. The latter in turn was determined partly by the number of workers and partly by their diligence. Chydenius believed that both assets and efficiency were created by nature herself 'where she is left untrammeled'. He therefore considered that in the absence of legal obstacles, every individual would spontaneously seek that place and that occupation in which he best increased the national profit. Chydenius wrote:

That labour always pays best, which has the highest value, and that which pays best is most sought after. So long as in the one trade I can manufacture goods for 6 *daler* per day, I am unwilling to go into the other which yields 4. In the former, both the nation's and my own profit are one third [*sic*] larger than in the latter.[12]

7

When anyone was compelled, or induced by rewards, to work in any occupation where he did not earn the maximum possible, this was at the nation's expense.

Chydenius endeavoured to show that manufacturing and export bounties worked to the nation's detriment. The former created an excess of labour and goods in the occupations receiving the manufacturing bounties, which would first reduce prices in those branches and second cause shortages of labour in other profitable branches of economic activity.

Export bounties would lead to the same result and additionally involve a double burden on the country in question for the benefit of other countries. It was assumed that because of the export bounties, individuals in the country in question had to pay the price which the exporter received when selling abroad, plus the export bounty. If the exporter did not receive this price he would regard this as a relative loss and not accept the transaction. The double burden thus consisted first of the financing of the fund from which the export bounties were paid, and second of the payment of a home market price which was fixed by reference to export prices and export bounties. Foreign countries benefited too, by virtue of their being able to buy the goods more cheaply and then re-export hem. All this took place at the expense of the country in question.

Chydenius thus advocated a system in which the division of labour would be accomplished entirely without restrictions. 'Freedom, free competition and the natural equilibrium of forces' were the absolutely crucial criteria in his scheme.[13] This applied both to conditions within a country and between different countries.

His work was also characterized by social fervour. His chief concern here was with the agrarian so-called lower orders, and it was expressed *inter alia* in the work he did from the end of the 1770s onwards in opposing the servants laws.

However, as Heckscher pointed out,[14] this social commitment ought to have led Chydenius towards a different position on the population problem from the one he adopted. For he accepted and advocated the mercantilists' view on the development of population, holding that this should be as vigorous as possible. His attitude is difficult to explain, but his natural optimism may have had something to do with it.[15] Among other possibilities it has been conjectured that there may have been a link with Chydenius's profession of pastor, with theological considerations playing a role.[16] From the same standpoint, it is also remarkable that Chydenius regarded the labour force as a commodity and wages as a cost, although it has to be observed that the terminology was unusual for those days and did not have the present-day Marxist connotations.

However, Chydenius's attitude may also be seen as a consequence of his radical liberalism. He contended that the poorest worker's sole property was his work and his capacity to work. If the value of that property was fixed by tariff, then the freedom which other citizens enjoyed was lost to him![17]

Chydenius does not seem to have been influenced by foreign writers but to have studied mainly Swedish socio-economic literature. In certain instances, consequently, as for instance with respect to his conception of the exchange rate, he simply took over another writer's theory (see below). His works contained in fact no original or detailed theoretical economic reasoning.

What, nevertheless, makes Chydenius interesting from the standpoint of economic history is his radical liberalism. He epitomized in his works various aspects of the liberal opinion of the day and drew a radical conclusion from it.

Even if Heckscher is right in saying that originality in economic theory was on the whole lacking among eighteenth-century authors and pamphleteers, two exceptions at least must be made to this generalization. This applies most of all to P.N. Christiernin and his works of the 1760s, but A. Wappengren's modern ideas on monetary theory in the 1790s also deserve notice.[18]

The works of both these authors were published during periods when Sweden's currency was in disarray. Chistiernin was writing at a time when a paper standard prevailed in Sweden (1745–76), and Wappengren during a decade when the specie standard was again out of action, i.e. during the 'credit-note epoch', as it has been termed.

A modern critic – Eagly – has not only described Christiernin, with justice, as Sweden's leading economist of the eighteenth century, but also ranked him among the best monetary theorists in eighteenth-century Europe by virtue of the analytical content of *Utdrag af Föreläsningar angående den i Swea Rike upstigne Wexel-Coursen* (*Abstract of Lectures regarding the Exchange Rate prevailing in the Land of Sweden*), published by Christiernin in 1761.[19] In this work and other writings supplementing it, Christiernin, from a standpoint grounded in the quantity theory of money, discussed the reasons for the then rapidly rising exchange rate, i.e. the fall in the value of

Swedish currency abroad, and the means by which to correct the situation. In Christiernin's view, the cause was to be found in too large an expansion of credit and the note issue in combination with the ban on metal exports. Internal prices had therefore risen and affected the exchange rate.

By virtue of its detailed analysis of the connections between domestic and foreign price levels, the values of currencies and thus the prices of countries' goods of export and import, Christiernin's 'Abstract of Lectures ...' was the first economic work which was able to show that a country's trade and payments balance was automatically corrected by totally flexible exchange rates given the freedom to export bullion. Nevertheless, Christiernin did not advocate a switch to flexible exchange rates as a practical policy, for he realized that such a move would also have serious negative effects.

As regards rising exports resulting from a rising exchange rate, these involved first a country's living standard, which could be expected to fall as a result of a reduced supply of goods on the home market, and second the concentration of wealth which would be the result. This would upset the equilibrium in the distribution of wealth, an equilibrium which Christiernin regarded as necessary in order to maintain order among a 'free people' and not to disturb the circulation of money in the community.

However, Christiernin believed that a fall – i.e. a rise according to 'modern' economic terminology – in the exchange rate would have even more serious effects on a country's economy. His emphasis on the close connection between the quantity of money and the price level caused him to draw the same conclusions as if the situation was merely one of a reduced money supply, despite the fact that earlier on in his work, he had identified a number of other factors which influenced the demand for a given country's currency. Christiernin held that a decrease in the money supply led to a diminution of aggregate demand, which in turn caused unemployment because of a lack of flexibility of prices and wages. Reduced demand, and therefore falling incomes, then caused demand for imported goods to decline and the exchange rate to fall. Christiernin considered this would have an unfavourable effect on exports because of higher prices in foreign currency, causing further unemployment, and so forth.

Thus Christiernin grasped early on, and sounded a warning against, the dangers of a policy aimed at lowering the exchange rate by withdrawing paper money. However, the person who emerged as the foremost critic of the deflationary policy of the 1760s was Chydenius, through the publication in 1776 of his *Rikets Hjelp genom en Naturlig Finance-System* (*A Natural Financial System as Help to the Nation*). From having earlier been a fierce critic of Christiernin, however, Chydenius had simply taken over Christiernin's views in his own work![20]

Christiernin's analysis of the structure, functioning and significance of the monetary system for a country's overall economy was very advanced, and in at least one field – exchange rate theory – he anticipated the works and views of later economists. Eagly declares: 'Had Christiernin's Lectures existed in an English translation by the 1790s, the work would very likely have gained an important place in the main stream of economic thought and certainly would have played an outstanding role in the English Bullionist Controversy.'[21]

Wappengren's works of the 1790s are not marked by the same rigour of theoretical economic reasoning as Christiernin's, his argument for a permanent paper monetary standard in a country merits mention when considering the economic conceptions of the age. It was presented most notably in *Grunderne till ett Naturligt Finance-systeme, i jämförelse med vårt nuvarande* (*The Foundations of a Natural System of Finance, in comparison with our present System*), which was published in 1792.

Wappengren was an advocate of the *riksgäldssedlar* (Treasury notes, which unlike the Riksbank notes also in circulation were not tied to the silver standard and consequently were exchangeable for the latter only at a discount on nominal value), which dominated the Swedish note circulation at this time. He started off from a quantity theory, non-metallist standpoint (cf. Christiernin), in which the value of money was determined only by its quantity and money merely represented goods, receiving its value solely from this relationship. He held that if the quantity of money was fixed at a particular volume, rising and falling prices of goods would be determined only by the supply of goods.

He thus proposed a paper monetary standard, but one in which the size of the note issue was fixed. This would create a monetary system wholly free from inflation or deflation. Wappengren's system was entirely static, however, taking no account of the consequences which the freezing of the note issue would have on the development of production. He also overlooked the importance of credit as an engine of circulation in an economy; and the velocity of circulation was put at one. In spite of his fundamentally anti-metallist approach, he was forced to accept metal coin for foreign trade. Thus he did not solve the problem of international exchange of goods via paper currency.[22]

Despite its defects, Wappengren's proposal for the introduction of a permanent paper standard and his contention that the paper currency would maintain a stable value, once society accepted it as a universal medium of payment, were original ideas for his day. As Heckscher pointed out, the fundamental superiority of the paper monetary standard over the metal standard had thereby been asserted for the first time in Swedish economic literature.[23]

The ideas of mercantilism became predominant in the world of practical politics during the eighteenth century. Swedish writers on economic subjects during the first half of the nineteenth century were probably also of a conservative social outlook for the most part. Nevertheless, Heckscher held that parallel with these authors' works, writings were also being published that showed some greater or lesser degree of affinity with liberal opinions.[24]

It is difficult to judge what importance the liberal elements in Swedish socio-economic literature during the eighteenth century had for subsequent developments, but they probably played a minor role. Nor was Adam Smith's *The Wealth of Nations* (1776) probably of any crucial significance in Sweden, even though works elaborating upon Smith's exposition were published during the Swedish debate of the 1790s. In fact, Smith's work was not available in Swedish translation until 1800, and even then it was re-translated from an abridged German translation.[25] Liberal ideas did not supplant mercantilist ones in Swedish economic policy until the middle of the nineteenth century. An explanation for this must be sought in factors other than a direct influence from the literature.[26]

NOTES

*   This chapter was originally published in *Ekonomisk-historiska vingslag. Festskrift tillägnad Gunnar Fridlizius och Lennart Jörberg* (Lund, 1987). Since that time Lars Magnusson has published an article, 'Corruption and Civic Order – Natural Law and Economic Discourse in Sweden during the Age of Freedom', *Scandinavian Economic History Review*, vol. 37, no. 2, 1989, which discusses the Swedish development in a more ideo-historical way. See also T. Vallinder, 'Adam Smiths genombrott i Sverige' (*Ekonomisk debatt*, 1987: 3), which more strongly than in this chapter asserts Smith's importance to the economic–liberal reforms in nineteenth-century Sweden.

1 Petander (1912, p. 76).
2 Heckscher (1949, II: 2, p. 816).
3 The 1732 translation was given the Swedish title *Englands Förkofring genom Utrikes Handel*, while the new translation of 1745 appeared under the title *Engelands Skatt-Kammare genom den Utländske Handelen*.
4 Heckscher (1949, II: 2, p. 829; 1963, p. 224).
5 Berch had been influenced chiefly by German so-called cameralistics, or cameralism. The latter's primary purpose was to serve the personal interests of the princes, whereas Berch emphasized the situation of the private individual. See Heckscher (1949, II: 2, p. 831). See also Liedman (1986) on the tension between individual liberty and the good of society.
6 On the title page, it is stated that the work is 'Translated from the French according to the Latest Edition, Which has been enlarged by Seven Chapters, and completed in those places which had been left open'.
7 The home trade in corn was liberated in two stages, in 1775 and 1780. In addition there was the customs policy introduced in 1776 with periodical adjustments of tolls and active state intervention in the form of bulk corn purchases and relief measures.
8 See Heckscher (1943, p. 9; 1949, II: 2, p. 872) and Herlitz (1974).
9 Scheffer (1770, p. 48, XXVI) and Heckscher (1949, II: 2, p. 874).
10 A. Wappengren, cited in this chapter as an original economic theoretician, presented certain physiocratically inspired ideas in *Grunderne till den Borgerliga Hushållningen* (*Foundations of Civic Housekeeping*), 1798. These lack scholarly value, however; see Heckscher (1943, p. 15; 1949, II: 2, p. 875) and Herlitz (1974, p. 9).
11 Chydenius (1765), *Den Nationnale* ..., p. 4.
12 Chydenius (1765, p. 7) and Petander (1912, pp. 256–7).
13 Petander (1912, p. 274).
14 Heckscher (1949, II: 2, p. 867).
15 Petander (1912, p. 275).
16 Heckscher (1949, II: 2, p. 868).
17 See Chydenius (1778, pp. 20–1) and Petander (1912, p. 266).
18 Heckscher (1949, II: 2, pp. 816–17) contended with respect to the history of economic ideas that it was possible to find 'at most' two original Swedish contributions: Chydenius – who scarcely dealt with 'economic ideas in any specific sense' – and Wappengren. In his *Svenskt arbete och liv*, however, Heckscher disregarded Wappengren completely. However, Heckscher (1963, p. 226) had a high opinion of Christiernin – 'aggressive and polemical' but possessing 'great clarity of thought within the bounds of his subject' – and described him in the capacity of economic writer as 'one of the most clearthinking and theoretically most practised minds of the Age of Freedom, and indeed possibly the one which in its own field, chiefly monetary theory, best understood the theoretical implications' (Heckscher, 1949, II: 2, p. 765). However, Heckscher does not seem to have ascribed any originality to him.

19 *The Swedish Bullionist Controversy,* 1971.
20 See Heckscher (1949, II: 2, p. 765). Petander (1912, p. 264) wrote: 'It is
    ... obvious that Chydenius knew of and studied Christiernin, and so it
    must also be regarded as highly probable, in the light of the consider-
    able resemblance which the above-mentioned text bears to Christi-
    ernin's, that Chydenius borrowed a fair number of ideas from it.'
21 Eagly (1971, p. 24). His summing-up of Christiernin runs as follows:
    'He rose well above the analytical competence of his contemporaries in
    Sweden, and the analytical content of his *Lectures* places him among the
    best monetary economists in eighteenth-century Europe.'
22 See, e.g., Andreen (1956, p. 20), Heckscher (1942, p. 133ff; 1949, II: 2,
    pp. 805ff), and Ohlin (1920, pp. 115–16).
23 Heckscher (1949 ET, p. 254).
24 Heckscher (1963, p. 305).
25 Heckscher (1963, p. 230; 1949, II: 2, p. 877).
26 Concerning the Swedish governmental debt policy, however, the
    classical liberal point of view was predominant from the 1820s. See
    Ahlström (1989).

REFERENCES

Ahlström, G. (1974) *Studier i svensk ekonomisk politik och prisutveckling 1776–1802,* Lund.
—— (1989) 'Riksgäldskontoret och Sveriges statsskuld före 1850-talet', in E. Dahmén (ed.), *Upplåning och utveckling. Riksgäldskontoret 1789–1989,* Stockholm.
Andreen, P.G. (1956) 'Det svenska 1700-talets syn på banksedlar och pappersmynt', *Historisk Tidskrift.*
Arnberg, J.W. (1868) *Anteckningar om frihetstidens politiska ekonomi,* I, Uppsala.
Berch, A. (1747) *Inledning till Allmänna Hushållningen,* Stockholm.
Christiernin, P.N. (1761) *Utdrag af Föreläsningar angående den i Swea Rike upstigne Wexel-Coursen,* Stockholm.
Chydenius, A. (1765) *Källan til Rikets Wan-Magt,* Stockholm.
—— (1765) *Den Nationale Winsten,* Stockholm.
—— (1776) *Rikets Hjelp genom en Naturlig Finance-System,* Stockholm.
—— (1778) *Tankar om Husbönders och Tienstehions Naturliga Rätt,* Stockholm.
Coleman, D.C. (1969) *Revisions in Mercantilism,* London.
Eagly, R.V. (1971) *The Swedish Bullionist Controversy,* Philadelphia.
Forsman, K. (1947) 'Studier i det svenska 1700-talets ekonomiska litteratur', in *Skrifter utgivna av Svenska Litteratursällskapet i Finland,* 312, Helsinki.
Heckscher, E.F. (1942) 'Moderna inslag i svensk ekonomisk diskussion mot 1700-talets slut', *Ekonomisk Tidskrift.*
—— (1943) 'Fysiokratismens ekonomiska inflytande i Sverige', *Lychnos.*
—— (1949) 'Riksgälds, en unik fas i det svenska penningväsendets historia', *Ekonomisk Tidskrift.*
—— (1949) *Sveriges ekonomiska historia från Gustav Vasa,* II: 2, Stockholm.
—— (1963) *Svenskt arbete och liv,* Stockholm.

Herlitz, L. (1974) *Fysiokratismen i svensk tappning, 1767–1770,* Gothenburg.

Jörberg, L. (1972) *A History of Prices in Sweden 1732–1914,* I–II, Lund.

Leuhusen, C. (1761, 1763) *Tankar om de rätta och sannskyldiga medel till Sveriges välmåga,* Stockholm.

Liedman, S.-E. (1986) *Den synliga handen. Anders Berch och ekonomiämnena vid 1700-talets svenska universitet,* Värnamo.

Magnusson, L. (1989) 'Corruption and Civic Order – Natural Law and Economic Discourse in Sweden during the Age of Freedom', *Scandinavian Economic History Review,* vol. 37, no. 2.

Melon, J.F. (1734) *Essai politique sur le Commerce,* in Swedish translation 1751 under the title *Et Politiskt Försök om Handel.*

Mun, Th. (1664) *England's Treasure by Forraign Trade, or the Balance of our Forraign Trade is the Rule of our Treasure,* London. In Swedish translations 1732 and 1745.

Ohlin, B. (1920) 'Kvantitetsteorin i den svenska litteraturen', *Nationalekonomiska studier tillägnade professor D. Davidson,* Stockholm. Also published in *Ekonomisk Tidskrift,* 1919.

Petander, K. (1912) *De nationalekonomiska åskådningarna i Sverige,* I, 1718–1765, Stockholm.

Quesnay, F. (1846) 'Maximes générales du gouvernement économique d'un royaume agricole et notes sur ces maximes', in *Collection des Principes Économistes,* Tome II, Paris, pp. 81–104.

Scheffer, C.F. (770) *Bref til Riksens Råd,* Stockholm.

Vallinder, T. (1987) 'Adam Smiths genombrott i Sverige', *Ekonomisk debatt,* 1987: 3.

Wappengren, A. (1792) *Grunderne till ett Naturligt Finance-Systeme,* Stockholm.

—— (1798) *Grunderne till den Borgerliga Hushållningen,* Stockholm.

2

PEHR NICLAS CHRISTIERNIN

Mats Persson and Claes-Henric Sivén

Political economy in Sweden prior to Wicksell makes for some very dull reading. Of course, it is possible to find economists who were considered prominent – indeed, brilliant in some cases – by their contemporaries, but it is difficult to grasp precisely *what* their contribution to our discipline might have been. In most cases they seem to have been good exponents of the conventional wisdom of their day, rather than scholarly pioneers and trailblazers. However, leafing through the annals, we do find *one* person who truly made an individual contribution, and what's more a contribution of fundamental importance. That person is Pehr Niclas Christiernin (1725–1799) of Uppsala University, who in 1760 formulated the quantity theory of money.

To be sure, the relationship between the supply of money and the level of prices had been discussed on the continent for centuries and had been given an authoritative formulation by David Hume in the essay 'Of Money' in 1752. But Christiernin's formulation, published in 1761, was decidedly clearer and more to the point than Hume's, and while Hume's analysis had assumed an economy with fixed exchange rates, Christiernin expanded the analysis to cover an economy with floating exchange rates. Thereby his analysis anticipated a famous discussion in England half a century later, and it is possible that *if* his writings had been made available to the international economic community in some world language, the history of economics might have looked different in the nineteenth century.

STUDIES IN UPPSALA

Pehr Niclas Christiernin belonged to a well-to-do family of clergymen and iron-works' owners in the Bergslagen mining district. As a

16

very young man, he came to Uppsala to study theology, law and philosophy in the 1740s. Owing the affluence of his family, he was under no pressure to finish his education quickly in order to support himself; instead, he let his intellectual curiosity lead him from one course to the next.

With his social background among mill-owners in Bergslagen, he also had a natural interest in economic subjects. At this time economic research and teaching at Uppsala University was run by Anders Berch (1711–74), who, at the age of thirty, had become the first professor of economics in the Nordic countries, and who had developed into a moderate mercantilist with close connections to the Hat Party.[1] He soon took notice of Christiernin and eventually became his mentor of sorts. After a field trip to Bergslagen in 1757 and a dissertation on the benefits to the country of having low interest rates, Christiernin was eligible to be appointed to a post as adjunct in economics in 1759. The following year he undertook another field trip, this time via Finland to St Petersburg. During the entire journey he kept a detailed diary, which is now in the possession of the Uppsala University Library, Carolina Rediviva. In it, we can follow how the curious adjunct day by day gathers information about the settlements he travels through: the population of cities and their businesses, observations about trade roads, price levels and exchange rates. However, he did not meet any prominent economists, and Daniel Bernoulli (1700–82) had left St Petersburg as early as 1733.

In 1760 he also gave the series of lectures that was published the following year under the title of *Föreläsningar angående den i Swea rike uppstigne wexel-coursen*[2] (*Lectures concerning the Increased Rate of Exchange in the Kingdom of Sweden*) – (Stockholm 1761). This book, which attracted a great deal of attention, is his major work on economics. Indeed, it could be said to be almost his *only* work on economics; his 1759 dissertation was a rather derivative piece of work, based primarily on British polemical pamphlets advocating the legislation of fixed rates of interest,[3] and his writings from the 1760s consist almost without exception of polemics resulting from the tremendous controversy surrounding his 1761 book. During the 1770s he shifted more and more towards philosophy, and by the time Adam Smith's *The Wealth of Nations* was published, he had left political economy for good.

Christiernin's career as an economist was thus a short one, encompassing less than two decades. It was followed by a long and tormented career as a philosopher, or more properly, as a reactionary third-rate philosopher, as an academic eccentric, notorious for his cantankerousness, his opinionation and his scandals. In other words, Christiernin's final decades were rather bitter, and he was provided with abundant opportunities to display poor judgement, although they cannot be said to overshadow the singular good judgement and, in his day, unique perspicacity he showed in his *Lectures* from 1761. In order to understand the significance of that book, it might be helpful to devote some space to tracing the background to the economic policies of the so-called Period of Liberty in Sweden.

ECONOMIC AND POLITICAL BACKGROUND

When Sweden finally achieved peace in 1721, after the wars of Charles XII, there was a twenty-year period of slow reconstruction under the leadership of Arvid Horn. However, during the 1730s successive Parliaments were marked by ever-increasing partisanship. Two parties emerged: the Hats and the Caps. Arvid Horn was ousted, and the Hats took power in the 1738–9 Parliament.

The Hats had two main points in their programme: on the one hand, to seek revenge (primarily against Russia), and, on the other, to develop Swedish industry in the spirit of mercantilism. These two planks in their platform required financial resources if they were to be realized. These resources came to be created by parliamentary control of the *Riksens Ständers Bank* (Central Bank of Sweden).

When Charles XII's emergency coins were discontinued, they were replaced mainly by slabs of copper bullion, the metal content of which was supposed to correspond to their value. This was a guarantee against a return to the inflation that marked the final years of the wars. However, the copper slabs were heavy and bulky. Eli Heckscher (1957, p. 106) relates a story about this: '... in Viborg it happened that some thieves who had broken into a cellar to steal a small sum of money had to abandon the attempt, because they could not lift it above knee-level.'

To make payments more convenient, so-called 'transport bills' were instituted in 1726. They were actually receipts for copper bullion which had been turned in to the Central Bank. Instead of transporting the heavy copper slabs when making payment, it was sufficient for the transport bills to change owners. However, ten years later the bank started to lend transport bills if they were secured by real estate and pig-iron. This lending assumed ever greater proportions in connection with the Hats' abortive revanchist war in Finland, 1741–3, and with the increasingly ambitious industrial policies of the 1740s and 1750s. In 1745 the bank stopped redeeming bills with copper bullion.

The year 1756 was a watershed. It was then that a coup was attempted with the aim of enhancing the power of the king at the expense of Parliament and the Council. The attempt failed. Its main perpetrators (with the exception of King Adolf Fredrik and Queen Lovisa Ulrika) were beheaded in July the same year.

In the excitement and relief following the thwarted coup attempt, the Hat government came to expand and strengthen its industrial policy. Lending was increased, the interest rate was lowered from 4– 5 per cent to 3–4 per cent, and a sizeable amount of gold was lent without interest to some needy industrialists. The theory was that an expansive economic policy would lead to increased national income and a surplus in the balance of payments. In reality, however, the general level of prices started to rise and the exchange rate went up, that is, the Swedish daler depreciated.

The following year the Pomeranian War broke out, and Sweden became involved in the Seven Years War. The purpose of the war was to recover those parts of Pomerania that Sweden had ceded to Prussia in 1720. But, apart from pledges of French subsidies, the Hat government may also have been tempted to teach the queen, Lovisa Ulrika, a lesson after the royal attempt at revolution. The queen was the sister of the king of Prussia, Frederick the Great.

The government financed the Pomeranian War by issuing even more bills, which, among other things, caused speculation against the exchange rate. People bought foreign currencies, expecting their value to rise in terms of Swedish dalers. (The exchange office tried for a time to maintain a fixed rate.) The general level of prices also soared.

The Hats' theory about the course of inflation was as follows: the rate of exchange rose as a result of a deficit in the balance of payments. This higher exchange rate led, in turn, to higher prices for imports and thereby to a higher general price level. The remedy was import restrictions instead of anti-inflationary policies. The Hats even advocated further increases in the volume of money in order to achieve equilibrium in the balance of payments by increasing domestic production and thereby, indirectly, exports (the Hats believed in increasing returns to scale).

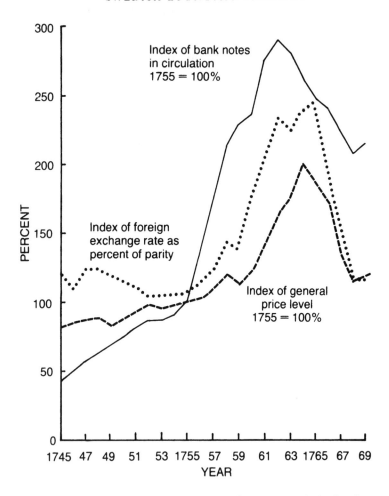

Figure 2.1 Price level, exchange rate and money supply in Sweden, 1745–69 (*Source:* Eagly (1971)).

The Caps were opposed to the Hats' policies of subsidization and control, maintaining that the cause of inflation and the fall of Swedish currency was the extensive issuance of bills. But the causal link was the acquisitiveness of those who borrowed from the banks. The Caps' foremost theorist of inflation was Anders Nordenkrantz. He was a well-read man who had published a mercantilist-inspired work on economics in 1730 which had attracted a great deal of attention. He once belonged to the Hat Party but had suffered losses from inflation, so he changed sides. He came to provide the Caps with the theoretical basis they needed to attack the Council. As Nordencrantz saw it, evil men, not impersonal economic forces, were responsible for the miserable state of the realm. There were also personal links between the trading houses, mill-owners and industrialists on the one hand, and the Hat Party on the other. Nordencrantz was an early public-choice theorist.

With the 1765–6 Parliament, people's patience with the Hat regime was exhausted. Inflation had led to declining real income for those with fixed nominal wages, including officials. The Caps now assumed power with the help of a deflationary platform which aimed to push prices back down to their pre-1747 level. They did not believe that this would lead to unemployment. Wealthy Hat merchants had profited from inflation; now those same individuals would suffer losses instead.[4]

The Caps' deflationary policies led not only to reductions in the level of prices and exchange rates, but also to extensive declines in production and employment. Bankruptcies were legion. The Caps' popularity faded quickly, and the Hats regained power in 1769. They abolished the deflationary policies and endeavoured to preserve the value of money, as Christiernin had suggested in 1761.

CHRISTIERNIN'S ANALYSIS OF THE COURSE OF INFLATION–DEFLATION

In the heated debate surrounding the rise and fall of the rate of exchange – its causes and cures – there was only one person with clear vision, the university adjunct in Uppsala, Pehr Niclas Christiernin.

Christiernin's 1760 lectures mainly treated the theory of money, but they also touched upon the current problems stemming from inflation. The following year he published parts of these lectures.[5] The book provoked a violent debate, with attacks from the Anders Nordencrantz camp, among others. In 1763 Christiernin published a reply to his critics. In a third work from 1769 he summed up the debate against the background of the actual course of events.

Christiernin's publication of excerpts from his lectures was of course prompted by his feeling that his analysis had direct bearing on the discussion that was then going on in Parliament. Christiernin's book was remarkable for several reasons. In the first place, even though it merely consisted of selections from lectures, it was a scholarly product. His book was completely different from the pamphlet-like works others were publishing about economic and political matters. This meant that the book was rooted in economic theory and *institutionalia* in a way that was uncommon elsewhere.

Second, Christiernin's book did not take the side of either party. His argumentation was directed at both Hats and Caps, although the latter were the main target. This impartiality can be interpreted in two ways. On the one hand, by Act of Parliament, the instruction in economics given in Uppsala was to be free from political considerations. In other words, Christiernin could satisfy this requirement by criticizing both of the main currents in the ongoing discussion between Hats and Caps. On the other hand, there is another, more probable interpretation. Intellectually, Christiernin was a thoroughly honest person. The acuity and intrepidness that characterized his arguments regarding political economy during the 1760s would later lead to entirely different consequences.

Below we shall briefly summarize Christiernin's discussion of exchange rates and the process of price increases, of the effects of inflation and deflation, and finally comment on his suggestions for designing stabilization policies.

In his analysis there are two systems to take into consideration: first, fixed exchange rates (or rather fixed parity rates) under a metal standard; second, free exchange rates with paper money. In both cases, the rate of exchange is assumed to create equilibrium between supply and demand for foreign currencies. The rate is influenced in principle by all transactions which result in supply or demand for currencies. With a metal standard, however, the rate cannot in the long run deviate from par value by more than the costs of exporting or importing the metal for coins.

If, instead, the rates of exchange are free (domestic bills are not redeemable by metal coin or there is a prohibition against importing or exporting coin metals), then there is no exogenously given limit to the rate. It is then determined by the monetary policies of the various countries. Christiernin emphasizes the fact that flexible exchange rates can provide a self-regulating mechanism:[6] a rising rate of exchange increases exports and reduces imports.

With this description of price formation in the currency market as a point of departure, Christiernin then analysed the reasons for the depreciation of the Swedish currency. The reasons, according to Christiernin, were the country's expansive monetary policy and the financing of the war with bank loans. Low rates of interest led to an increase in the price of real property, and some people were fooled into selling real estate for daler bills. The demand for luxury items rose. Sweden's demand for imports (imports consisted to a large extent of foodstuffs and luxury goods at this time) went up, which, with a paper monetary standard, entailed rising exchange rates; that is, more and more Swedish dalers were needed to purchase one unit of foreign currency.

Christiernin's analysis of the causes of the rising rates of exchange and the rising level of prices was thus directly at odds with both the Hats' and the Caps' pictures of what had brought about the situation. After all, the Hats maintained that the deficit in the balance of trade was the driving force behind the problem, while Christiernin stressed that Sweden's trade was largely in a state of balance. Instead, the great demand for imports led to a higher equilibrium level for the rate of exchange. As opposed to the Caps, Christiernin emphasized the fact that impersonal economic forces lay behind the course of events. The depreciating Swedish currency, for example, was not the result of a cartel between the sellers of foreign currency. He claimed that monopoly can only raise the price of certain goods, while a general rise in the price level was due to an increase in the supply of money.

Christiernin discussed not only the causes of the rising exchange rate but also analysed its effects. First of all he emphasized – polemicizing above all against the Caps – that a high or low exchange rate is in itself of no particular significance. It merely reflects *nominal* quantities. Goods are bought and sold between countries as if there were no rate of exchange; money is just a veil. In other words, a country cannot be said to benefit or lose from a low or high rate of exchange. On the other hand, individuals can either suffer losses or profit from changes in the rate of exchange.

Variations in the exchange rate do play an important role in creating equlibrium in foreign payments, but what is gained by exporting industries when the rate of exchange goes up might disturb the equilibrium as regards distribution which is necessary to maintain law and order among a free people. At the same time, he stressed that a falling rate of exchange (with deflation) was even worse.

DEFLATION AND UNEMPLOYMENT

Decreased circulation of bills, with a consequently lower rate of exchange (that is, an appreciation of the currency), also entails a redistribution, but it tends moreover to disrupt trade and production; after all, the price system has been adapted to the previously high exchange rate. When the exchange rate now falls, some prices will change more than others. It is more difficult to adjust prices downward than upward.

If the supply of money declines, then the number of purchases decreases, stocks pile up and production falls. This leads to pessimism, increased demand for liquidity, declining velocity in the money supply and a further reduction in demand for goods. Falling prices would create expectations for more falling prices. Declining income leads to a further reduction in demand.

Even if all prices could be immediately adjusted to the lower rate of exchange, some problems would arise anyway. The most important problem is that price increases and price decreases do not have symmetrical effects. While it is true that lenders do lose money when prices rise (unexpectedly), they still have a positive net wealth. When prices fall, it is not certain whether borrowers will be able to pay back their loans. Cumulative effects might occur after a succession of bankruptcies. Production declines and the masses become unemployed.

Christiernin's conclusion regarding all this was that it was imperative to prevent continued inflation, but also to stabilize prices at the current high level and not try to press price and exchange rates back down some earlier level, as the Caps proposed.

Since inflation was caused by excessive issuance of bills, further increases in printing bills must be avoided. The bank should not be allowed to lend more than a sum corresponding to ten times its reserves. Deflation can be brought about by raising the rate of interest for lending. If the goal, however, is to achieve a stabilization of the value of money, it is better to sell government bonds with a high rate of interest or to open interest-yielding accounts for deposits in the bank.

How original were Christiernin's analysis and conclusions? To start with, it can be established that he was familiar with the international economic discussion. In the two books from 1761 to 1763 he refers to David Hume, Richard Cantillon, John Locke and Thomas Mun, for example. The quantity theory of money was therefore not his own invention, nor was the notion that there is a self-regulating mechanism for foreign payments (cf. Hume's specie-flow mechanism).

John Eagly, who has studied Christiernin's contributions and translated his most important writings into English, maintains, however, that Christiernin comes across as a more sophisticated theorist of money than Hume and Smith; for example, that he was the first to put forward a theory of floating exchange rates as an equilibrium-creating mechanism, and that he clearly anticipated the British debate on the price level and rate of exchange ('The Bullion Debate') in the early 1800s.[7]

However, Christiernin's analysis of the ramifications of deflation should also be ranked high. He predicted its negative effects in his book as early as 1761. It should be stressed, however, that in this respect Christiernin actually had a precursor in his own country.

Emanuel Swedenborg, in his *Oförgriplige tankar om myntets upphöjande och nedsättande* (*Humble Thoughts on the Rising and Falling of Coinage*) (1722), had analysed the effects of inflation during the last years of Charles XII and the effects of deflation with the aim of restoring prices to their original levels. Apart from the fact that Swedenborg was touching upon the distributional and terms-of-trade effects of inflation and deflation respectively, he emphasized that prices were less flexible downward than upward and that deflation would therefore have damaging effects on production and employment. Swedenborg ends his work with the following con-clusion:

> For the reasons presented above it should be possible to establish that a rise is extremely damaging to a country; as is a decline if it has been too high for a time and thus become part and parcel of the nation's economic fabric: there clearly follows, as was said at the beginning, that to tamper with and disturb the coinage would be the same thing as tampering with everyone's dearest possession and disturbing the most precious thing people can own, as well as altering the entire nation's commerce, and consequently, making oneself blame-worthy to each and every person in the chain of those who would be made to suffer from it.[8]

While it is thus possible to find forerunners, it is also evident that Christiernin's analysis of the stabilization problems of the 1760s exhibited great independence and perspicacity. He was a brilliant economist. But why did he end his career in economics shortly thereafter?

ACADEMIC CAREER

In 1767 Anders Berch was granted a leave of absence from his chair, and adjunct Christiernin was appointed to serve in his stead. A couple of years later Berch was named university treasurer, with the task of straightening out the academy's tangled economy, and he permanently vacated his professorship. The choice of a successor might appear to have been rather simple, but it was complicated by two things. First, Christiernin had made a number of powerful enemies[9] during the stabilization debates of the 1760s, both in the government and among the opposition, who were eager to put an end to his career. Second, the honourable Anders Berch had divided loyalties in this matter: he wanted his son, Krister Berch, to have the desirable post.[10] After some plotting, Christiernin was nevertheless appointed by the king on 24 October 1770.

He remained in the post for only a year, however, leaving to become professor of theoretical philosophy. The story behind this switch would prove to be fateful for Christiernin, and as it also tells us a great deal about the relative positions of science and politics even in those days, it might be worth relating here.

Henrik Frosterus was the name of a legal scholar whose slight academic merits were more than offset by strong political credentials. During the 1760s he had established valuable ties with the Hat Party, and both the party and Frosterus himself thought it would be beneficial to them if he were to be granted the title of professor. The government had made an attempt in this matter as early as 1762, but Uppsala University had so forcefully rejected the idea of such an arrangement that it came to nothing. In 1769, when the Hats had regained power after the four-year Cap regime, the time was ripe for a new attempt.

The first chair to fall vacant was Anders Berch's professorship in economics. Since it formally belonged to the law faculty, Frosterus's candidacy was not unreasonable; he was, after all, a legal scholar. But it turned out that his rivals (that is, the younger Berch and Christiernin) were so obviously more qualified that not even the Hat government could do anything about it. Towards the end of 1770, however, the chair in theoretical philosophy became available. While it was true that Frosterus had no knowledge of theoretical philosophy, the competition here was much feebler, and the government eventually succeeded in giving him the post, against the suggestion of the panel of experts charged with filling the vacancy.

The university now had two newly appointed professors on its hands: a professor of economics with a good knowledge of economics and with considerable knowledge of (and a great interest in) philosophy and theology, and a professor of philosophy with no knowledge of philosophy, but with some knowledge of economics and law. It was only natural that the idea was floated that the two gentlemen should simply swap their chairs, and this was done in December 1771.

To everyone involved, the exchange seemed like a clear Pareto improvement. Frosterus was able to devote himself to a subject of which he had some knowledge, and Christiernin got the opportunity to apply his incisive analytical abilities to a field which had been close to his heart ever since his adolescence. Over the long term, however, it became apparent that he had definitely wound up in the wrong place in life. Philosophy at that time, just like economics, was undergoing tremendous change and was facing a major upheaval. The only difference was that, in economics, Christiernin had been fortunate enough to act as a representative of the new emergent ideas and to be on the winning side. In philosophy, he happened to land on the conservative, losing side, and his final decades were wasted in a hopeless struggle against the new ideas.

THE EMBITTERED PHILOSOPHER

From the middle of the 1770s Christiernin phased out his economic writing and employed his best energies partly to academic disputes and scheming and partly to a no-holds-barred struggle against the philosophical ideas of Immanuel Kant, which were beginning to reach Sweden at that time. In many cases, these two activities were one and the same. He considered Kantian philosophy unrealistic, irrational and downright injurious to society, and in the history of Swedish philosophy, the so-called Kant controversy, which raged throughout the decades surrounding 1800, constitutes a voluminous chapter.

The academic disputes and scandals – which did not revolve around philosophical principle alone, but also had purely practical or sometimes personal backgrounds – seem to have been a product of Christiernin's dialectical and analytical powers, his reluctance to compromise and his passion for the truth, which bordered on dogmatism. When one reads Claes Annerstedt's history of Uppsala University in the eighteenth century,[11] one continually encounters

Christiernin as a notorious quarreller and malcontent. Especially infamous instances are his inaugural lecture in 1771, in which he did not mince his words in puncturing the prevailing physiocratic doctrines, and his life-long animosity toward Daniel Melanderhjelm, the astronomer. He seems often to have been more or less right as regards the issues at hand, like, for example, the time he mounted a major attack on the university librarian in 1780 for alleged carelessness and negligence, or when he spent years wrangling about his salary – but the way in which he carried out his crusades often hurt himself as much as others.

One piquant example is the scandalous disputation that took place at the theological faculty in 1777. Christiernin had sought the chair in theology as it was more remunerative than the one in philosophy, and on 5 May he met his foremost rival for the post, the theologian L.G. Palmberg, in a debate concerning the role of the Holy Ghost in converting sinners. The two antagonists, who had been enemies even before this point, grew more and more heated and aggressive. The chairman tried to calm them down several times but failed, and when they eventually abandoned Latin – with the boisterous approval of the audience – and started slinging insults at each other in home-grown Swedish, it became a full-blown scandal. The episode brought ridicule upon the university, and King Gustav III personally intervened in the matter. He decided that neither Christiernin or Palmberg would get the theology professorship, but that it would instead be granted to the person who had been suggested as a third candidate. The king's justification of his decision is worth pondering: 'His Majesty finds that learning alone is not a sufficient qualification for a post; rather morals and demeanor should also be taken into account, that young people may receive the edification that is right and proper.'

To the long list of misfortunes that were visited upon Christiernin, we must add his love life. After several failed courtships, he finally married Elisabet von Kiörning, a clergyman's daughter, in 1767. Their marriage was an unhappy one, however, and tradition has it that the bride entered into it against her will.[12] Hugo Hamilton relates an anecdote about the Christiernin's life together in his memoirs:[13]

> He and his wife must have been rather odd people if we can trust a story my grandmother used to tell. They despised each other like the plague and lived separately, each in one half of

the house. But at the stroke of eight every morning, they opened their respective doors to a room between their apartments and – stuck out their tongues at each other, to relieve their hearts.

Despite all his misfortunes and scandals, Christiernin was outwardly a rather successful person. For example, he was a precursor of Keynes and Bertil Ohlin in that he created a respectable fortune through clever speculation, primarily in grains. He lived grandly and elegantly in the beautiful Julinsköld House, which he had purchased when University Treasurer Peter Julinsköld went bankrupt – an event that created a stir in the Uppsala of the 1760s. The house still stands; it is the so-called Dean's House between Trinity Church and the Cathedral, now owned by the Faculty of Theology.

Here he put together a large scholarly library of 5000–6000 volumes, which were auctioned off in March 1800, after his death. The 240-page auction catalogue provides interesting information about what literature an eighteenth-century professor of economics had on his shelves. Unfortunately, most of the space was devoted to theological and philosophical works, while economic opuses were in the minority. The latter consisted primarily of practical textbooks on agriculture, industry and managing iron-works, all in the spirit of the Englightenment, but there were also some books which correspond to our definition of specialist literature in economics: one finds both Thomas Mun's *England's Treasure by Forraign Trade* and David Hume's collected works. Adam Smith is represented by *The Theory of Moral Sentiments* in a German translation from 1770. *The Wealth of Nations* is conspicuous by its absence, however; by 1776 Christiernin had strayed so far from economics that he no longer bothered to keep abreast of the latest scholarly literature.

The last scandal in Christiernin's life also proved to be the greatest, and today it is probably primarily for this event that his name is remembered in Uppsala. According to tradition, the university appointed a new *rector magnificus* (vice chancellor) every year, and the office circulated among the professors according to a fixed schedule. In 1795 the elderly Christiernin's turn came round. He had earlier served as rector twice, namely in 1780 and 1786, and both times he had caused considerable commotion by over-zealously attempting to rectify either real or imagined wrongs at the university.

The third time around he was firmly determined to exploit the powers of his high office to intervene in the ongoing Kant controversy. He was convinced that the French Revolution was a consequence of Kant's detrimental influence, a connection which we might find surprising today but which was nevertheless a reality for Christiernin and many of his contemporaries. Nor can it be denied that quite a few of Kant's disciples in Uppsala nursed revolutionary sympathies, and they came to be regarded by the conservative camp as dangerous 'Jacobins'.

By 1795 the French Revolution had degenerated, and it could truly be said that what would become of the dawning nineteenth century depended on how the left managed to cope with its disappointment. In Sweden the rightist winds blew strong; the Reuterholm regime, with its censorship and harsh ideological control, gave Christiernin his cue: he would take action against Kantianism in Uppsala.

During the autumn there were a number of confrontations between the rector and students. Christiernin made several speeches to the students, exhorting them to mend their ways. The students replied with contemptuous oaths, and Christiernin lost control and called them 'young wolves' and 'puppies'. Other mutual provocations made the situation more and more tense.

In the dark of night between 25 and 26 October, a large crowd of students gathered outside Christiernin's house, shouting '*pereat, pereat*'.[14] Beside himself with fury, he pulled on his clothes, called the university's own police force, and ordered it to attack the students, egging the officers on with cries like 'Slash and jab at them! Beat them or arrest them!' The students were dispersed, but Christiernin had nine people arrested during the course of the night. Eight of them later proved to be innocent, only one of them having had anything to do with the uproar. The incident created a tremendous stir, and Christiernin was forced to resign from the rectorship.

The story of Pehr Niclas Christiernin is interesting in many ways. On a superficial plane, it teaches us something about the history of economic doctrine. If we feel that the history of doctrine is a key to understanding our discipline, it is also important to shed light on how the quantity theory developed in the eighteenth century. On the human plane, we are faced with the paradox of a brilliant economist choosing to leave economics to become a mediocre philosopher. Finally, Christiernin's behaviour in various situations brings up the perennial question of how strongly one should believe in, and fight for, one's convictions. It was Christiernin's tragedy that he always dared to stand up for his opinions and to struggle against phenomena he felt were harmful – not out of wickedness, but rather out of consideration for the students and for society.

Dean Mattias Floderus, who was Christiernin's contemporary, sums up his person in the following lines: 'A versatile man and rather zealous regarding both the instruction and the morals of young people, but, being ornery and quarrelsome, he led a troubled life. He wanted to do good, but always exaggerated the means to achieve it.'[15]

NOTES

1 Cf. Liedman (1986).
2 'The Increased Rate of Exchange' means that the number of Swedish dalers needed to purchase one unit of foreign currency has increased, that is, Swedish currency has fallen or depreciated.
3 See Petander (1912).
4 Cf. Wicksell's programme for a monetary policy for the years following the First World War.
5 Christiernin's work is most readily available in an English translation of parts of the book, published by Robert V. Eagly in 1971.
6 Cf. Hume's parallel discussion of the self-regulating mechanism under a metal standard.
7 See also Ohlin (1919) and Myhrman (1976).
8 Swedenborg (1722), p. 15. 'Rise' means 'inflation' here, 'decline' means 'deflation'.
9 On a couple of occasions the government even tried to have him prosecuted for his writings. Cf. Segerstedt (1971, pp. 123–5).
10 This procedure was not without precedents which had attracted considerable attention. Just a few years prior to this, in 1763, Carolus Linnaeus had arranged to have *his* son succeed him as professor of botany.
11 Annerstedt (1913).
12 Carlquist (1922).
13 Hamilton (1928, p. 67).
14 If the student rebels of 1968 had been as well-versed in Latin as these students from 1795, we would have stood outside the American Embassy chanting: '*pereant, pereant*'.
15 Carlquist (1922).

LIST OF LITERATURE

There is still no biography of P.N. Christiernin. The only summing up of his life and works consists of B. Boethius's article in *Svenskt Biografiskt Lexikon* (*Swedish Biographical Dictionary*) (1929). An impressionistic depiction of

Swedish economics during the 1700s, and of Anders Berch in particular, is found in Liedman (1986). Christiernin's economic theories are thoroughly discussed in Eagly (1971).

Annerstedt, C. (1913) *Uppsala Universitets historia*. Tredje delen, Almqvist & Wiksell, Uppsala.

Berch, A. (1747) *Inledning til almänna hushållningen*, Stockholm.

Boethius, B. (1929) 'Pehr Niclas Christiernin', *Svenskt Biografiskt Lexikon.*

Carlquist, C. (1922) 'Prosten Mattias Floderus' teckning av Uppsala-professorerna 1809', *Personhistorisk Tidskrift*, vol. 23.

Christiernin, P.N. (1759) *Rikets Nytta af Låga Penningräntor*, Uppsala.

—— (1761) *Utdrag af Föreläsningar Angående Den i Swea Rike upstigne Wexel-Coursen, Til dess Beskaffenhet, Orsaker och Påfölgder, Samt Botemedel emot Wexel-prisets ytterligare uplöpande*, Stockholm.

—— (1763) *Svar til några påminnelser, som utkommit emot hans föreläsningar, angående den i Svea Rike upstigne wexel-coursen*, Uppsala.

—— (1769) *Nordencrantzes finance system, utdragit utur herr commerce-rådets skrifter och med några anmärkningar lämpade til närwarande tid*, Uppsala.

Eagly, R.V. (1971) *The Swedish Bullionist Controversy*, American Philosophical Society, Philadelphia.

Hamilton, H. (1928) *Hågkomster*, Bonniers, Stockholm.

Heckscher, E.F. (1957) *Svenskt arbete och liv. Från medeltiden till nutiden* (1941), 3rd edn.

Liedman, S.-E. (1986) *Den synliga handen*, Arbetarkultur, Stockholm.

Myhrman, J. (1976) 'Experiences of Flexible Exchange Rates in Earlier Periods: Theories, Evidence and a New View', *The Scandinavian Journal of Economics*, vol. 78, pp. 169–96.

Nordencrantz, A. (Backmansson) (1730) *Arcana oeconomiae et commercii eller handelens och hushåldnings - wärkets hemligheter*, Stockholm.

Ohlin, B. (1919) 'Kvantitetsteorin i den svenska litteraturen', *Ekonomisk Tidskrift*, vol. 21, pp. 99–146.

Petander, K. (1912) *De nationalekonomiska åskådningarna i Sverige sådana de framträda i litteraturen*, Part I, 1718–1765. P.A. Norstedt & Sons, Stockholm.

Segerstedt, T.T. (1971) *Den akademiska friheten under frihetstiden*, Uppsala.

Swedenborg, E. (1722) *Oförgriplige tankar om myntets uphöjande och nedsättande*. Quoted from reprinted edition, Edman, Uppsala 1771.

3

THE EXISTENCE OF A POSITIVE RATE OF INTEREST IN A STATIONARY STATE: A WICKSELLIAN ENIGMA

Björn Hansson

INTRODUCTION

This essay analyses the following Wicksellian enigma:

> Is it possible that capital, under stationary conditions and neutral time preferences, can be a permanent source of income, that is to say can a positive rate of interest exist in a stationary state?
>
> (cp. Wicksell 1934, pp. 146, 154)

Wicksell does not give a formal or an explicit solution to the problem but he gives bits and pieces as an answer. Our purpose is to use these fragments as a basis for the construction of a formal solution, which should be located within a Wicksellian framework.

To provide a basis for a Wicksellian solution, the analysis starts from Wicksell's procedure of dividing the question into two parts: (1) the existence, the cause or the origin of the rate of interest, which is based on the idea of round-about processes of production and the productivity of capital; (2) the determination of the level of the rate of interest, which takes into account the given amounts of labour and capital. It is then shown that the productivity of capital is, under certain assumptions, a sufficient cause for a positive rate of return.

ROUND-ABOUT PROCESSES OF PRODUCTION

To analyse *the origin of the rate of interest*, capital should, according to

Wicksell, be treated in the same manner as labour and land, which means that capital is a homogenous factor of production. Labour and land can be measured, at least in principle, in their *technical units* – labour time and hectares respectively – and their marginal products would then determine the wage and the rent. This procedure is followed by Wicksell when he determines the wage and the rent as marginal productivities in *an economy without capital* or where capital is a free good (cp. Wicksell 1934, p. 108). However, capital has no common technical unit and it is not appropriate, for Wicksell's purposes, to treat capital as *a bundle of heterogenous capital goods* – the Walrasian solution – since that only gives the rents for different capital goods and does not allow us to derive a common rate of profit. Neither can capital be measured as *a sum of exchange values*, which is then used to determine the marginal productivity of capital and the rate of profit, since the sum itself depends on the rate of profit.

Wicksell opts for the Austrian solution, where the basis is to take *labour and land as the common origin of capital.* This implies a *longitudinal section* through social production:

> we can refer everything back to the original factors of production in conjunction with waiting (or preferably time). . . . If we proceed thus, the indirect demand for the factors of production from the consumers' side becomes a mere metaphor, and we also cease to take capital–goods into consideration; adopting the scheme of Jevons and Böhm-Bawerk, everything is resolved into a continuous production directed towards the future.
>
> (Wicksell 1919, p. 237)

Sraffa characterizes this approach as 'a one-way avenue that leads from "Factors of production" to "Consumption goods"' (Sraffa 1960, p. 93). Walras, on the other hand, takes 'a *cross-section* through social production at a moment of time, and thus considers only the co-operation of the factors of production existing at the moment' (Wicksell 1919, p. 236; original emphasis). The advantage with the Austrian approach is that the *time-element* is explicitly taken into account, and Wicksell praises Böhm-Bawerk's conception:

> Already in his Introduction [to the book *Positive Theorie des Kapitals*] we find the brilliant suggestion that we should regard the *capitalistic process of production* ('the adoption of wisely-

chosen round-about methods') as the *primary* concept and the capital itself as the *secondary* – 'the complex of intermediate products emerging at the various stages of the round-about process of production taking time'.

(Wicksell 1934, p. 168; cp. Hicks 1983, p. 100; original emphasis)

The longitudinal section of social production is used to dissolve the whole capital stock, fixed capital as well as circulating capital, into original factor inputs with two dimensions: amount and date. Sraffa calls this operation 'reduction to dated quantities of labour' (Sraffa 1960, p. 34). However, it is in *general* not possible to use this procedure when fixed capital exists (cp. ibid., p. 58). Hence, if Wicksell's formulation is to be used, it is necessary that the structure of production has the following characteristic:

In effect it is of the essence of such a Reduction that each commodity should be produced separately and by only one industry, and the whole operation consists in tracing back the successive stages of a single-track productive process.

(ibid.; cp. Hicks 1983, pp. 98–9)

It will be seen below that Wicksell's production function fulfills this condition.

Capital is defined as saved-up or accumulated labour and land which have taken on a different form from current labour and land. To simplify the exposition we will from now on only deal with current and saved-up labour, although Wicksell considered his inclusion of saved-up land as a development of Böhm-Bawerk's approach. Capital or saved-up labour is supposed to be more productive than current labour:

this difference [between current and saved-up labour] is suffi-cient to justify the establishment of a special category of means of production, side by side with labour and land [the only *original* factors of production], under the name of capital; for, in the interval of time thus afforded, the accumulated labour and land have been able to assume forms denied to them in their crude state, by which they attain a much greater efficiency for a number of productive purposes.... In this circumstance is also to be found the whole explanation of the value-creating power of capital, or its so-called productivity.

What emerges is simply the importance of the *time-element* in production.

(Wicksell 1934, p. 150; original emphasis)

This is the general principle that the *productivity of capital*, 'the value-creating power of capital', is related to round-about processes of production.

The rate of interest has the following relation to the productivity of capital:

> this increase in efficiency is a necessary condition of interest; it is the source from which it flows (just as the fruitfulness of the earth is the source of rent and the productivity of labour the source of wages); but it does not, on that account, regulate the *rate* of interest. Some part of this increase in productivity accrues, and must accrue, to the other factors of production, for their co-operation is essential and is indeed itself a part of the application of capital.

(ibid.; original emphasis)

Hence, the *existence* or the *cause* of the rate of interest can be explained by the productivity of capital, i.e. a physical explanation, which is Wicksell's reason for considering time preferences, Böhm-Bawerk's first two grounds, to play a secondary role (cp. below). However, in order to determine the *actual level* of the rate of interest, it is also necessary to take into account the available amount of labour and capital.

THE MAGNITUDE OF THE RATE OF INTEREST

To analyse the determination of the level of the interest rate, we will apply Wicksell's model of capital stratification, which describes the given capital stock in a stationary state (see Fig. 3.1). During the current year, year 0, L_0 is the amount of current labour which is used together with the machines L_1, the fruit of one-year-old labour, and L_2, the fruit of two-year-old labour, to produce the output. The machines will be completely worn out during the production period, which implies that the production process is flow input–point output. L_{01} and L_{02} are current labour which are invested during this year – and mature during year 1 and 2 respectively – to reproduce the capital with the same stratification. The economy has a given amount of current labour L^*, which can be used to produce current output and reproduce the capital stock: $L^* = L_0 + L_{01} +$

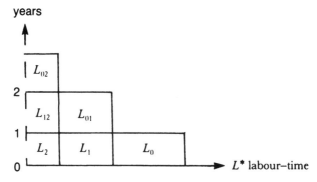

Figure 3.1 Wicksell model of capital stratification.

L_{02}. L_{12} is a machine in progress which was produced during the last production period and then transferred to the current period; it is assumed that this half-finished machine is just left to 'mature' during the current period. Consequently no current labour is expended on this machine. In a stationary state, where the capital structure is kept intact, the following must be true: $L_{01} = L_1$ and $L_{02} = L_{12} = L_2$, i.e. the same amount of labour but of different ages.

The economy produces only one commodity (Q). The following production function is homogenous of degree one:

$$Q = f(L_0; \ L_1; \ L_2)$$

The production function is taken from Wicksell:

> We consider the total amount of a commodity produced as a function ... of all the quantities of labour and land employed (i.e. anually consumed) both *current* and *saved up*.
>
> (ibid., p. 203; original emphasis)

However, the arguments of the function are 'only those parts of capital which are annually consumed' (ibid., p. 204) plus the part of current labour which directly produces the consumption good. It is also assumed that, within the relevant range for Q, the marginal productivities of current and saved-up labour are falling: $\delta^2 Q / \delta L_0^2 > 0$, $\delta^2 Q / \delta L_1^2 > 0$, etc.

Wicksell also analyses the case with several commodities, all of which are consumption goods, where it is necessary to determine relative prices. A single commodity is produced as 'a one-way avenue' from current labour to the output. Each production process is like a completely separate and fully vertically integrated industry, i.e. 'successive stages of a single-track productive process' with no trade in half-finished machines (cp. the quotations from Sraffa above). In fact, Wicksell's notion is very much like 'Ricardo's corn-rate of profit': any consumption good could be taken as the numeraire in which to measure the wage rate (W), which is equal to the marginal productivity of current labour (L_0), and the rate of profit (π) is a pure number. The function of the relative prices is to equalize the wage rates and the rates of profit between the industries. The extra complication of relative prices does not change the exposition of our problem and a one-commodity world is therefore taken for granted.

Euler's theorem, which holds since the production function is homogenous of degree one, gives the following expression:

$$Q = L_0 \cdot W + L_1 \cdot \delta Q/\delta L_1 + L_2 \cdot \delta Q/\delta L_2$$
$$\text{where } W = \delta Q/\delta L_0$$

The terms, $\delta Q/\delta L_1$ and $\delta Q/\delta L_2$, define the *gross* profit of the economy. The value of the *net* profit (P) is found by deducting the value of the current labour necessary to reproduce the capital stock, $L_1 \cdot W = L_{01} \cdot W$ to reproduce L_1 and $L_2 \cdot W = L_{02} \cdot W$ to reproduce L_2, from the value of the total output (Q):

$$P = L_1 \cdot (\delta Q/\delta L_1 - W) + L_2 \cdot (\delta Q/\delta L_2 - W) = Q - L^* \cdot W$$

The rate of interest is determined at the margin of production – Wicksell being a true marginalist – and all capital goods must *in* equilibrium give the same uniform *rate* of profit or interest (π):

$$\pi = (\delta Q/\delta L_1 - \delta Q/L_0)/(\delta Q/\delta L_0) = (\delta Q/\delta L_2 - \delta Q/\delta L_1)/(\delta Q/\delta L_1)$$

$$\delta Q/\delta L_0 = W \Rightarrow \delta Q/\delta L_1 = (1 + \pi) \cdot W$$
$$\text{and} \quad \delta Q/\delta L_2 = (1 + \pi)^2 \cdot W$$

This expression is not true for all production functions which are homogenous of degree one, but it is enough for our purpose if a class of production functions is to exist for which the relation holds.

We follow Wicksell in assuming that the time structure or round-aboutness of production is already fixed outside the equilibrium model. The maximum length of saved-up labour or the age of the oldest machine (L_n) is decided during the process towards equilibrium. Thus, in the example above, it is taken for granted that only up to two-year-old labour is used, which implies that three-year-old machines are not productive enough:

$$(\delta Q/\delta L_3 - \delta Q/\delta L_2)/(\delta Q/\delta L_2) < \pi \Leftrightarrow \delta Q/\delta L_3 < (1 + \pi)^3 \cdot W$$

Although it is still more productive than a two-year-old machine $(\delta Q/\delta L_3 > \delta Q/\delta L_2)$ which follows from the assumption about round-aboutness of production. This is an example of the truncation problem (cp. Hicks 1983, pp. 100–1).

The following system of equations gives the necessary relations for an equilibrium:

1 $\delta Q/\delta L_0 = W$
2 $\delta Q/\delta L_1 = (1 + \pi) \cdot W$
3 $\delta Q/\delta L_2 = (1 + \pi)^2 \cdot W$
4 $L^* = L_0 + L_{01} + L_{02} = L_0 + L_1 + L_2$
5 $K^* = (1 + \pi) \cdot W \cdot L_1 + [(1 + \pi) \cdot W \cdot L_2 + (1 + \pi)^2 \cdot W \cdot L_2]$

Equations 1, 2 and 3 imply that the capital has an efficient time structure which must be true in a stationary state. Equation 4 implies full employment which is guaranteed via a flexible wage. The relation between the amounts of current labour and saved-up labour, which holds in the stationary state, is used for the second equality in equation 4. The model has five variables L_0, L_1, L_2, W and π. L_0, L_1 and L_2 represent the time structure of the production or the technical side of the problem, while W and π represent income distribution or the value side of the problem. There are only four equations so the system is underdetermined. Wicksell solves this problem by assuming that the *value* of the capital stock (K^*) is given at the beginning of the period, which is shown in equation 5, i.e. there are five equations and five endogenous variables.

Wicksell explicitly warns us that a given value of the capital stock K is only true *in* equilibrium:

In equilibrium, the capital employed in production has already assumed a certain technical dimension and composition, as well as a certain exchange value.... It can now be asserted that, so long as capital of this magnitude and composition, or even of this exchange value, is maintained and utilized from year to year, equilibrium cannot be disturbed if, from the beginning, the other conditions of stability are fulfilled. But it would clearly be meaningless – if not altogether inconceivable – to maintain that the amount of capital is already fixed *before* equilibrium between production and consumption has been achieved.

(Wicksell 1934, p. 202; original emphasis)

Hence, it is *not* implied that the value of capital is constant while the system is adjusting towards equilibrium. This problem is due to the fact that capital, even if it is regarded as 'a certain quantity of labour and land accumulated in different years' (ibid.), is not 'an *original* factor of production [like current labour and current land or "man and nature" (ibid., p. 150)] which can exist (even hypothetically) independently of, or antecedently to, production' (ibid.).

To sum up: the model provides the necessary relations between the rate of profit, the wage rate and the efficient time structure of capital for a given amount of current labour and a given value of the total capital.

BÖHM-BAWERK'S THIRD GROUND AS A SUFFICIENT CAUSE

Böhm-Bawerk's third ground for a positive rate of interest relates to the technical superiority of round-about processes of production. It was in Wicksell's view the most important one and might be a sufficient cause, a point of view which he even reiterated in his last paper which was published after his death (cp. Wicksell 1928, p. 205). In this section, we will present Wicksell's arguments for his analytical position: the choice of a stationary state, the exclusion of time preferences and the effects of a given amount of capital. The next section shows a possible formal proof.

His attempt is to exclude all references to positive time preferences, which are related to Böhm-Bawerk's first two grounds, since the major problem that presents difficulties is to explain the existence of a positive rate of interest in a *stationary* state:

The real theoretical difficulty is rather to explain how, under stationary conditions, the possession of capital can remain a permanent source of income. The application to *non-stationary* conditions offers no difficulty in principle.

(Wicksell 1934, p. 154; original emphasis)

40

This is strictly speaking not correct since positive time preferences are a sufficient cause for a positive rate of interest even in an economy without capital (cp. Samuelson 1943, p. 67), which has in fact been pointed out by Wicksell himself:

> He [Böhm-Bawerk] ... puts forward the doctrine that interest is originally an exchange phenomenon (and thus no longer exclusively the result of production and distribution) – it is the *agio* which arises in the exchange of present against future goods. This treatment may be justified, in so far as interest is undoubtedly a broader concept than productive capital itself. It can arise in a mere exchange of present against future goods or services without any intervening production and thus *without* any real accumulation of employment of capital.
>
> (Wicksell 1934, p. 169; original emphasis)

Wicksell is not completely satisfied with this explanation since the available future supply of goods is indeterminate (cp. ibid.).

Wicksell gives further reasons for his concentration on a stationary state instead of a dynamic economy. The first and second grounds may namely be very important as determinants of capital accumulation, although *the proper analytical procedure* is to start the analysis without these causes:

> these considerations play a very important role in the actual *accumulation of capital*; and in its converse, the unproductive consumption of capital, as in loans for consumption purposes. Both logically and for purposes of exposition, it would seem right to begin by examining the effects of a given supply already accumulated, and *then* to inquire the causes which influence, and eventually alter, this supply.
>
> (ibid., pp. 154–5; original emphasis)

At the same time, the first two causes are already implicitly present in the stationary case:

> In reality, the amount of capital is not determined by physical conditions, but by the equilibrium between psychical forces which, on the one hand, drive us to save and accumulate capital and, on the other, to consume already existing capital. In other words, *the accumulation of capital* is itself, even under

stationary conditions, a necessary element in the problem of production and exchange.

(ibid., pp. 202–3; cp. p. 207; original emphasis)

This does not imply that Wicksell accepts the solution put forward by Walras and endorsed by his followers Pareto and Barone:

If conditions are assumed to be *stationary*, Walras's seemingly so meaningful formula reduces itself to the simple relation $F(i) = 0$ where $F(i)$ is the total of new savings as a function of the rate of interest, i. In other words, the equation now says that under such circumstances the incentive to construction of new capital must have disappeared. This is correct, but insufficient, for we also want to know why and how a given total amount of capital warrants a certain definite rate of interest. We can find the answer to that question only by following a particular line of thought: by considering *the effect of time* on production and distribution, by considering the effect of a virtual lengthening of the production process. This is what is really new in the theory of capital, and an absolutely indispensable element of every rational theory of capital.

(Wicksell 1913, p. 172; cp. Wicksell 1934, p. 171; original emphasis)

Once again, Wicksell places the emphasis on the time element in production, which cannot be reduced to just an indirect exchange of productive services against each other and a relationship between the direct marginal utility of the service and its indirect marginal utility.

The proposition boils down to the following formulation: is Wicksell's proposition valid for a stationary economy with capital but where time preferences are neutral, that is to say is the productivity of capital a sufficient cause for a positive rate of interest under capitalistic conditions?

THE SOLUTION TO THE ENIGMA

The physical formulation of the problem has a major weakness: why does accumulation not proceed until the rate of interest or profit (π) is zero? Wicksell denotes such a situation a *technical maximum of production* (Q_{max}), which would be reached in a collectivist society. In a capitalist society where the capitalists control the accumulation

42

process it seems that this technical maximum will not be reached.

The question is situated within an analysis which is strictly comparative statics and there is no attempt to explain or describe the process between adjacent stationary states with different age structures. This analysis is possible since it is irrelevant what happens to K^*; the important relationship is not the absolute size of W and π but the signs of their changes for different age structures of the capital.

Unfortunately Wicksell gives no formal identification of the barrier for the accumulation process in a capitalist society. But he mentions that the limit to the round-aboutness of production follows from the following reason:

> What really limits the length of productive processes ... is not this [Böhm-Bawerk's first two causes], but simply the circumstance that a longer period of production, even if technically more productive, would yield to entrepreneurs ... with the available supplies of labour and capital, a smaller *profit* than the productive processes actually begun.
>
> (ibid., pp. 170–1; original emphasis)

This is an assumption that capitalists maximize net profit (P):

$$P = \sum_{t=1}^{n} L_t \cdot (\delta Q/\delta L_t - \delta Q/\delta L_0) = Q - L^* \cdot W$$

Hence, the capitalists just compare the size of the net profit (P) in different stationary states. This assumption seems more relevant than the alternative assumption that capitalists maximize the rate of profit (π), since π is a pure number, it can hardly play a role in a utility function while P is directly measured in the consumption good Q.

Wicksell makes a further strategic assumption of the nature of the accumulation process. When capital grows, while L^* is constant due to the stationary state, the following happens:

> It is the peculiarity of capital that, when it grows, it grows in height [t in L_t is increasing] as well as in breadth [more current labour is used to reproduce the capital stock], and in this there is a counter-weight to the tendency for an increase of capital to raise wages and rents.
>
> (ibid., p. 163)

This implies that growing capital will always lead to less current labour (L_0) in the production function, since $\sum_{t=1}^{n} L_t$ will always increase despite the fact that less machinery of younger ages ($L_t(t < n)$) will be used to produce Q. Growing capital means that current labour is more thinly spread in producing the consumption good and the machinery of younger ages. Capital accumulation in a Wicksellian world will always imply that machinery of an older age is being used, i.e. t in L_t must increase, since different stationary states are being compared and each stationary equilibrium already employs the optimum amount of the oldest machinery (L_n). Thus, it is never the case that accumulation will just mean that more of the oldest machinery (L_n) is being used.

The effect of the capital accumulation is the following: when output (Q) increases, the wage (W) rises and the rate of profit (π) falls since we have assumed falling marginal productivity. In the example above, capital accumulation to three-year-old machines implies that $\delta Q/\delta L_3 = (1 + \pi)^3 \cdot W$, but W is higher than before and π must therefore be lower. This is independent of what happens to K^*! It is important to notice that net profit (P) may increase even if the rate of profit (π) falls. The crucial result used below is that capital accumulation, in the sense that t in L_t increases, leads to a lower rate of profit (π).

The problem is finally to show that the technical maximum of production (Q_{max}) and the maximum amount of net profit (P_{max}) are reached for different age structures of the capital stock, i.e. for different values of t in L_t. The condition for Q_{max} is that the marginal productivity of current labour is equal to the marginal productivities of the machines:

$$\delta Q/\delta L_0 = \delta L/\delta L_t \quad t = 1, 2, \ldots, n$$
$$\Leftrightarrow \pi = 0 \Rightarrow P = \sum_{t=1}^{n} L_t \cdot (\delta Q/\delta L_t - \delta Q/\delta L_0) = 0$$

At the technical maximum (Q_{max}) the rate of profit (π) as well as the net profit (P) is equal to zero; the wage bill ($L^* \cdot W_{max}$) is equal to the whole net product, that is to say what is left of the gross product when all depreciations have been covered and the capital stock is kept intact.

The rate of profit is greater than zero ($\pi > 0$) in a stationary state where the oldest machine is younger than what is true for Q_{max}, since less capital leads to a higher rate of profit. It is obvious that in such a case net profit is above zero: $P > 0$. The exact maximum of the net profit function $(P = Q - L^* \cdot W)$ is irrelevant for our purpose; the crucial fact is that P is greater than zero before Q_{max} is reached. The final conclusion: P_{max} is certainly reached before Q_{max}, which means that the accumulation will come to a halt when the rate of profit (π) is still positive.

CONCLUSION

We have thus been able to construct a formal solution to Wicksell's proposition: the rate of interest, based only on the physical productivity of capital, can be positive in a stationary state. The solution leans heavily on certain strategic assumptions which are all clearly located within a Wicksellian framework: capital is treated as saved-up labour; the production function is homogenous of degree one with falling marginal productivities of current labour (L_0) and machines (L_t); the process of capital accumulation is characterized by less current labour being used to produce the output (Q) and the younger machines $(L_t(t < n))$.

BIBLIOGRAPHY

Hicks, John (1973) 'The Austrian Theory of Capital and its Re-birth in Modern Economics', in Hicks and Weber (eds), *Carl Menger and the Austrian School of Economics*, Oxford: Oxford University Press. As reprinted in Hicks (1983) *Classics and Moderns*, Oxford: Blackwell.

—— (1983) *Capital and Time: A Neo-Austrian Theory*, Oxford: Oxford University Press.

Samuelson, Paul (1943) 'Dynamics, Statics, and the Stationary State', *Review of Economics and Statistics*, vol. 50, pp. 58–68.

Sraffa, Piero (1960) *Production of Commodities by Means of Commodities*, Cambridge: Cambridge University Press.

Wicksell, Knut (1913) 'Vilfredo Pareto's *Cours D'Economie Politique*', review in *Zeitschrift für Volkswirtschaft, Sozialpolitik und Verwaltung*. As reprinted in Knut Wicksell (1958) *Selected Papers on Economic Theory*, London: Allen & Unwin.

—— (1919) 'Professor Cassel's System of Economics', *Ekonomisk Tidskrift*. As reprinted in Wicksell (1934).

—— (1928) 'Zur Zinstheorie', in Hans Mayer (ed.), *Die Wirtschafstheorie der Gegenwart*, vol. 3, Wien.

—— (1934) *Lectures on Political Economy*, vol. 1. London: Routledge & Sons.

4

KNUT WICKSELL ON FORESTRY: A NOTE

Torun Hedlund-Nyström, Lars Jonung, Karl-Gustaf Löfgren and Bo Sandelin

Knut Wicksell is probably Sweden's best known economist. Around the turn of the century, he provided an excellent summary of the most important contributions to economic theory during the previous decades. He left about 100 unpublished, mostly topical, manuscripts, primarily intended as contributions to the current debate in the press. This collection contains some relatively advanced works as well. A translation of one of those is published here for the first time. The Swedish original is kept in the rich Wicksell Archive in the library at the University of Lund.[1]

In this comment, we will first try to date the manuscript. Next, we will compare Wicksell's solution and the Faustmann solution to the optimal rotation problem in forestry. Following the comment, Wicksell's manuscript is presented.

DATING THE MANUSCRIPT

The manuscript was probably written no earlier than 1898 and no later than 1902. The treatment of interest, average period of investment and capital suggests that it was not written before 1898.

In the manuscript, Wicksell develops a capital model of the flow input–point output type, which among others is also found in his *Value, Capital and Rent* (1893), *Finanztheoretische Untersuchungen* (1896) and *Interest and Prices* (1898).

Except for some notes, Wicksell uses simple interest in these older works, whereas in the manuscript published here, he uses compound interest. In the older works, the average period of investment is determined as the input weighted average of the time distance between input (or costs of inputs) and output. In the stationary case of flow input–point output, where continuous input during, say, t years results in an output that is available in its entirety immediately after the t years, the average period of investment will consequently be $t/2$.

In this manuscript, the average period of investment, T, becomes approximately equal to $t/2$ only for small values of t and the rate of interest, ρ.

It should be observed that there is a rationale for this difference; the average period of investment is not independent of the choice between simple and compound interest. The following pattern of reasoning, which is implicit in Wicksell's older works, is explicit in the manuscript. The capitalized value of input costs occurring at different points of time during the process of production is equal to a given amount. The average period of investment, T, may be conceived of as a period of such length that if all input costs were capitalized over this period, the same amount would be obtained.

Adopting this reasoning, using simple interest, and denoting the annual input cost by a,

$$a \int_0^t (1 + \rho x)\,dx = at(1 + \rho T)$$

Solving this equation for T, we find

$$T = t/2$$

i.e., the average period of investment, T, is exactly equal to half the time that elapses between the beginning of the input flow and the output. Using compound interest instead, we get the following equation:

$$a \int_0^t e^{\rho x}\,dx = at\, e^{\rho T}$$

i.e.

$$\frac{e^{\rho t} - 1}{\rho t} = e^{\rho T}$$

In this case, the solution for T is more complicated,

$$T = \frac{\ln(e^{\rho t} - 1) - \ln \rho t}{\rho}$$

For positive ρ, this implies that $T > t/2$.

The discussion of the nature of capital is, perhaps, the clearest indication of a new direction. In the older works, Wicksell referred directly to Böhm-Bawerk's refined version of the old wage fund theory (although he did prefer to speak of the wage and land rent fund rather than the wage fund). Thus, in *Interest and Prices* (p. 130) he states: '*K* itself, the value of the whole of the "circulating" capital, can be regarded as the *aggregate* wages-and-rent fund, although it is not all free and liquid at any one moment, but becomes so only over a period of time' (original emphasis).

Against this background, he formulates the following equation

$$K = (A \cdot l + B \cdot r) T$$

where A is the number of workers, l the wage rate, B the amount of land, r the land rent, T the average period of investment (as defined in the older works), and K the capital, or the wage and land rent fund. In this particular case, there is an exact correspondence between the amount of capital invested during an average of T years and the sum of wages and land rent paid out during the same period of time. However, in the manuscript presented here, we find:

As regards the total stock of social capital, K, we should now be able to equate that to T years of wages and land rent, *including accrued interest on capital* [our italics], i.e.

$$K = (A \cdot l + B \cdot r) \int_0^T e^{\rho t} \, dt \ldots$$

(Note the new implication of t; here it does not denote the period of time between the first input and output.)

Given the values of A, l, B and r as well as the longest possible period of investment, the capital stock is now greater than the total wage and land rent fund, according to the analysis found in the works written between 1893 and 1898. This is partly due to the fact that capital is now assumed to increase through accrued interest, and partly to the fact that the average period of investment, according to the new definition, is somewhat longer.

Compared to the concept used in the works published before 1899, Wicksell now formally uses a modified concept of capital. However, as already suggested, he also expresses himself quite differently. The term wage fund, or wage and land rent fund is not used in the manuscript. Instead, he talks about 'the total social capital, K' and about 'K as the national wealth, or its productive part less the actual value of land, etc.'

It is therefore likely that the manuscript was written no earlier than 1898. (The preface to *Interest and Prices* is signed in January of that year.) This is, however, not quite certain.

We are, on the other hand, certain that it was written no later than 1902. The reason for this is Wicksell's claim about the production function in connection with the derivation of the equation

$$AP'_A + BP'_B = P$$

where P represents the size of the annual production, and P'_A and P'_B are the marginal products of labour and land, respectively. In two different places in the manuscript, he claims that 'this equation shows that P must be a homogeneous and linear function in A and B'.

He expresses himself similarly in an article in *Ekonomisk Tidskrift* from 1900, entitled 'Marginal Productivity as the Basis of Distribution in Economics' (translated into English and reprinted in his *Selected Papers on Economic Theory*, 1958) as well as in the first Swedish edition of the first volume of his *Lectures on Political Economy* (1901, pp. 156–7).

However, he soon realized that this claim was wrong, and devoted the article 'On the Problem of Distribution' in *Ekonomisk Tidskrift* (1902) (translated and reprinted in *Selected Papers on Economic Theory*, 1958) to an explanation of his error and a further investigation of the matter. In this article, he states (A and B are replaced by a and b):

> In the special case considered by Wicksteed and me, where production on a large scale and production on a small scale give the same return, it is easy to see that the above equation is *identically* satisfied, i.e. it is valid for all possible values of a and b. In the general case, it is only valid as a *maximum condition*. It is satisfied for those values of a and b which correspond to the most advantageous production arrangement, but not otherwise [original emphasis].

The equation may, in other words, be satisfied without P being a linearly homogeneous function. Wicksell was aware of this in 1902, and it is therefore hardly likely that the manuscript was written later than that date.

WICKSELL'S SOLUTION AND THE FAUSTMANN SOLUTION

There is another interesting aspect of the manuscript. Wicksell's analysis of the wine ageing problem in the second Swedish edition of his *Lectures*[2] is generally considered to be the closest he gets to an examination of the optimal rotation problem in forestry. The wine ageing solution,[3] where the wine is ready for sale when its relative value growth coincides with the interest rate, was known to Swedish foresters at the beginning of this century from an earlier discussion of the optimal rotation problem in Germany. The school that advocated this solution applied to forestry was called *Geldreinertrags-wirtschaft*. During the 'Swedish profitability war' in forestry 1907–13,[4] Eli F. Heckscher was a leading Swedish proponent of this school.[5]

As is now well known, Wicksell's wine ageing solution applied to foresty will result in a longer growth period than the Faustmann solution. In the manuscript presented here, on the contrary, the optimum solution is under certain conditions equivalent to the Faustmann solution, as we will now demonstrate.

In this manuscript where the model is of a flow input–point output type, Wicksell explicitly mentions forestry. His first equation (1) reads:

$$f(t) = r \frac{e^{\rho t} - 1}{\rho} \tag{1W}$$

where

$f(t)$ = the value of trees of age t on a hectare of land
r = the constant land rent to be paid each year
ρ = the rate of interest.

Wicksell maximizes the internal rate of interest.[6] It is, however, possible to show that his solution is consistent with an approach where an infinite number of rotations are considered, and where the present value is maximized.

To see this, let us first introduce Wicksell's condition for a maximum of ρ. He writes that 'one of the conditions for a maximum of ρ' is:

$$\rho = \frac{f'(t) - r}{f(t)} \qquad (2W)$$

Substituting for r, it can be transformed into:

$$f'(t) - \rho f(t) - \rho \frac{f(t)}{e^{\rho t} - 1} = 0 \qquad (2W1)$$

Let us now consider a forest where we can neglect regeneration costs, as Wicksell does, and the cost and benefits of other silvicultural measures. Given a perfect capital market with interest rate ρ, the present value PV of a hectare of forest land – the value of the capital – is equal to the sum of the infinite series

$$f(t) e^{-\rho t}, (f(t) e^{-\rho t}) e^{-\rho t}, \ldots$$

or

$$PV = \frac{f(t) e^{-\rho t}}{1 - e^{-\rho t}} = \frac{f(t)}{e^{\rho t} - 1}$$

$$\left. \right\} \qquad (1)$$

The optimal rotation period is now determined by maximizing the value of the capital with respect to t. Direct calculations show that the first-order condition

$$\frac{\partial}{\partial t} \left(\frac{f(t)}{e^{\rho t} - 1} \right) = 0 \Leftrightarrow f'(t) - \rho f(t) - \rho \frac{f(t)}{e^{\rho t} - 1} = 0 \qquad (2)$$

is satisfied if equation (2W1) holds for the given ρ.

To understand the 'dual' connection between the internal rate of return maximization at a given land rent, and the maximization of the present value of the forest capital (or the land rent = interest on the capital) at a given interest rate, let us solve the Wicksellian problem using a 'modern' approach.

Wicksell solves the problem

$$\max_{t, \rho} \rho$$

subject to

$$\frac{\rho f(t)}{e^{\rho t} - 1} - r = 0$$

The Lagrangian is

$$L = \rho + \mu \left(\frac{\rho f(t)}{e^{\rho t} - 1} - r \right)$$

and the first-order conditions (given $\rho \neq 0$) are:

(i) $\dfrac{1}{\rho} \dfrac{\partial L}{\partial t} = \mu [f'(t) - \rho f(t) - \rho PV(\rho, t)](e^{\rho t} - 1)^{-1} = 0$

(ii) $\dfrac{\partial L}{\partial \mu} = \rho PV(\rho, t) - r = 0$

(iii) $\dfrac{\partial L}{\partial \rho} = 1 + \mu [f(t)(e^{\rho t} - 1) - \rho t\, e^{\rho t} f(t)](e^{\rho t} - 1)^{-2} = 0$

Equation (i) is, for any given ρ, the equivalent to the Faustmann–Pressler–Ohlin (FPO) theorem[7] (equation 2 above). At the optimal rotation age, the rate of change in the stand value with respect to time is equal to the interest on the value of the stand plus the interest on the value of the forest land. By using (ii) to solve ρ as a function of t and r, $\rho(t, r)$, one can after direct substitution into (i) solve for the rotation period, which maximizes the 'yield energy' as Wicksell would have expressed it. Finally, μ, the increase in the 'yield energy' from a decreased land rent, follows from equation (iii) as soon as the optimal values of ρ, and t are known.

A perfect market for land would force the person who rents the land to choose an optimal rotation period, since competitive bidding would result in a land rent, r^*, that solves

$$r^* = \frac{\max}{t} \frac{\rho f(t)}{e^{\rho t} - 1} = \rho \frac{\max}{t} PV(\rho; t) \qquad (3)$$

which, since it maximizes the interest on the capital at a given interest rate, gives the same rotation period as the one which maximizes the value of the capital.[8]

Putting $r = r^*$ in the Wicksellian optimization problem, that problem is obviously solved by an internal rate of interest equal to the market rate of interest, and the Wicksellian optimal rotation period will coincide with the FPO-rotation period.

Wicksell would not himself have chosen a Lagrangian technique to solve his problem, although the Lagrange method had already been developed in the eighteenth century. He would probably have used the constraint (ii), i.e. (1W), to establish the existence of a function $\rho = \rho(t, r)$ and used the fact that at the optimal[9] t,

$$\frac{\partial \rho}{\partial t}(\cdot) = 0$$

By differentiating the constraint totally with respect to ρ and t and solving for

$$\frac{\partial \rho}{\partial t} = 0$$

he would end up with an expression analogous to (i), 2W, which together with the constraint could be used to determine ρ and t. The details are left to the reader.

CONCLUSIONS

The manuscript is interesting not because of its revelation of some hitherto unknown results in capital theory, but because of the fact that it was written during a period of, if not upheaval, then at least modification in Wicksell's approach to capital theory. It may be seen as a link between his approach in the works from the 1890s and that used in the second edition of his *Lectures* and later.

We recognize the foundation – a model of the flow input–point output type – from his earlier works. The change in the treatment of capital, the average period of investment and the rate of interest is, nevertheless, an indication of a more modern approach.

It is also interesting to note that forestry on valuable land serves as his example, and that, as a result of the approach adopted, he arrives at the correct optimum condition for the rotation period in an area in which many prominent economists have stumbled. For details see Samuelson (1976).

The manuscript, which is not signed, is handwritten and full of revisions and additions. In the middle of the manuscript, Wicksell seems to start from the beginning again, repeating the preceding analysis. Maybe, he was not content with the first formulation and wished to replace it? Anyhow, this accentuates the preliminary character of the manuscript. Wicksell himself would probably not have had it printed without a thorough revision. It finishes in the middle of a sentence.

In which context was this manuscript written? We have found no answer to this question. Contextually, it might fit into volume 1 of his *Lectures*, in the section on capitalistic production. The first lines suggest that it was intended as a part of something. Could it be that Wicksell originally meant it to be included in the first edition of his *Lectures*, but changed his mind, because he found it too difficult for the students? The famous wine example was introduced in a formal model of the point input–point output type in the second edition in 1911. The analysis there is at approximately the same level of technical difficulty. This suggests that he might previously have thought of including something similar.

In conclusion, the manuscript combines some of Wicksell's older approaches with some of his newer. The former are represented by the choice of a problem of the flow input–point output type, as well as by the structure of the system of equations used. The latter are represented by his treatment of capital, interest and the average period of investment. The manuscript may thus be viewed as a link in the development of his theory of capital. This link should, in turn, be seen as an indication of the fact that the development was a continuous process.

NOTES

1   It was presented in Swedish in the *Ekonomiska Samfundets Tidskrift*, nos. 3 and 4, 1987, see Wicksell (1987).
2   Published in 1911.
3   The wine ageing solution was known to Wicksell from Jevons. See *Lectures*, part I.
4   The dating is somewhat arbitrary, based on an early article by Uno Wallmo (1907), which started the debate in Sweden, and a late article by Tor Jonsson published in 1913.
5   Heckscher actively participated in the annual discussions at the Society for Foresters. He also published a paper in *Ekonomisk Tidskrift* in 1912 on forestry; see Heckscher (1912). It is not unlikely that Heckscher was inspired by Wicksell rather than by the German discussion.
6   The assumption that entrepreneurs maximize the internal rate of interest is not unique to the manuscript under consideration. It appears in all Wicksell's major works on capital theory, from *Kapitalzins und Arbeitslohn* (1892) to *Real Capital and Interest* (1923) (included in the

English edition of *Lectures* I), usually alternatively with maximization of the wage rate.
7 See Johansson and Löfgren (1985) and Löfgren (1983).
8 See Samuelson (1976) and Johansson and Löfgren (1985) on the generation of the FPO first-order condition.
9 'When ρ reaches its maximum, it behaves as a constant' (*Lectures*, p. 278; cf. *Value, Capital and Rent*, p. 123).

SELECT BIBLIOGRAPHY

Heckscher, E.F. (1912) 'Skogsbrukets räntabilitet' ('The Profitability of Forestry'), *Ekonomisk Tidskrift*, pp. 139ff and 253ff.
Johansson, P.O. and Löfgren, K.G. (1985) *The Economics of Forestry and Natural Resources*, Oxford: Blackwell.
Jonsson, T.C. (1913) 'Omloppstidens inverkan på skogsbrukets ekonomi' ('The Influence of the Rotation Period on the Profitability of Forestry'), *Svenska skogsvårdsföreningens tidskrift*, 11, 69–112.
Löfgren, K.G. (1983) 'The Faustmann–Ohlin Theorem: A Historical Note', *History of Political Economy*, 15, 261–4.
Samuelson, P.A. (1976) 'Economics of Forestry in an Evolving Society', *Economic Inquiry*, 14, 466–92.
Wallmo, U. (1907) 'Uthålligt skogsbruk' ('Sustainable Forestry'), *Svenska Skogsvårdsföreningens tidskrift*, 5, 305–24.
Wicksell, K. (1892) 'Kapitalzins und Arbeitslohn', *Jahrbücher für National-ökonomie und Statistik*.
—— (1893, translated 1954) *Value, Capital and Rent*, London: Allen & Unwin.
—— (1902) 'Till fördelningsproblemet' ('On the Distribution Problem'), *Ekonomisk Tidskrift*, 3.
—— (2nd edn 1911, 3rd edn translated 1934) *Lectures on Political Economy. Vol. I: General Theory* L. Robbins (ed.) (London).
—— (1958) *Selected Papers on Economic Theory*, edited with an Introduction by Erik Lindahl, London: Allen & Unwin.
—— (1987) 'Ett opublicerat manuskript av Knut Wicksell' ('An Unpublished Manuscript by Knut Wicksell'), *Ekonomiska Samfundets tidskrift*, no. 3, pp. 123–36, with a foreword by T. Hedlund-Nyström, Lars Jonung and Bo Sandelin. Errata are corrected in no. 4, 221.

APPENDIX: AN UNPUBLISHED MANUSCRIPT BY KNUT WICKSELL

Proceeding to the general problem of production, we shall now deal with a case in which productive power, although still of only one kind, is applied *repeatedly* during the same period of production in a technically (or naturally) predetermined order. *Forestry*, on *valuable* land, will serve as our example. Let us assume that a certain individual, or firm, holds the right of disposal of a piece of forest land for an unlimited amount of time, for which a certain annual rent per acre, r, must be paid. If, for the sake of simplicity, the amount of labour that must be spent on the maintenance of the forest is ignored, the annual land rent will represent the firm's sole capital outlay. Consequently the sole objective of the firm will be to find the forest rotation time that will maximize the return on its capital. If we call the value of one acre of t-year-old standing forest $f(t)$, the following equation may easily be derived:

$$f(t) = r \frac{e^{\rho t} - 1}{\rho} \tag{1}$$

where ρ represents the so-called 'yield energy' (i.e. the continuously compounded rate of interest) together with one of the conditions for a maximum of ρ, namely

$$\rho = \frac{f'(t) - r}{f(t)} \tag{2}$$

from which the most advantageous value of t is obtained through the elimination of ρ.

The problem may, however, be seen from a different angle: if the entire forest area amounts to B acres, the annual felled area (by continuous land utilization) will amount to $B : t$, while $B \cdot f(t) : t$ will constitute the value of annual production. The firm must, on the other hand, pay an annual land rent amounting to $B \cdot r$. The former of these quantities may be seen as the result of the latter, capitalized over a certain period of time, T, where T represents the average (economic) age of the forest as defined by

$$B \cdot \frac{f(t)}{t} = B \cdot r \cdot e^{\rho T}$$

or using (1)

$$e^{\rho T} = \frac{e^{\rho t} - 1}{\rho t} \tag{3}$$

By eliminating ρ between this equation and (1), T may be derived as a function of t alone, or conversely, t as a function of T. It is thus possible to view the annual production per acre as capitalized over this particular period of time through

$$P = (Al + Br)\, e^{\rho T} \tag{1}$$

where P denotes the size of the annual production, and the remaining symbols the quantities mentioned above. A and B represent the available amounts of labour and land which, for the time being, we shall consider to be constant. All other quantities are variable, *although not mutually independent*. Once the general conditions of production, the technological level of the society in question, and the level of its capital power, or what ultimately amounts to the same, the individual's ability and inclination to save is given, the above-mentioned quantities will also be determined (although not always *unambiguously*). Any one of these quantities may, in other words, be used as an independent variable. The entire social production situation will, therefore, be determined the moment this variable assumes a certain value. Thus it must be possible to express all other quantities (except A and B) as functions of T, if we select T as our independent variable. It should certainly be possible to write P as an explicit function in T alone. Of course, P is also a function of A and B. Accordingly:

$$P = F(A, B, T)$$

Equation (1) above should, of course, not be seen as an identity. The expression on its left-hand side must be thought of as a known function of A, B and T alone, while that on its right-hand side is a function of l, r and ρ as well. Equality is not obtained until l, r and ρ assume the values assigned to them by the economic equilibrium values for A, B, and T respectively. If T is changed, equality will not be obtained unless l, r and ρ change correspondingly at the same time.

The following conditions must be met if the above equation is to characterize economic equilibrium. No single entrepreneur, or group of entrepreneurs, whether workers, land-owners or capitalists, will be capable of altering the production situation to his or their advantage (unless they all stick together, in which case free competition ceases), since each of the quantities l, r and ρ now has its greatest value with both of the other quantities at constant values. Nor should it be possible for an entrepreneur who does not belong to any of the above-mentioned categories and who consequently must pay for the use of labour, land and capital at the going market prices, to gain any profit from an increase (or a reduction) of the amounts of labour, land or capital used in his firm.

Such a change would, however, to the extent it were possible, *ceteris paribus* imply a small increase (or reduction) of A, B or T (or of two, or all three of these quantities simultaneously) and thus also a small variation δP of the annual production P. Since this does not provide the entrepreneur with any profit (nor, with caution, with any loss), it must be of the exact same magnitude as the change occurring on the *right*-hand side of equation (1), since changes in the amounts used of labour, land and capital must be paid for at going market prices.

In other words, it must be possible to differentiate equation (1) with respect to A, B or T, while l, r and ρ are regarded as constants (or what amounts to the same thing: while two of them are regarded as constants, and the third as having reached its maximum value, at which point its variation, or first derivative = 0). Differentiating, we obtain

$$P'_A = l \cdot e^{\rho T} \tag{2}$$

$$P'_B = r \cdot e^{\rho T} \tag{3}$$

and

$$P'_T = \rho \cdot P \tag{4}$$

The third equation is Jevon's interest formula, which states that the rate of interest (based on time units) is equal to the relative change in annual production, when the average investment period is extended or shortened by one unit of time (actually $\rho \, dt = P' dt : P$). The first and the second equations state that wages and land rent, respectively, are equal to the annual production increase that would have come about as a result of an increase of one unit of labour or land *T years ago, discounted* over this time period by an interest rate of ρ. In other words, the production increase will be equal to that which a worker, or owner of one unit of land would have received, had he *waited* for his compensation for a period of T years. Multiplying equations (2) and (3) by A and B, respectively, and adding the terms, we obtain

$$AP'_A + BP'_B = P$$

which shows that P must be a homogeneous and linear function in A and B, but not in T. This is of course obvious since our argument actually presupposes the relative outcome of total social production to be independent of its volume *at every level of capital intensity*, which – as we have already seen – is a condition for total economic equilibrium.

As regards the total social stock of capital, K, we should now be able to equate that to T years of wages and land rent, including accrued interest on capital, i.e.

$$K = (Al + Br) \int_0^T e^{\rho t}\, dt = \frac{P - (Al + Br)}{\rho} \tag{5}$$

or

$$\rho \cdot K = P - (Al + Br)$$

This must necessarily hold, since one year's interest on the *entire* stock of capital will (under stationary conditions) be equal to the entire annual production less wages and land rent paid out *during the same year*.

The practical implication of this argument (if, indeed, there is one) should be that it enables us to investigate *the nature of the social productivity function*, P, using statistical data, related to population, labour, production and banking. Most of the quantities we have dealt with as being 'unknown', l, r, ρ (or i) etc., may – more or less approximately – be derived from statistical information. This is also the case when we deal with P, which represents the total national income. K represents the national wealth, or its productive part, less the actual value of land, etc. T is a mere conceptual magnitude, or rather, a mathematical magnitude (which does not prevent it from always having a certain computable value). Little is known about the *functional form*, P: although we do know that it grows with A, B and T (or K), we know little about how, or by which laws it grows. Assuming production without capital, we may give it the following (provisional) form:

$$P = kA^{\alpha} \cdot B^{\beta},$$

59

where k is a constant and α and β are fractional exponents, the sum of which must be 1. The conditions of capitalistic production require the addition of in all cases a new factor, a function in T, the general characteristics of which should be that it grows more slowly than a geometric progression, as T grows arithmetically. Tentatively, we might have

$$P = k \cdot A^\alpha \cdot B^\beta \cdot e^{k_1(T^\tau)}$$

where k_1 is a new constant and τ a new, fractional exponent which, however, in no way is related to α or β. If the *real* functional forms were that simple (and the remaining conditions approximately met), statistical observations for one single year would suffice to determine that the four constants (as well as T) by means of equations (1)–(5). It hardly needs saying that, even under the most advantageous conditions, it is a great deal more complex than that.

However simple or complex it may be, it is to the study of this functional form that the disciplines of Economics and Statistics must devote themselves, if they are to accomplish anything at all. Therein lies the answer, from an economic point of view, to most of society's problems, and certainly to the great and important population problem – although the latter has yet to be recognized as such.

[Here Wicksell recommences]

$$t \cdot L \cdot e^{\rho T} = L \int_0^t e^{\rho t} dt \quad \text{or} \quad e^{\rho T} = \frac{e^{\rho t} - 1}{\rho(t)}$$

An expansion of the exponential function gives us

$$T + \rho \frac{T^2}{2} \cdots = \frac{t}{2} + \rho \frac{t^2}{6}$$

so that for small values of ρ and not too great values of t, T becomes approximately equal to $t/2$, i.e. independent of ρ.*

If we invest a certain amount of capital (in the form of labour, land or both) in a durable object, such as a home, a boat etc., which during T years continuously yields a series of utility effects at an

---

*This is also *generally* valid if, like Böhm-Bawerk, we use simple interest; however, only in this particular case, and not in the following.

annual value of a (i.e. $a \cdot dt$ under each moment of time) the rate of interest ('yield energy') may be derived from the following equation:

$$K = a \int_0^t e^{-\rho t} \, dt = a \frac{1 - e^{-\rho t}}{\rho}$$

Subsequently, we may derive the average period of investment, T, from

$$t \cdot a = K e^{\rho T}$$

which states that our capital would have achieved the same rate of interest, had the total production outcome, $t \cdot a$, been sold at T. By elimination of K (and thus also of a) and by expanding the exponential functions, we obtain

$$T - \rho \frac{T^2}{2} \cdots = \frac{t}{2} - \rho \frac{t^2}{6} + \cdots$$

so that, once again, sufficiently small values of ρ and t render T equal to $t/2$, i.e. independent of ρ.

The average period of investment, T, is, as mentioned before, more or less dependent upon ρ, the rate of interest obtained in economic equilibrium. It is also greatly dependent upon the relative sizes of wages and rent: if, for instance, a certain amount of labour and land were invested in and for the same production, but at different points in time, the average investment period would depend upon the relative sizes of wages and land rent. However, it should be possible to temporarily *define* our T in such a way that the exchange value of the annual production outcome amounts to the sum of wages and land rent paid out during one year, as a known function in T, $\phi(T)$. Thus we may write

$$\phi(T) - \frac{f(t)}{t} = r e^{\rho T} \tag{3}$$

The maximum value of ρ obtained from this is

$$\rho = \frac{\phi'(T)}{\phi(T)} \tag{4}$$

which is *formally* independent of *r* and naturally must correspond with the value obtained from equation (2), as can easily be seen. If, on the other hand, we let ρ be known and *r* unknown (assuming that the *land-owner* borrows and consumes an annual amount, *r*, which he subsequently repays with compounded interest at some previously agreed upon rate by felling), the most advantageous value of *t* or *T* (i.e. that which maximizes *r*) may be obtained from exactly the same equations. Finally, if we let both *r* and ρ be determined by the common quest for the greatest possible profit, i.e. assuming perfect competition, while the value of the available *capital* intended for forestry, or what amounts to the same thing, the time periods *t* and *T*, assume a constant value, the mathematical solution to the problem will, obviously, still be found in equations (3) and (4), or (1) and (2).

However, in the latter case, we might also have viewed the size of the total annual production, *P*, as a function of the total land area used for forestry, *B*, and written

$$P = F(B, \ T) = B \cdot \phi(T) = Br \ e^{\rho t}$$

Partial differentiation with respect to *B* gives us

$$P'_B = \frac{d}{dB} F(B, \ T) = \phi(T) = r \ e^{\rho T}, \quad \text{or} \quad r = P'_B \cdot e^{-\rho T}$$

so that the land rent for one acre of land becomes the partial derivative of the annual production with respect to the size of the land area, discounted over time period *T* by the rate of interest ('yield energy') ρ. In other words, this partial derivative becomes the land-owner's compensation for *waiting* during period *T* (i.e. *not* during period *t*).

It now becomes quite easy to approach the general problem in which there are different kinds of primary productive forces (land and labour – in reality, a great number of different kinds of labour and land which do not compete directly with each other), and in which the sequence of their application is not always technically determined, but may vary occasionally for economic reasons as well. Let us write

$$P = (A \cdot l + B \cdot r) \ e^{T\rho} \tag{1}$$

where P represents the size of society's total annual production, A the (annual) total available amount of labour, l wages, and the remaining symbols, the quantities mentioned above. T, which now represents the average period of investment for one year's wages *and* land rent, is now – precisely as before – a purely mathematical (or economic) concept, the *definition* of which should be sought in the equation above. We may, nevertheless, choose to view this T as an *independent variable*; the entire production situation becomes fixed and determined the moment that it is assigned a certain value. All of the relevant quantities (except A and B) are, in other words, functions of T. This is true of P as well; the size of the annual production may be seen as a function of T alone, along with A and B, the moment the technical conditions of production are given. Let us therefore write

$$P = F(A, B, T)$$

through which equation (1) above becomes identically solved, the moment l, r and ρ obtain their appropriate values expressed in T (as well as in A and B).

However, it should also be possible to partially differentiate this equation with respect to A, B or T, *with l, r and ρ treated as constants.*

This is merely a statement of the fact that in economic equilibrium, no single entrepreneur, whether he is a worker, land-owner or capitalist, is capable of altering the production situation to his advantage or, put differently, no entrepreneur as such is capable of achieving any profit (nor should he, if cautious, suffer any loss) by increasing, or reducing the amounts of labour, or land used by him, or the capital investment period which, *ceteris paribus*, would imply a small change in A, B or T. (The individual production and investment periods are the same for everyone, if the production involves only one good, and will naturally vary, if more than one good is produced; however, a change in one of them must, in any case, result in a change in T.)

Carrying out the differentiation, we obtain

$$P'_A = l \cdot e^{\rho T} \tag{2}$$

$$P'_B = r \cdot e^{\rho T} \tag{3}$$

and finally

$$P'_T = \rho \cdot P, \quad \text{or} \quad \rho = \frac{P'_T}{P} \tag{4}$$

Obviously, the last equation is Jevon's interest formula as applied to the average time, T. The two preceding equations state that the conditions pertaining to wages and land rent are the same as those previously found for land rent alone. By multiplying these equations with A and B respectively, we may then add the two and obtain

$$A \cdot P'_A + B \cdot P'_B = P$$

which shows that P must be a homogeneous and linear function in A and B (but not in T). This should actually be obvious, since we assume that similar increases of the amounts of labour and land will result in purely proportional increases of P at any given value of T, or level of capitalistic production; this, as we have already seen, is one of the fundamental conditions for economic equilibrium.

It should now be possible to express the size of the entire social capital, K, as the sum of T years of wages and land rent, including accrued interest on capital, i.e.

$$K = (Al + Br) \int_0^T e^{\rho t} \, dt = (Al + Br) \frac{e^{\rho T} - 1}{\rho}$$

or

$$\rho \cdot K = P - (Al + Br) \tag{5}$$

since, after wages and land rent have been paid out and assuming stationary conditions, the surplus from the annual production must constitute one year's interest on the entire capital. In other words, if K is known, or assumed to be an independent variable, everything else may be expressed as functions of A, B or K (although these will be more complex than those shown above).

The productivity function $P = F(A, B, T)$ has, assuming production *without capital* (i.e. $T = 0$), been given the following tentative form:

$$P = kA^\alpha \cdot B^\beta; \quad \alpha + \beta = 1,$$

where k is a constant and α and β are two fractional exponents, the sum of which must be 1; the latter to indicate that production increases with both A and B and that large- or small-scale production (in *relative* terms) is equally profitable. Returning to capitalistic production, we must – in all cases – include a new function which depends on the time, T, the general nature of which is dictated by the above-mentioned fact that production, generally, must grow less than geometrically as the length of the investment period grows arithmetically. This condition is met, when we write

$$P = kA^{\alpha} \cdot B^{\beta} \cdot e^{k_1 T^{\tau}}$$

where k_1 is a new constant and τ is a similarly fractional exponent of T, and where the sum of α and β must still be 1.

If the function really were as simple as this, one single year's statistical observations of wages, land rent and interest on capital as well as the numerical value of P, which is equal to the national income, would suffice to determine, using equations (1)–(4), the four constants k, k_1, α (or β) and τ, including T (assuming, of course, that the remaining conditions relevant to this problem, i.e. a stationary state and goods production at predetermined prices, were approximately met). A further verification is possible through equation (5), the left-hand side of which may be obtained by estimating the size of the total social capital, i.e. the total national wealth, or its productive part less the actual value of land.

It hardly needs saying that the function P actually must be a great deal more complex, and that the expressions suggested here should be seen as nothing more than the first of an entire series of similar terms, each containing new constants. However, a closer study should, of course, not be considered to be futile. It may, for instance, be undertaken in a country with a relatively small number of essential industries – like our own.

Now that A and B are assumed to be given, the nature of the problem allows us to select one of the remaining quantities as our independent variable. If we choose T, all other quantities, including P, become functions of T. Furthermore [manuscript ends].

[The Wicksell manuscript is translated from the Swedish by Henrik Lutzen with financial support from the Gothenburg Business School Foundation.]

5

THE SWEDISH ECONOMISTS, THE LABOUR MOVEMENT AND THE 8-HOUR DAY*

Marianne Sundström

The view that reductions in working hours are an efficient means of reducing unemployment seems to have as many lives as a cat. Although repeatedly refuted, it pops up again and again. The trade unions of the European Community (ETUI 1979) and the Nobel laureate Wassily Leontief (1979, 1982) have been eager proponents of this policy proposal. In Sweden, however, it has never won many adherents either among trade unions, academic economists or in the public opinion. In this chapter, I argue that the clearsightedness of Swedish unions may to some extent be attributable to the thorough analysis of this issue by Swedish economists, to their view of the causes of unemployment and to the fruitful intellectual exchange between academic economists and labour leaders. Extending over the period 1889–1935, this chapter starts with an account of the early labour movement's demand for the 8-hour working day and the criticism of the demand delivered by Knut Wicksell. The actual reductions in working hours that took place during the period, including the introduction of the 8-hour day, are then discussed. Next, the analyses by Swedish economists of the effects of the 48-hour week are presented. Finally, I discuss why the Swedish unions did not embrace reduced working hours as a remedy against unemployment.

KNUT WICKSELL AND THE CAMPAIGN FOR THE 8-HOUR DAY

In 1891 the average working week in the Swedish engineering industry exceeded 62 hours and was even longer among domestic and farm workers (Johansson 1977, p. 144). Reduced working hours, thus, became the principal demand of the rising Swedish labour movement since it was considered a necessary means to achieve goals such as higher wages and universal suffrage. As a similar situation prevailed in other industrializing countries, the demand for the 8-hour working day was put at the top of the agenda at the founding of the Second Socialist International in 1889.[1] Moreover, the first of May was selected as a workers' international holiday to campaign for this goal and in the following years large May Day demonstrations were held all over the world, including Sweden. This great involvement of the international labour movement attracted the interest to Brentano (1891) and Schäffle (1890, 1891) on the continent, and in Sweden that of Knut Wicksell.

Returning to Sweden from studies abroad in 1890, Wicksell gave lectures in Malmö and Stockholm in which he took up the issue with the labour movement. As he criticized and opposed the 8-hour day, his talk caused dismay among the audience.[2] Wicksell's behaviour on this point may serve as a good example of his total lack of opportunism; he even ventured to deliver his critique of the demand as a speaker at the May Day meetings in Stockholm in 1892 and 1893, which deprived him of the little popularity he enjoyed among Stockholm workers (Gårdlund 1956, p. 153). In the years to come, his position on this issue was to bring about his alienation from the labour movement.

Wicksell developed his view on the 8-hour day in the completed but unpublished manuscript *Normalarbetsdag* (*The Standard Working Day*) (1892). In principle, he concurred with the labour movement on the desirability of reduced working hours, but found such a large reduction unfeasible at the time (p. 5); the size of the cut in hours would be conditional on the rate of growth in labour productivity (p. 33) and exchangeable for improvements in wages or other working conditions (p. 28). In particular, he opposed the idea of reduced working hours as the way to improve workers' living conditions in the long run. Instead Wicksell, as a neo-Malthusian, believed that workers' living standards could only be permanently raised through extensive use of birth-control measures, and his attack on the labour movement was essentially motivated by his fear that the 8-hour demand would divert labour's interest from this issue (Gårdlund 1956, pp. 152–3), His deep commitment to the campaign for population control originated partly in his alarm at the rapid rate of population growth[3] with accompanying high levels of poverty in nineteenth-century Sweden, and partly in his highly pessimistic view on the chances of future productivity increases to keep up with population growth. His treatment of the effects of reduced working hours was, however, advanced and clearsighted. In particular, I would like to draw attention to his analysis of three problems, which are also central to the contemporary debate on reduced hours.

First, there is the issue of how productivity and total production is affected by a reduction in working hours. Will productivity: (i) increase in proportion to the cut in hours; (ii) increase but less than the cut in hours: (iii) be unaffected; or will it (iv) decrease? In modern terminology, outcomes (i) and (ii) imply decreasing returns to hours of work; the elasticity of hours with respect to output being zero in case (i) and less than one in case (ii); while in case (iii) we have constant returns to hours, i.e. the elasticity of hours with respect to output being equal to one; and if (iv) is the case, returns to hours are increasing and the elasticity of hours is greater than one.[4] Whereas the most eager proponents of the 8-hour day maintained that (i) would be the outcome, Wicksell argued that (ii) was the most likely result and that positive productivity changes were more likely if the working day had previously been very long (p. 11). In particular, he pointed to the inconsistency in claiming both that (i) would be the outcome of a cut in hours and that a law was necessary to initiate the 8-hour day (p. 16). If a cut in hours would raise productivity to the extent that total production remained constant, it could only be, argued Wicksell ironically, prejudice or ill-will that prevented employers from having a benefit which did not harm them in the least (p. 10). Hence, if case (i) prevailed, competition between employers would ensure a reduction in hours. Today there is unanimity among researchers that the effect on productivity of reduced working hours would be greater, the longer the working week prior to reductions.[5] Moreover, empirical research from our days points to the limited positive or zero effect of reduced hours on productivity, i.e. the elasticity of hours with respect to output is close to or slightly below one.[6]

Second, Wicksell argued against the belief held by parts of the labour movement that reduced working hours was an efficient means to raise wages; the argument being that as the supply of labour was reduced, its price would increase (p. 21). Instead, Wicksell demonstrated with an example from agriculture (p. 24), that if the reduction in hours was not counterbalanced by increased productivity, total production would fall and even if hourly wages rose, this rise would fall short of the cut in hours. Consequently, weekly wages were likely to decrease and, thus, even if labour's share of national income was to increase, its absolute size would shrink (p. 22). Wicksell pointed out that the popularity of the 8-hour day was based on the delusion, not refuted thoroughly enough by economists, that reduced hours would increase both employment and wages at the same time (p. 2).

Third, he argued against the view that the introduction of labour-saving machinery would give rise to a stock of redundant labour (p. 31) that could be decreased through a reduction in working hours.[7] The oft-heard statement that the long working hours which ten workers now endure deprive the eleventh worker of a job is untrue, Wicksell observed. On the contrary, the long working hours of the ten workers is the cause of the eleventh getting work and bread at all. Moreover, he maintained that the savings which arise in consumption through the introduction of machinery must create new jobs elsewhere in the economy in sufficient numbers to absorb redundant labour. To the question, which was often posed, whether the European industry of the time would be able to employ more workers without machinery, he replied that the only correct answer could be that without machinery, industry would not exist to any extent similar to that of the day and it would certainly not be able to employ the same number of workers, far less employ more workers.

REDUCTIONS IN WORKING HOURS IN 1890–1918

The intense campaign for the 8-hour day and the large May Day demonstrations brought about an upswing for the labour movement in the early 1890s, which in the mid-1890s was turned into its opposite; disruption, stagnation and passivity (Lindgren 1938, p. 85). In spite of its being pushed to the forefront, the demand for the 8-hour day was not to be realized for a long time.

At its congress in 1897, the Swedish Metalworkers' Union demanded a clearer definition of overtime work and restrictions on the length of the working day on weekdays from the usual 11 hours (shorter on Saturdays) to a maximum of 10 hours as well as higher wages. Standardization of the working week, i.e. reductions in the differences in length of the working week among firms across the country, was also emphasized (Johansson 1977, p. 12). While their wage demands were partly successful in the local collective bargaining during 1898–9, their success was limited when it came to overtime and reduced hours; only in certain cases, when the working week exceeded 60 hours, was it reduced. Under the influence of this partial success, the Metalworkers' Union in 1899 revised its demand to a 54-hour working week. However, in the following years, the demand met with greater resistance from employers and it was not until the central wage agreement of 1905 that weekly hours were reduced to 57, 10 hours on weekdays and 7 hours on Saturdays (op. cit., pp. 25–32).

As there were almost no changes in working hours from 1905 to 1917, the labour movement in 1917 had obtained a standard working day, not of 8 hours but of 10 hours. In fact, most of the major modern engineering workshops had already reduced their working week to 57–60 hours in the early 1890s and consequently had a working day on weekdays of the same length in 1917 as in 1891 (op. cit., p. 32).

During the First World War, food shortage brought about a rapid rise in prices, which was followed by local labour disputes all over the country, since wages did not keep up with prices. Through widespread discontent, social unrest and riots, Sweden was brought to the verge of revolution. In 1917 a coalition government of Liberals and Social Democrats came to power, undertaking to carry through both the 8-hour day and universal suffrage. Hence, instead of a revolution, Sweden got an official government committee on working hours in the autumn of 1918. Meanwhile, the negotiating parties on the labour market, expecting hours to be reduced, entered into a one-year agreement on reducing the standard working week from 57 to 52 hours at the end of 1918 (op. cit., p. 20).

THE INTRODUCTION OF THE 8-HOUR DAY

The Committee on Working Hours had worked less than a year when in August 1919, it proposed a law on a 48-hour working week to apply from 1 January 1920.[8] As soon as the proposal was presented, the Metalworkers' Union demanded higher hourly wages in compensation for the reduced hours, which led to central negotiations between the union and the Engineering Industries Employers' Association. The negotiations continued into 1920 but were broken by industrial conflict, which resulted in a special agreement on the 48-hours' law with a certain amount of compensation for the reduction in hours.[9] However, in the autumn of 1920, Swedish manufacturing industry was hit by the world depression which deepened in the course of 1921 and led to demands from employers on wage concessions. In the following year, nominal wages were reduced by 4o per cent on average and it was not until the recovery in 1924 that conditions returned to normal in manufacturing industry.

During the period from Wicksell's 1892 paper to the appointment of the Committee on Working Hours, reductions in working hours were little discussed by Swedish economists. When the 8-hour day was in sight (March 1919), Gösta Bagge (see Chapter 7 by Wadensjö in this volume) held a lecture at the Swedish Technologist Association in which he delivered a discerning theoretical analysis of the effects of the 8-hour day. On the issue of how productivity, hourly wages and weekly wages would be affected he took the same position as Wicksell. The lecture is notable for its comprehensive account of factors determining the effects on production of a reduction in working hours (with increasing hourly wages), namely: (a) the size of productivity increases; (b) labour's share of total production costs; (c) the possibility of shifting rising labour costs to consumers through higher prices, i.e. the price elasticity of consumer demand; (d) the degree of substitutability between capital and labour; and (e) the extent to which capacity utilization could be increased through introduction of shiftwork.[10] As these factors vary across industries, the impact of the 8-hour day will differ from industry to industry. Hence, the changes and adjustment within and between firms and industries will be of considerable proportions, albeit temporary. Hence, according to Bagge quite a long period of transition was necessary when introducing the 8-hour day. Regarding the non-temporary effects on national income and real wages, Bagge concluded that the most significant factors were the size of productivity increases and the extent of improved capacity utilization (factors a and e).

In August the same year, Wicksell expressed the same view on the 8-hour day as he had previously done in the unpublished *Arbetarfrågen* (*The Worker Question*) and argued that the bill was ill-timed since the uncertain economic prospects made the time unsuitable for social experiments. Moreover, he suggested that workers in certain occupations should be given guarantees against income losses in case they could not attain a sustainable wage at a 48-hour working week.

SWEDISH ECONOMISTS ON THE EFFECTS OF
THE 48-HOUR WEEK

When the Bill on the 8-hour day had been passed, Wicksell commented on it in *8-Timmarsdagen* (*The 8-Hour Day*) (1920). While still wishing to postpone the law's coming into force, he launched the idea of disarmament as a way to compensate workers for the expected fall in earnings as hours were reduced. Evidently, he had great faith in the then recently founded League of Nations, since he believed that Swedish membership would make disarmament possible. Further, his polemics against the view that the 8-hour day would cause inflation bear witness to the differences that exist between contemporary society and economic thought and that of Wicksell's day. Wicksell maintained that even though a shortage of goods could be expected, a productivity increase would not suffice to offset the cut in hours. A shortage would not necessarily lead to higher prices. It might be the case that goods prices remain constant while nominal wages decrease, since the Central Bank determines whether or not there will be inflation.

Criticizing the Committee on Working Hours for using legislation to enforce increases in hourly wages of 17 per cent, Brisman (1921) manifested a highly 'dismal' view of the likely effects on wages and productivity of the 8-hour day.[11] Contrary to Wicksell and Bagge, he ruled out the possibility of productivity increases and maintained that national income would fall almost in proportion to the cut in hours. Consequently, a rise in hourly wages would raise unemployment, although the wage share of national income would not increase, possibly decrease, Brisman claimed.

A couple of years later, when the effects of the 8-hour day began to be observable, several official evaluation studies were carried out (SOU 1922:33, SOU 1925:45). These studies provided the data for the numerous analyses produced by economists which were to appear in the course of the 1920s. The effects of a reduction in working hours was the topic for the papers with which Erik Lindahl and Bertil Ohlin competed for a position as professor at the University of Copenhagen in 1924. The two papers differed both in content and in size. Lindahl's 35-page essay dealt mainly with the relation between work capacity and the length of the workday, but also predicted and explicitly discussed the substitution of land and capital for labour that would follow a reduction in hours. Lindahl was fairly optimistic about the chances of the negative effects on wages being offset by extended shiftwork and increased productivity.

Ohlin's paper resulted in two articles (Ohlin 1924, 1925) of which the first began by observing how odd it was that a question of such significance as the recent reduction in working hours had not been the subject of theoretical treatment which aimed to assess its impact on national income. He then proceeded to discuss the factors governing the productivity effects of reduced hours in a highly penetrating fashion. Reporting the results of Australian, English, American and German studies, Ohlin compared the productivity effects of different types of jobs, the effects of general versus firm-based reductions as well as both smaller and larger reductions in working hours. He observed, for example, that productivity increases were less likely to arise in work governed by machinery and in high-quality work. Furthermore, there were cases where reduced hours in individual firms were combined with unchanged output. However, Ohlin pointed out that these cases were unsuitable for purposes of general inference, since workers were more interested in avoiding output losses in the one-firm case.

Ohlin presented Swedish data from SOU 1922:33 which indicated that there was a large dispersion across industries in the percentage reduction in hours between 1919 and 1920, from 31 per cent in sugar refineries to 7 per cent in electricity and water power, and 12.6 per cent on average. (Less, thus, than the 17 per cent assumed by Brisman.) Further, he pointed out that not only was the surveyed period unduly short for observing the effects of the reduction, since adjustments would take longer, 1920 was also unsuitable for purposes of comparison due to the recession. These circumstances in combination with the wage compensation paid to workers could explain the failure to observe any general increase in work intensity. On the other hand, he demonstrated that in those cases where productivity had been increased, it was mainly due to an increased proportion of efficient hours to paid hours.[12]

In his second article, Ohlin argued that the fall in capacity utilization that resulted from the large-scale reorganization of the production process induced by the cut in hours, could be counteracted through extended shiftwork. This was also a means of avoiding a decline in production and wages. A modern economist equipped with computers and econometrics would undoubtedly have difficulties in assessing the effects of the 8-hour law, since so many factors other than working hours varied; Ohlin found it 'impossible'. Finally, he struck a positive tone as regards the long-run impact of increased leisure for workers:

> Experience indicates that high technical standards and productivity in a country's industry is associated with a well-educated working class. The opportunities for further education promoted through the increase in leisure should therefore be expected to have long-run favourable effects on the nation's productivity.
>
> (Ohlin 1925, p. 24; my translation)

The gauntlet thrown down by Ohlin was taken up by Åkerman (1925, 1926). His first article was mainly devoted to a rather pointless discussion of the effects of the 48-hour week when there is depreciation of productive capital, analysed in terms of the rate of usage as compared to time depreciation. His second article, however, presented interesting results based on SOU 1925:45 regarding the effects of the 48-hour week. Conducted in 1924, this was more useful than SOU 1922:33 for purposes of inference. According to this study, working hours had been reduced by 14.8 per cent between 1919 and 1924; 12.6 per cent for non-shift workers and 23 per cent for shiftworkers. Like Ohlin, Åkerman emphasized the difficulty of assessing what was due to the 8-hour day and what was due to other influences. For example, the rise in productivity reported in the study may have been the result of increased work

Table 5.1 Productivity effects of the reduction in working hours 1919–24

	Output increased				Output decreased			
	> 15%	15–10%	< 10%	Output unchanged	< 10%	10–15%	> 15%	Sum
Production/hour Average change (%)	+18	+13	+6	0	−5	−12	−17	
% of workers	16	19	18	19	21	0	7	100
Production/week Average change (%)	+17	+12	+5	0	−6	−13	−18	
% of workers	1	2	2	31	9	14	42	100

Source: Åkerman (1926, p. 171).

intensity as well as of the introduction of labour-saving machinery, which in turn may have been induced by the rise in wages. In order to determine the productivity effects, he subtracted from the data reported by SOU 1925:45, the firms which had not been subject to a reduction in hours and those which had made such large alterations in machinery (except increasing the speed) that productivity had been raised by more than 15 per cent. The results, presented in Table 5.1, show that productivity increased in the majority of firms but the increase was not sufficient to prevent weekly output from falling.

Further, the SOU 1925:45 report contained interviews with the labour inspectors of 49 firms. As summarized by Åkerman, the results showed that an increase in work intensity had certainly occurred which might compensate for 25–33 per cent of the reduction in hours. Although the reduction in hours was the most important source of increase in work intensity, it was however not the only one. Other significant factors reported by Åkerman were the decline in the frequency of labour disputes and management's improved scheduling of working hours through which 'unnecessary' breaks were avoided.

Regarding the effects on national income, Åkerman (1926) estimated that if hours had not been reduced and if productive capital and the number of workers had been the same as in 1924, total production would have been 10 per cent higher. Further, he revealed an early understanding of the different roles of hours and workers in the production process, i.e. that they are not perfect substitutes. This insight was reflected, for example, in his observation that the fall in total production would be larger when daily hours were cut for all workers than if the same reduction in hours was obtained through a decrease in the number of workers employed, since in the former case capacity utilization would decrease.

WILL SHORTER HOURS REDUCE UNEMPLOYMENT?

As we have seen above, the work of Swedish economists on reduced hours in the 1920s dealt mainly with the effects on productivity, production and national income. By contrast, the European debate in the late 1920s and early 1930s was focused on the effects of a shorter working week on employment. A widespread view, supported particularly by the European unions and the International Labour Organization (ILO) was that reduced working hours was an efficient way of combating unemployment (Cuvillier 1984, p. 27; Anxo 1987, p. 4). Such a reduction was regarded as the logical consequence of the enhanced productivity in manufacturing, which was believed to be the major cause of the mass unemployment (ILO 1935, p. 35). Consequently, demands that the working week should be reduced to 40 hours to combat unemployment were adopted at the International Labour Conference in 1935. In the following years, the 40-hour week was introduced in France, New Zealand and in the US. The Swedish Confederation of Trade Unions sided with the ILO but without enthusiasm and without believing that this would be an efficient way to achieve full employment. In fact, during the 1930s only one article putting the blame for mass unemployment on technological change appeared in *Fackföreningsrörelsen*, the main paper of the Swedish Confederation of Trade Unions.[13] It was to take another 40 years before the working week was shortened to 40 hours in Sweden.

Why did the Swedish labour movement refuse to embrace the opinion of the European unions? Without underrating the wisdom of Swedish union leaders, it seems likely that the analyses conducted by economists of this issue and the close relationship between economists and labour leaders contributed to this clearsightedness. Thus, as was seen above, the view that a reduction in working hours is a cure for unemployment had already been refuted by Wicksell and had found no support among his successors. The views of economists had also appeared in newspapers and were popularized and disseminated to the labour movement, e.g. by the journalist Axel Uhlén, who wrote several articles in the daily labour paper *Arbetet.* He also wrote a book in which one chapter (Uhlén 1928, ch. 8) was devoted to demonstrating that a shorter working week would not reduce unemployment, especially as a reduction was likely to be followed by increased hourly wages.

An even more important explanation for the attitude of the Swedish unions is perhaps to be found in the analysis of the causes and remedies of unemployment which was evolving among economists and labour leaders of the time. As shown by Wadensjö (1991), The Committee on Unemployment, appointed in 1927, played a significant role in forming the new view on unemployment which was later to be associated with the Stockholm School. Many distinguished economists were involved in the work of the

Committee, e.g. Dag Hammarskjöld, Alf Johansson, Erik Lindahl, Gunnar Myrdal, Bertil Ohlin, Gösta Bagge and Gustaf Åkerman, several of whom had analysed the reduction in working hours seen above. The Committee also became an important forum for fruitful intellectual exchange between economists and labour leaders, not least due to the efforts of Ernst Wigforss and Alf Johansson. As pointed out by Rehn (1990), Alf Johansson was important as a teacher and a link between the academic world and the labour movement. One chapter of the Committee's final report, written by Hammarskjöld, was titled 'Reductions in working hours as a means against unemployment' and demonstrated why it could not be regarded as such a means (SOU 1935:6, part II, ch. 8). No doubt Gösta Rehn has continued Alf Johansson's mission as bridge-builder and, interestingly, as a young student in the spring of 1935 he presented a paper at Alf Johansson's seminar at the Stockholm University with the same title as Hammarskjöld's chapter (Rehn 1988, p. 11). Moreover, in the following years, Rehn wrote several articles firmly criticizing the ILO idea of a 40-hour working week as a cure for unemployment.[14] A point (repeatedly) made by Rehn was that the size of unemployment is uncorrelated with the length of the working week; the unemployment rate could very well be the same with a working week of 40 hours (or 35 hours) as at 48 hours.

SUMMARY

In 1889, the 8-hour working day became the chief demand of the Swedish labour movement. Knut Wicksell, who held a highly pessimistic view on future productivity increases and population growth, repeatedly criticized the demand and thereby alienated himself from the labour movement. However, it was not until 1920, and then as a result of the social unrest at the end of the First World War, that the 48-hour working week was introduced in Sweden. A few years after the reform, several official evaluatory studies were carried out, which provided the data for the economists' thorough analyses of the reduction in working hours during the 1920s. However, in contrast to the Swedish economic debate which focused on the effects on productivity, production and national income, the European discussion dealt mainly with the effects on unemployment. Among European unions reduced hours were widely believed to be an efficient cure for mass unemployment. Consequently in 1935 the ILO adopted a resolution demanding a 40-hour working week to combat unemployment. In Sweden this view on the relation between working hours and unemployment did not gain much support from unions. In this chapter, three main reasons for this clearsightedness of the Swedish unions have been pointed out. First, it had been carefully explained by Wicksell, as well as by his successors, why reduced hours were not an efficient means to combat unemployment. Second, there already existed among Swedish economists in the late 1920s a more sophisticated view on the causes and remedies of unemployment. Third, the analyses conducted by economists were popularized and disseminated to the labour movement by Alf Johansson, Axel Uhlén and others. The Committee on Unemployment also played an important role as a forum for intellectual exchange between economists and labour leaders.

NOTES

* This work has benefited from the useful suggestions of ˙Dominique Anxo, Gösta Rehn, Lena Schröder and Eskil Wadensjö.

1 For a presentation of the historical background of the demand, see Langenfelt (1954).

2 The content of his lectures is known through a report in *Social-demokraten*, 2 and 4 October 1890. See Gårdlund (1956, pp. 152 and 388).

3 Due to the fall in the death rate, mainly among women and children, natural population growth increased strongly in the period 1810–70 and remained high until 1910 (Guteland *et al.* 1983, pp. 28 and 236; Holmberg 1970a, b).

4 Assume we have the production function $Q = Q(C, U, N, H)$ which can be written $Q = C^a \, U^b \, N^c \, H^e$, where Q is output, C is the stock of capital, U is the degree of capacity utilization, N is the number of workers and H is the average number of hours per worker. We then say the returns to hours are decreasing if $e < 1$, increasing if $e > 1$ and constant if $e = 1$.

5 See for example Leveson (1967) and Owen (1979, p. 68).

6 See Anxo (1987, ch. 4) and Hart (1987, p. 147). It appears that increasing returns to hours is obtained when the degree of capacity utilization is not properly accounted for in the production function. Analysing data for Sweden over the years 1963–82, Åberg (1987) obtained $e < 1$, but approaching 1 over the period as weekly hours were reduced. Also, long-run e was larger than shortrun e and closer to 1.

7 Wicksell also polemicized against this view in an article in the journal *Samtiden*, Bergen 1980.

8 See Arbetstidskommittén (1919). The Bill was presented on 17 August 1919 and was adopted on 27 September.

9 Johansson (1977, pp. 20–1), Lindgren *et al.* (1948, p. 708) and Styrman (1946, p. 177).
10 In fact, Bagge mentioned all of the factors (parameters) that a modern researcher would include except the size of fixed labour costs. See, for example, Anxo (1987, ch. 5).
11 As the average working week prior to the reduction was estimated to 56.4 hours by the Committee, a 48-hour working week with real income constant would imply a 17.5 per cent increase of the hourly wage (Brisman 1921, p. 26).
12 Johansson (1977) demonstrates in great detail that the employers made intense efforts and also succeeded in increasing efficient hours in proportion to paid hours in order to offset the cost effects of the 48-hour week.
13 Fehlinger (1932). See also Schröder and Sehlstedt (1984, p. 25).
14 See, for example, Rehn (1937a, b, 1985).

LITERATURE

Åberg, Y. (1987) *The Impact of Working Hours and Other Factors on Production and Employment*, Aldershot: Avebury Publishing.
Åkerman, G. (1925) 'Teoretiska anmärkningar rörande 8-timmarsdagen' ('Theoretical notes regarding the 8-hour day'), *Ekonomisk Tidskrift*, pp. 251–69.
—— (1926) 'Den industriella utvecklingen och 8-timmarsdagen' ('The industrial development and the 8-hour day'), *Ekonomisk Tidskrift*, pp. 161–97.
Anxo, D. (1987) *Sysselsättningseffekter av en allmän arbetstidsförkortning* (*Effects on Employment of a General Reduction in Working Hours*), Economic Studies no. 20, Department of Economics, University of Gothenburg, Gothenburg.
Arbetstidskommittén (1919) *Betänkande med förslag om begränsning av arbetstiden* (*Report from the Committee on Working Hours*), Stockholm: Civildepartementet.
Bagge, G. (1919) 'Lagstadgad arbetstid' ('Statutory working hours'), *Teknisk Tidskrift*, vol. 49, pp. 237–43.
Brentano, L. (1891) 'La question de huit heures en angleterre', *Revue d'Économie Politique*, pp. 981–92.
Brisman, S. (1921) Åttatimmarslagen' ('The 8-hour law'), *Nationalekonomiska ekonomiska Studier*.
Cuvillier, R. (1984) *The Reduction of Working Time*, Geneva: ILO.
European Trade Union Institute (1979) *Reduction of Working Hours in Western Europe*, Brussels: ETUI.
Fehlinger, H. (1932) 'Teknologisk arbetslöshet' ('Technological unemployment'), *Fackföreningsrörelsen*, no. 13.
Gårdlund, T. (1956) *Knut Wicksell*, Stockholm: Bonniers.
Guteland, G., Holmberg, I., Hägerstrand, T., Karlqvist, A. and Rundblad, B. (1975) *Ett folks biografi* (*Biography of a People*), Stockholm: Liber.
Hart, R.A. (1987) *Working Time and Employment*. Boston: Allen & Unwin.

Holmberg, I. (1970a) 'A study of mortality among cohorts born in the 18th and 19th century', in *Cohort Mortality of Sweden*. Statistics Sweden: Statistiska meddelanden, Serie Be.

—— (1970b) Mortality, fertility and reproductivity. An outline of Swedish population development during 200 years. Mimeo. University of Gothenburg.

ILO (1935) *Report of the Director*, International Labour Conference, 19th Session, Geneva: ILO.

Johansson, A. (1977) *Den effektiva arbetstiden (The Efficient Working Time)*. Uppsala Studies in Economic History 17. Acta Universitatis Upsaliensis and Stockholm: Almqvist & Wicksell International.

Langenfelt, G. (1954) *The Historic Origin of the Eight Hours Day*. Kungl. Vitterhets Historie och Antikvitets Akademiens Handlingar del 87. Stockholm: Almqvist & Wicksell.

Leontief, W. (1979) 'Is technological unemployment inevitable?', *Challenge*, Sept–Oct.

—— (1982) 'The distribution of work and income', *Scientific American*, Sept.

Leveson, I.F. (1967) 'Reductions in hours of work as a source of productivity growth', *Journal of Political Economy*, vol. 72, pp. 199–204.

Lindahl, E. (1925) *Arbetsdagens förkortning (Reduction of the Workday)*, Malmö, Skrifter utgivna av Fahlbeckska stiftelsen.

Lindgren, J. (1938) *Svenska Metallindustriarbetarförbundets historia (History of the Swedish Metalworkers' Union)*, Part I, Stockholm: Tiden.

Lindgren, J., Westerståhl, J. and Tingsten, T. (1948) *Svenska Metallindustriarbetarförbundets historia (History of the Swedish Metalworkers' Union)*, Part II. Stockholm: Tiden.

Ohlin, B. (1924) 'Åttatimmarsdagens ekonomiska verkningar del I' ('The economic effects of the eight-hour day, part I'), *Ekonomisk Tidskrift*, pp. 193–218.

—— (1925) 'Åttatimmarsdagens ekonomiska verkningar del II' ('The economic effects of the eight-hour day, part II'), *Ekonomisk Tidskrift*, pp. 65–94.

Owen, J.D. (1979) *Working Hours*, Lexington, Mass.: D.C. Heath & Co.

Rehn, G. (1937a) '40-timmarsveckan' ('The 40-hour week'), *Clarté*, vol. 14, no. 7, pp. 4–7.

—— (1937b) 'Kring 40-timmmarsfrågan' ('About the 40-hour question'), *Metallarbetaren*, no. 32, p. 2.

—— (1985) 'Is job sharing and the shortening of working hours an alternative to the payment of unemployment benefits?', Symposium on the Grants Economy, Augsburg Sept./Oct.

—— (1988) *Full sysselsättning utan inflation ·(Full employment without inflation)*, *Skrifter i urval* av E. Wadensjö, Å. Dahlberg and B. Holmlund (eds), Stockholm: Tiden.

—— (1990) 'Reminiscences of the Stockholm School' in L. Jonung (ed.), *The Stockholm School of Economics Remembered*, in preparation.

Schäffle, A.E.F. (1890) 'Zur Theorie und Politik des Arbeitserschutzes', *Zeitschrift für die gesamte Staatswissenschaft*, vol. 46, pp. 611–94.

—— (1891) 'Zur Theorie und Politik des Arbeiterschutzes', *Zeitschrift für die gesamte Staatswissenschaft*, vol. 47, pp. 68–135.

Schröder, L. and Sehlstedt, K. (1984) *Vad händer med jobben?* (*What is Happening with Jobs?*), Stockholm, Rabén & Sjögren.

SOU 1922:33. *Förslag till reviderad lag om arbetstidens begränsning jämte utredningar rörande arbetstidslagstiftningens verkningar inom vissa yrken* (*Proposal of a Revised Law on Working Hours*), Stockholm: Socialstyrelsen.

—— 1925:45. *Statistiska undersökningar angående åttatimmarslagens och bageri-lagens verkningar* (*Statistical Analyses of the Effects of the 8-hour Day*), Stockholm: Socialstyrelsen & Kommerskollegium.

—— 1935:6. *Arbetslöshetsutredningen.* Stockholm: Socialdepartementet.

Styrman, G. (1946) *Verkstadsföreningen 1896–1945* (*The Swedish Engineering Industries Employers' Association*), Stockholm.

Uhlén, A. (1928) *Löner, arbetstid och arbetslöshet* (*Wages, Working Hours and Unemployment*), Stockholm: Tiden.

Wadensjö, E. (1990) 'Gösta Bagge', Chapter 7 in this volume.

—— (1991) 'The Committee on Unemployment and the Stockholm School of Economics', in L. Jonung (ed.), *The Stockholm School of Economics Revisited*, Cambridge: Cambridge University Press.

Wicksell, K. (1892) *Normalarbetsdag* (*The Standard Working Day*), unpublished manuscript, The Wicksell Archives, Lund.

—— (1919) *Arbetarfrågan* (*The Worker Question*), unpublished manuscript, The Wicksell Archives, Lund.

—— (1920) *8-Timmarsdagen* (*The 8-Hour Day*), unpublished manuscript, The Wicksell Archives, Lund.

The manuscripts by Knut Wicksell (1892), (1919) and (1920) will be published in a volume containing previously unpublished manuscripts by Wicksell.

6

THE ECONOMIST AS POPULARIZER: THE EMERGENCE OF SWEDISH ECONOMICS 1900–30

Lars Magnusson

In his review of Gunnar Myrdal's *The Political Element in the Development of Economic Theory* (Myrdal 1954; first Swedish edition 1929) the Swedish economist Sven Brisman presented a snapshot picture from a gathering of *Nationalekonomiska klubben* (the Political Economy Club) in 1928. Brisman was a slightly younger colleague of Eli Heckscher at the *Handelshögskolan* in Stockholm and was, along with Knut Wicksell, Gustav Cassel, David Davidson and Eli Heckscher, one of the leading economists in Sweden of the older generation before the emergence of the Stockholm School in the 1930s. According to Brisman (1930):

> One day about two years ago, a remarkable meeting was held at our political economy discussion club in Stockholm. Here we elder economists had gone for years, basking in our own splendidness, full of an unfeigned mutual admiration, convinced that we had finally found the only True and Correct economic viewpoint. And then came Gunnar Myrdal, who was a young docent at that time, about whom I knew little more than that he had defended a brilliant dissertation. Figuratively speaking, he turned all of us upside-down. His presentation was one long glowing sermon from the mouth against everything we had considered most valuable in our economic education. And it was apparent that he had a group of enthusiastic followers among the even younger, who were indignant over the writings of Cassel, Heckscher and myself. All our old and beloved concepts, especially 'maximum welfare' and 'efficiency', not to mention 'population

optimum' and the 'economic correct distribution of productive forces', 'national income', 'price level' and much more – all these were blown away like straw in the wind, until we didn't know if we stood on our heads or on our feet.[1]

In the long enduring debate regarding the intellectual roots of the Swedish crisis policy of the 1930s, it has often been emphasized that the rise of the Stockholm School from the late 1920s implied a radical break with the 'neo-classicism' of an older generation.[2]

Although this might be true with regard to theoretical developments – albeit this remains a controversial issue largely due to Björn Hansson's (1982) attempt to reconstruct the stages in the development of the 'new' economics in Sweden during the 1920s and early 1930s, which clearly showed that there is *also* a case for continuity in a theoretical and methodological sense – there is another aspect to this question which has been rather neglected in the debate. It is clear that the Stockholm School economists were to a considerable extent able to profit from the efforts of an older generation of economists to build up a reputation for the discipline of economics as both a *scientific* and highly *practical* subject. To put the question another way: in his book *Monetary Policy and Crises: A Study of Swedish Experience* Brinley Thomas (1936) first introduced the scholarly writings of the Stockholm School for an international audience. As a foreign visitor Thomas was above all impressed by the influence that the professional economists seemed to have on politicians both of right and left, on banking and business people as well as on the lay public. Economists in Sweden, he stressed 'seem, moreover as a class, to have a better public reputation than elsewhere' (Thomas 1936, p. ixf).

If Thomas is correct in his assertation – and this is the hypothesis we start out from in this chapter – the question of course arises: how was this made possible? Public influence is of course not an automatic consequence of analytical rigour or theoretical sophistication, although many economists would perhaps prefer it to be so. Rather, it should be regarded, first, as a consequence of successful popularization, the successful manufacturing of an image of the economist as an expert, the work to establish channels through which the economist was able to reach a certain audience, etc. Thus, in short, such a state must be historically developed and achieved through the efforts laid down by an earlier generation of economists. As argued here, it is also in this sense that the first generation of

Swedish economists had an important impact upon subsequent developments. Through successful popularization, they were able to launch economics as a prestigious scientific subject. The picture that was presented to the lay public in order to achieve this goal was primarily one of an economics discipline that was politically neutral and purely scientific. The practical character of economics was also emphasized; it was manifestly a box of tools in the Schumpeterian sense available for the professional economist in order to solve practical problems within the economic realm.

This argument does not imply that the picture they presented was an accurate one. On the contrary, Cassel for example can hardly be described as 'neutral' in policy matters. He was without doubt often used by different interest groups to pursue their special aims. Unfortunately, the important relationship between Swedish economics and the role of special-interest groups has not yet been subject to much detailed research.[3] However, the important point here is not whether an economist like Cassel was neutral – which of course he was not. Rather the question that must be raised instead is why it seemed so important for politicians, bankers and others to take help from professional economists (including Cassel) to pursue their own special policy suggestions. A precondition must have been that the economists were able to present themselves to the public as experts who were able to examine relevant issues on the basis of a sound theoretical approach. Thus in order to understand the influence of the Stockholm School in the 1930s and the development of Swedish economics as such during this period, it is essential to take a closer look at the process of popularization during the earlier decades of the twentieth century; how the view of the economist as a professional scholar was presented and to some extent accepted during this period. It is the aim of this essay to examine this issue in a Swedish context – dealing mainly with the first three decades of this century.

II

Not only in Sweden have economics and the economist made a great impact during the twentieth century. In order to understand this phenomenon, historians of economic thought have perhaps paid too much attention to analytical progress as such, to the leading scientists in the field and on the successive perfection of the economist's 'box of tools'. To be able to understand the success of economics during the twentieth century and its remarkable influential position within social thought and in society at large, one must certainly look more closely into the more mundane course of development taken by economic pedagogy and examine carefully the discipline's most influential propagandists and popularizers. The successive perfection of analytical tools and theoretical progress as such is probably not the only reason – or even the most profound one – why economics rose to a central position in the hierarchy of social sciences in this century. Moreover, an important question which has still not received much attention concerns the readiness of audiences to listen to the prophecies of economists and to accept their claims of having access to a body of scientific knowledge that contains certain principles which may be practically useful. As a professional economist himself, George Stigler may feel that the public has not listened carefully enough to the economists (Stigler 1982, p. 57f). However, on the whole, the success story of economics during this century cannot be denied.

Within the sociology of science, a new set of classificatorial concepts has been developed in recent years in order to understand scientific progress and the acceptance of science as a privileged form of knowledge within the community at large. For example, Richard Whitley (1984) stresses that the function of scientific facts is 'a highly socially contingent process of creating cognitive order out of disorder'.[4] However, this does not only denote – as an older sociology of knowledge in the tradition of Mannheim used to stress – that the scientific process is influenced by ideology and class consciousness. On the contrary, Whitley (1984) regards the different 'scientific fields' as being controlled by different scientific 'craft groups' – with their own distinctive masters, journeymen and apprentices – which use their special skills as exclusion devices with regard to other specialists or the common public. Whether they are successful or not as a socially organized craft group in upholding a monopoly of knowledge and specialist advice in their field depends to a large extent upon what Whitley defines as 'the grade of technical task uncertainty'. In cases where such uncertainty is prevalent and a subsequent ambiguity surrounds the scientific results, leaving them open to conflicting interpretations, the craft of a certain field will have great problems in sustaining such control – and hence their status as scientists will tend to be low. This will be even more marked where the use of technical methodology is flexible and not rigidly defined. Hence at every instance 'amateurs' from outside are threatening the scientific curriculum cherished by this craft. On the other hand, where 'technical task uncertainty' is low there will be 'a well-established set of research techniques' to which only the experts in this field have access through procedures of formal training. At the same time, these techniques will be fairly straightforward, quite well defined and have a certain rigidity. Thus, in this case as well, the research results will be 'more predictable, visible and reliable' (Whitley 1984, p. 119f).

As an example within the social sciences of a field with a relatively low task uncertainty. Whitley especially mentions 'Anglo-Saxon economics after 1870'. Its characteristic feature is, according to the same author:

> a high degree of uniformity in the analytical skills and outlook of economists, strong consciousness of the boundaries of economics and what are, and are not, economic problems, a highly rule-governed set of research practices which are strongly oriented to theoretical and analytical goals and a highly formal symbol system for communicating and co-ordinating task outcomes
>
> (Whitley 1984, p. 184)

In the case of economics, 'craft' control is thus achieved through a high degree of standardization of procedures and interpretation of results as well as by a rigid delineation of legitimate 'field' problems. However, another important feature of economics is a strong separation between its central theoretical core and its application at the periphery. Only to a minor extent are empirical results of this process of application allowed to influence the hard core. According to, for example, Phyllis Deane (1981), this insulation of the core functions, works in a way that 'whatever the intractability of the problems posed in the applied areas of their discipline, they were building on virtually impregnable analytical foundations' (Deane 1981, p. 8).

Nevertheless, neither Whitley nor most other sociologists of science provide an answer to how this process of insulation was made possible in the first place. How and by which methods could the economists during this century convince their audiences – politicians, businessmen and the lay public – that they were in possession of an analytical 'Pandora's box' which would be useful in regard to certain problems defined as 'economic'? In an influential article, Arjo Klammer (1984) draws attention to the importance of how economists communicate with and try to convince one another. Such an aspect is also at the core of Donald McCloskey's (1985) argument regarding the significance of rhetoric in economics. However, it is important to note that economists do not only talk to each other. It is clear that they use different rhetoric for different audiences. The choice of rhetoric does not only influence the public's preparedness to accept what the economist has to offer but also defines the position of the economist within the scientific community at large. Thus in this sense, the choice of rhetoric will give rise to profound differences – as for example a rhetoric of the McCloskey or Samuelson brand most definitely does.[5]

I will argue below that in order to understand the success of economics during the twentieth century, it is crucial to discern how rhetoric was used by economists for the purpose of communicating with their audiences in order to convince them of their general usefulness and their access to a set of analytical principles – taught as economics at universities. This is also what the rest of this chapter will consider using the example of Sweden during the first decades of the twentieth century. On the one hand, it will deal with the economist as a popularizer of a certain conceptual framework, a problem-solving toolkit, a 'language' which insists on the scientific character of this methodology. On the other hand, we must also look at the 'demand side' examining how and why audiences became receptive to the messages channelled by the professional economists. This of course has to be done in a historical perspective and from the standpoint that such receptiveness is historically transient. Thus the same rhetoric does not apply over time in order to be successfully absorbed.

A lot more research must be carried out before it is possible to draw any definitive conclusion about the role of such rhetoric and popularization in general. Hence in relation to the specific Swedish situation we will have to confine ourselves to a number of important problems and the presentation of certain tentative hypotheses.

III

According to Heckscher (1953), the most striking feature of the Swedish economic debate during the last quarter of the nineteenth century was its overwhelming *laissez-faire* character. In the eyes of the general public the subject of economics even came close to being regarded as a theoretical justification for free trade and against protection. The influential *Nationalekonomiska föreningen* (The Economic Society) especially sang the gospel of free trade. According to its statutes of 1877, it was launched in order to 'support the study of economics and by means of lecturing, discussions and publication of texts contribute to the solving of such problems which are raised within this science' (*Nationalekonomiska föreningen* 1927, p. 19). At that time such *laissez-faire* economists as the American Carey and the Frenchman Bastiat seems to have been overwhelmingly influential: at least according to Heckscher, the preacher of universal economic harmony, Bastiat was the single most influential economist in Sweden during this period (Heckscher 1953, p. 109f).

Already in the same year it came into existence, the Economic Society had 160 paying members. By 1890 this number had increased to 494 and during the following decades it retained approximately this membership number; in 1925 there were 492 paying members of the Society. During the first period it was dominated by senior governmental officials and politicians. In 1880 this group outnumbered by far any other single group with a total of 124 persons (43 per cent). The second most important group consisted of trade-and-industry people, 90 persons in all (31 per cent), while the number of intellectuals and university employees was as low as 21 persons (7 per cent). In fact the number of bank directors was almost as numerous, 19 in all (6 per cent). By 1925 this situation had changed to some extent but not at all fundamentally. Government officials and politicians were predominant (36 per cent) followed by trade and industry (19 per cent), bank directors (14 per cent), privately employed officials (9 per cent), etc. By and large, scholars were still absent; in 1925 their share was only a mere 6 per cent (28 individuals including medical doctors, etc.) (*Nationalekonomiska föreningen* 1927, p. 25f).

Hence, this was an organization mainly for senior officials, leading businessmen and bank directors. Performing as a meeting place and discussion club for the higher echelons of official society, it had an immense influence on the political scene as well as on the general public discussion regarding economic matters. In the debates during the 1880s and 1890s, it acted in practice as a pressure group for free trade and against increased protection and tariffs. The subject most eagerly discussed was tariffs and protection. The list of lectures given before 1914 shows quite clearly how this issue dominated the discussions. It was followed in importance by themes dealing with banking and credit, 'the social question', etc.

(*Nationalekonomiska föreningen* 1927, p. 220ff). In 1877, when the Society was set up, strong voices were raised in order to create a Free Trade society instead, along the lines of the Cobdenite club in England. However, in order to guarantee a more scientific status and to appear less partisan, it was decided to keep the Society open to anyone regardless of political opinion (*Nationalekonomiska föreningen* 1927, p. 78). As noted above, this did not hinder its general outlook from being manifestly devoted to *laissez-faire* and free trade well into the beginning of the twentieth century (*Nationalekonomiska föreningen* 1927, p. 20; Heckscher 1953).

As indicated above, the academic economists do not seem to have seriously engaged themselves in the debates organized by the Economic Society. Apart from Johan Leffler's lectures on Marx and the German *Kathersozialismus* in the middle of the 1880s and some minor contributions by Knut Wicksell at the beginning of the 1890s – before Wicksell had become an academic economist – the first professional economist to appear was David Davidsson. In 1898 he held a lecture on 'Bank reform and commercial life' followed by the first more 'theoretical' lecture by Wicksell during the same year, presenting a summary of his book *Geldzins und Guterpreise* which had just been published. It would be quite erroneous to state that nineteenth-century academic economists were separated from the general public. Many of them (especially Karl-Gustaf Hammarskjöld and Per-Erik Bergfalk in Uppsala as well as Agardh in Lund) played an important political role. It was common that they served the state and its bureaucracy as ministers, held appointments in committees, etc. – at least after the turn of the century. However, in contrast to the twentieth century, they were not in the first place appointed as experts because they were professional *economists*, relying on a certain expertise. It was rather in their capacity as professors in law and jurisprudence – and hence in Sweden traditionally defined as civil servants – that they were chosen. Economics before the turn of the nineteenth century was largely a part-time job for the economist professors; they were appointed to chairs which contained both economics and law – and sometimes also finance (see below). Thus to the extent 'pure economics' was taught, it was mainly in a crude version closely following Bastiat (for example Hamilton in Lund) (Heckscher 1953, p. 110).

The post-1850 period had inherited two chairs in economics from the eighteenth century: one in Uppsala and one in Lund. In general it seems that the subject had a fairly low status both within the academic curriculum as well as in society at large. In Uppsala, Lars Georg Rabenius had been professor in jurisprudence, economics and commerce within the faculty of law during most of the first half of the nineteenth century (1807–37). In his textbook on economics, Rabenius (1829) tried to build a bridge between old and new visions of the economic order. In the introduction, he presents the 'three different economic systems': mercantilism, the physiocratic system and the industrial system (mainly Adam Smith). After criticizing the first two, he praises the 'industrial' system for being the most logical and for rending a 'true' model of economic reality (Rabenius 1829, p. 10f). It is also evident from one of his pupil's lecture-notes that Rabenius was most sympathetic to Smith. The student quoted Rabenius (probably in 1827) in saying 'that Smidt [sic] has laid a proper foundation for the study of this subject'.[6] But being an eclectician (as well as a professor supposed to defend the policies of the state) Rabenius was cautious to emphasize that: 'Freedom is of course the most valuable right Man possesses, but it must be regulated by law so that it does not degenerate and become pernicious' (Rabenius 1829, p. 6).

After Rabenius, there was an even greater emphasis in Uppsala on jurisprudence and economic legislation. In 1837 Per Eric Bergfalk was appointed professor in *Nationaleconomie, oeconomie- och finansrätt* (National Economy, economic and finance law). Besides some works mainly dealing with economic history (on gold and trade cycles), he hardly published anything touching upon the subject of economics (Bergfalk 1853a,b). Although he primarily lectured on jurisprudence, he did give some courses in what he himself described as 'theoretical economics'. However, in these courses, he was mainly concerned with a history of economic thought starting with Aristotle and ending with an exposition of the ideas of 'modern' socialist thinkers such as Owen and Proudhon. In passing, he discussed theoretical questions concerning value and distribution. His commentaries were heavily influenced by the 'last of the German cameralists', Karl Henrich Rau, from whom he quoted repeatedly.[7] By and large this situation continued with Bergfalk's two successors, Gustav Knut Hamilton (1859–62), Olof Rabenius (1862–77) and Karl Gustav Hammarskjöld (1877–88).

What has been emphasized with regard to Uppsala can also, by and large, be said about Lund. Before 1842 its economics chair had been placed within the faculty of natural science and its more famous holder had been Carl August Agardh (professor in 'Practical

Economy and Botany'). After this date it was placed – as in Uppsala – within the faculty of law. The implication was that its holder had to teach jurisprudence and law besides economics. The first occupant of the new chair was Jacob Lundell and he was succeeded by Olof Rabenius (1852–62) and G.K. Hamilton (1862–99) – the latter two also in Uppsala.

It was only with David Davidson in Uppsala (1890–1919), Knut Wicksell in Lund (1901–16) and Gustav Cassel at the newly established chair in Stockholm (1904–33) that Sweden achieved its first generation of academic economists who were able to devote themselves full time to the subject of economics. However, the emergence of such a narrow obligation to teach only 'pure' economics took time. Davidson in Uppsala, especially, was still obliged to lecture in law – and this was the situation in Uppsala until the chair was moved from the faculty of law to the faculty of philosophy in 1948. In Gothenburg a chair in economics and sociology was also inaugurated in 1904 but was held by Gustaf Steffen – hardly an economist by training or general outlook. However, the general trend was clear. Further additions to this list of academic 'pure' economists include Eli Heckscher at *Handelshögskolan* (he was professor in national economy and statistics 1909–29 and subsequently professor in economic history at *Handelshögskolan*), Sven Brisman at *Handelshögskolan* (in national economy and banking 1917–46) and Emil Sommarin who succeeded Wicksell in Lund after 1916.

Thus by the turn of the century, economics had emancipated itself and had become an independent scientific field in its own right within the Swedish academic community. This had important consequences. First, it implied a rapid professionalization of Swedish economics. In relation to what has been previously said, the newly established subject strived to establish its 'craft control' through the establishment of certain minimum criteria and scientific standards. In order to be an economist, the young student increasingly had to go through a curriculum of courses on theory and methodology. In this sense it is also clear that the standards and quality of Swedish economics rose considerably during this period. Second, this first generation of true academic economists also had a tremendous impact as popularizers. In contrast to the previous period, the academic economist and the influential economic popularizer (this function was previously upheld to a large extent by the Economic Society) were not different persons. This first generation of academic economists was to a great extent able to combine both these roles. In relation to earlier conditions, they were no longer seen as partisans for one political doctrine only (free trade). On the contrary – as we shall see – they used their position as neutral scientists to launch their programme of 'pure economics'. This was part of the rhetoric they used and to which we will now turn.

IV

In this section, we will look briefly at some of the leading first-generation professional economists and their function as popularizers. Popularization was of course only one of the roles performed by the leading economists of the day. In fact they could have one, several or perhaps even all of the following five functions or roles: (a) predominantly an innovative scientist who produces new theories and methods; (b) a pedagogue who teaches their own and others' theories; (c) an applied expert who uses his methodology for mainly practical economic purposes (for state committees, parliamentary commissions, etc.); (d) a popularizer of the theories of other economists for the general public; and (e) a popularizer of the 'scientific' hard-core methodology of economics. Clearly, some of the leading economists were quite able to combine many of these different roles, including that of being a successful popularizer. Others still were more specialized to a certain role or function.

Generally, the economist who devoted his time mainly to the propagation of the ideas of others is a highly underrated figure in the annals of the history of economic thought (cf. Tribe (1988)). In the Swedish context, the importance of such popularizers as Gunnar Silfverstolpe (a very influential propagator of neo-classical orthodoxy during the 1920s and 1930s who was especially widely read by social-democrats, trade unionists and members of the Swedish cooperative movement) and Emil Sommarin in Lund can hardly be exaggerated. However, it is especially popularization in the second sense that seems to have been even more pertinent during this period. In order to grasp the importance of popularization relating to the scientific claims of economic methodology more concretely, we will give a brief description of certain leading first-generation economists who seem to have been especially energetic popularizers in this sense: we will concentrate mainly on the three Stockholm economists Cassel, Heckscher and Brisman.[8] As their biographies are supposed to be generally known, we will present only a brief characterization of each before we deal with the rhetoric aspects of their work in the sense we have discussed earlier. In addition to these three, there are also others who would have been worth attention in this context, most importantly Wicksell. However, the further treatment of Wicksell as well as other economists as popularizers will have to await more research in the field.

Gustav Cassel (1866-1944)

More than anybody else of the first generation of Swedish economists Cassel has the reputation of being a popularizer. In this function he was not only well known to the Swedish public. According to Schumpeter he was in fact the 'most influential leader of our science' as a whole during the 1920s (Schumpeter 1972, p. 1154). Further according to Seligman (Seligman 1962, p. 562), Cassel

> exerted a remarkable influence not only on Sweden's monetary policy, but on other Nations as well. A long flow of articles, reviews, speeches, pamphlets, and commentary came from his pen. ... He wrote reports for the League of Nations, toured the United States lecturing on money, and offered his views to the House of Representative's Committee on Banking.

Although influential on the international scene, he undoubtedly also played an important role during the 1920s and early 1930s as an adviser on monetary issues for several Swedish governments. He was, for example, the main architect behind the dramatic devaluation of the Swedish krona in 1931 and the subsequent rejection of the gold standard soon after.[9]

He wrote articles on economic issues in *Svenska Dagbladet* almost once a week for the Swedish public over a period of forty years (in all about 1500 articles). However, he also wrote for numerous other newspapers and journals, especially *Skandinaviska bankens kvartalstidskrift* (100 articles), *Ekonomisk Tidskrift* (30) and the Swedish Taxpayers' Association's journal *Sunt förnuft* (30).[10] According to his autobiography, he also seems to have been an oft-invited lecturer to meetings, conferences, etc. organized by businessmen, bankers and learned associations. Thus, for example, he held lectures on several occasions at the annual meeting of *Svenska Bankföreningen* (Cassel

1940–1; cf. Carlson 1988, pp. 11ff, 26ff, etc.).

Hence, Cassel was more than willing to play a public role. On every occasion, he took the opportunity to use his position as a professor in economics in order to popularize his own or others' theories (although he has been commonly criticized that he was reluctant to admit and give credit for using others' ideas). In fact, employing the typology of the economist's functions introduced above, he seems to have been busy performing all of these roles at the same time. It must undoubtedly be admitted that Cassel was a teacher, expert adviser and popularizer – but also to some extent he was an innovative scientist (Brems 1989).

Although Cassel might still be acknowledged as a great popularizer and as a politically very influential economist, his reputation as a theorist has steadily diminished. There are probably several reasons for this: (1) many have emphasized that his role as a great and innovative thinker was highly overestimated and dramatized during his lifetime, especially by himself; (2) his tendency to boast has made this even more evident over the years; (3) especially in the 1930s, he became perhaps too politically partisan in a conservative direction which undoubtedly also affected his 'theoretical' work during this period; and (4) especially with the coming of the Keynesian revolution, his simplistic and explicitly static version of economics became rapidly obsolete.[11]

Whichever of these explanations one uses to account for the decline of his theoretical reputation – an issue which does not really concern us here – we still have to ask why Cassel became such an apparent success during his lifetime. Of course, his own campaigning explains quite a lot. Especially during his period as an international monetary expert he seems to have spared no energy whatsoever to get his message through to the public. To this extent, his autobiography probably gives an accurate picture of the tremendous amount of work he must have put down travelling, giving lectures, writing articles, publishing shorter pamphlets for popular audiences, etc.

However, his efforts to this effect can only explain one side of his popularity. Obviously, his audiences' apparent acceptance of what he had to say must also be added to the picture. Certainly this acceptance may to some extent be simply explained by stating that someone like Cassel was what governments and businessmen needed during the 1920s. Hence his popularity was caused by the fact that he presented himself as an able 'expert' on complicated monetary matters – a policy issue which completely dominated the economic debate during this chaotic decade of collapse in the international monetary system. Here a professor of economics appeared – coming from a neutral country which was believed to imply that he would be less partisan than economists belonging to nations which had recently fought a bloody war – who spoke clearly and loudly 'in the service of reason' (as he titled his autobiography a decade later); who would not have listened?

There is also another side to this question which seems even more relevant in the present context. Especially during the 1920s, Cassel became – probably to a greater extent than anybody else at the time – an explicit spokesman for scientific economics. It was two particular fundamental propositions he presented to the general public. First, he exclaimed that the economist must be – and also was – a neutral observer, a professional 'expert', who dealt with the problem of finding optimal means for the solution of problems which were identified by politicians or other laymen. Thus he claimed that the professional economist was able to raise himself above party politics or any kind of special interest. Neither would these ends in any fundamental way interfere with the means – or vice versa.[12] Second, and of course related to this, Cassel proposed that scientific economics could be equated with pure reason and rationality. At its core, it was basically a praxis of rational human behaviour. Thus it was the task of the scientific economist to find out and present to the public the rational solution to different economic problems.

This was also emphasized in a short article by Sven Brisman to celebrate Cassel's sixtieth anniversary. Here Brisman specifically discussed Cassel's role as 'tutor of the people'. First he stressed that Cassel's popularity – both in Sweden and also apparently on the international scene – stemmed from his ability to make clear and simple propositions: 'He always writes in a clear and simple way and always meets the problem straight on without any unnecessary abbreviation.' As a popularizer of complex theories, like Walras's equilibrium theory, he had no real counterpart, according to Brisman. As far as Brisman was concerned, Cassel's work on convincing the public of the scientific and rational aspect of the subject of economics was also important. In his article he explicitly discussed the important effects of this popularization activity by Cassel:

Probably the most important effect of Cassel's tutorial activities has been that he has made the general public aware that there are objective economic laws and that it is not possible to willy-nilly 'wish' either this or that with regard to a given economic state – which is so common for example in politics. His achievement to this effect is especially impressive as people's natural instincts with regard to economic issues are almost always quite the opposite of what the economic scientists have found to be objectively true. This is especially the case regarding the basic principles of the goals and means of economic life as such: the principle of the maximization of need-satisfaction and the efficiency principle.

(Brisman 1926)

Further, Brisman especially picks out Cassel's (1908) pamphlet *Riksbanken under krisen 1907–1908* as a classical piece of economic popularization. Not only because it demonstrated Cassel's ability to write clear and distinct prose or that the ideals were put forward in a straightforward manner – according to Brisman, this was probably the first text of its kind 'presenting the role of a national bank for the general economic situation in a country' (Brisman 1926).

It is clear that Brisman touched upon a very important aspect of Cassel's popularization activities. While he is seldom very explicit about methodology in his theoretical works – although he of course mentions his method of gradual approximization in *Theory of Social Economics* (Cassel 1935a, part I, p. 94; cf. also Cassel 1935b, p. 5ff) – he is almost always ready in his more popular writing to emphasize such aspects. For the general public, he mostly propounds an extreme rationalist view of the scientific process. Economics is the language of pure rationality and reason, he maintains. Without doubt, such statements can be exemplified by almost any popular text flowing from Cassel's pen during his active period. For example in the above-mentioned *Riksbanken under krisen 1907–1908*, he already sets the tone in the introduction maintaining that the Swedish discussion regarding the role of a central banking system has been very inadequate so far and that it is his humble task to put it on the right track again (Cassel 1908, foreword). In one of his lectures for *Exportföreningen* which was later published, he starts out by exclaiming that it is 'crucial to see through the veil of confusion which the monetary system is always entangled within' (Cassel 1908, p. 39). No reader can here escape the message that such an act of unravelling the hidden truths of the monetary system can only be carried through by the neutral and scientifically equipped professional economist. Or lastly, his discussion concerning this in his central small booklet *Dyrtid och sedelöverflöd* (1917) where he first presented his version of the purchasing-power-parity principle and at the same time bombastically castigated the European governments for not trying to hold down inflation during the war:

> Science cannot be silent with regard to what happens at this very moment in the name of economic policy. There will come a day when people will be astonished by the low standards of economic knowledge among governments and the public which have led to such catastrophic mistakes and misconceptions. ... Hence the task set out in this book is obvious. Its aim is to bring light to questions which are of the utmost importance for the community as such, but which have in a systematic fashion been obscurely and falsely presented to the general public
>
> (Cassel 1917, p. viii)

Eli Heckscher (1879–1952)

Although definitively among the first generation of professional 'pure' economists, Heckscher was much younger than the famous trio Wicksell, Davidson and Cassel. Furthermore, his main contribution to science came in the field of economic history rather than in theoretical 'pure' economics. In 1929, he actually became the first holder of a chair in economic history at *Handelshögskolan* in Stockholm. This chair was established in order to allow Heckscher to make research in this field. From then on and up to his death, he was mainly preoccupied with Swedish economic history – a line of study which he summarized in his monumental work *Sveriges ekonomiska historia sedan Gustav Vasa* (Heckscher 1936–49) in four volumes. His life-long interest in doctrinal history was also manifested in the international classic *Merkantilismen* (Heckscher 1931) in two parts. From the point of view of economics, he has become most famous for the so-called Heckscher–Ohlin theorem – first made public in an article in Davidson's *Festschrift Heckscher* (1919). Like other Swedish economists especially in the 1920s, he was a keen writer on monetary issues (mainly for Davidson's *Ekonomisk Tidskrift*). Some of these articles were subsequently published in a small book (Heckscher 1926).[13]

In spite of certain erratic attempts to make contributions to the theoretical discussion in economics during his period as professor in economics at *Handelshögskolan* in Stockholm (1909–29), in the field of economics, Heckscher is probably best described as a pedagogue and popularizer. Through the small booklet *Nationalekonomins grundvalar* (Heckscher 1910), which is in fact a short and stylized summary of his lectures notes in 'pure' economics, one gets a glimpse of his teaching activities in Stockholm, mainly during the 1910s. It shows Heckscher's ability to systematize and to present a skeleton version of 'modern' economics which was in most respects up to date. At *Handelshögskolan* he also taught courses in applied economics, statistics and the history of economic thought while at the same time carrying out administrative work. In the 1920s he served as *rector* Hallendorff's second man and stand-in at *Handelshögskolan* which of course presupposed a close involvement in the day-to-day affairs of the university bureaucracy (Henriksson 1979, p. 511f).

In economic terms, Heckscher was a stern liberal. In his political outlook during his early period, however, he is better characterized as a conservative than a liberal. To this effect he was especially influenced by the famous history professor in Uppsala, Harald Hjärne. Together with another economist colleague in Stockholm of conservative inclinations, Gösta Bagge, he started *Svensk Tidskrift* in 1911. While Cassel, who had started out as a mild radical, became increasingly conservative over the years, Heckscher made progress in the other direction. During the 1930s, he especially became much more openly liberal than before in his political and social outlook.

Perhaps to an even greater extent than his older colleagues Wicksell and Cassel, Heckscher (but perhaps not Davidson who was a regular member of governmental boards and investigation committees) was used as an expert and adviser by several governments. He served on advisory boards and wrote a number of Committee reports for investigatory committees, including the politically important *Tull-och traktatkommittén* (1921–4) as well as *Arbetslöshetskommittén* (1926–8). During the First World War he served as an adviser to the Hammarskjöld government, as a member of the politically powerful *Krigsberedskapskommittén*. After the war he became the Swedish editor and main contributor to the international project initiated by the Carnegie foundation for international peace. His work within this ambitious project led to a monumental monograph on the Swedish economy during the First

World War (Heckscher 1926). In 1933 he served as one of the experts on the committee on monetary issues which proposed that Sweden should depreciate its currency, leave the gold standard and defend the internal value of the krona.

However, Heckscher was a very busy popularizer of economic science. He published several short books on popular economics, for example *Gammal och ny ekonomisk liberalism* (Heckscher 1921). He wrote hundreds of articles on economic themes for the daily Stockholm newspaper *Dagens Nyheter*. The journal which he himself (with Bagge) had started and served as an editor during the 1910s, *Svensk Tidskrift*, published many of his articles. In these articles he dealt with a broad set of popular economic issues; the state versus the market, socialism, monetary policy, the benefits or disadvantages of state monopolies, etc. Like Cassel, he was often invited to lecture. However, Heckscher added another new dimension in order to put over his message: he reached a huge public by broadcasting lectures over the new radio media.

Without doubt this hectic activity led to an increased public acceptance of scientific economics during this period. Although very different in terms of personal appearance and theoretical outlook, Heckscher shared at least one view with Cassel; namely that it was an important task for the economist to educate the lay public, including governments, in the true principles formulated by modern scientific economics. However, in order to play this important role, the economist had to develop his pedagogical abilities. In order to persuade the public to follow a correct policy, Heckscher emphasized that the economist must present his principles as simply as possible. Otherwise it is possible, as he stated, that the public would instead lend their ears to practical businessmen and others who have had no training in scholarly economics (Heckscher 1921, p. 99). As with so many others of his generation, he was optimistic about the possibility of developing a true scientific economics based on objective grounds and on a few (rationalist) principles. Neither is there any sign – at least not in his popular writing – that he ever doubted the position of the economist as a neutral observer. For example in 1912 he emphasized, before an audience of iron-and steel-industry managers and technicians, that the economist

> would be able to help the practical men in two ways. First, that he was able from his more neutral position to point out the general traits of the development process as well as its speed.

Secondly, and perhaps more importantly, he was in the elevated position of being able to consider this development process from the viewpoint of the common interest.

(Heckscher 1912, p. 3f)

His general statement in a short popular brochure discussing the causes underlying the apparent unequal distribution of incomes in the modern industrialized society is particularly typical:

My aim here in all modesty is to treat this question from the point of view of economics, i.e. without any presuppositions to the extent that this is possible. Thus, the aim is to show *how things really are constituted* [Heckscher's italics], and not whether these circumstances are good or bad

(Heckscher 1913, p. 3f)

However, this optimism hardly survived the 1930s – and the attack from the young Turks of the new generation of Stockholm economists. But however it is judged, this untiring rhetoric was without doubt of great importance for the increased status of scientific economics in the previous period.

Sven Brisman (1881–1953)

Brisman also belonged to the first generation of scholarly economists in Sweden. In contrast to Cassel and Heckscher, he was much more narrow in scope and perhaps also in ambition. Although he published several theoretical articles in *Ekonomisk Tidskrift* (for example, in relation to wage formation, business cycles, inflation and loan rent, prices, etc.),[14] he did not delve deeply into these subjects. Accordingly in the history of Swedish economic thought, he may not deserve more than a footnote.[15] He was mainly a teacher and popularizer of economic science while his scholarly work was almost totally concerned with banking history. Unfortunately, it has become increasingly clear over the years that his work in this field suffers from the fact that he was not a historian by profession and lacked a sense of historical imagination.[16] However, he presented his findings in several voluminous works, first in *De moderna affärsbankerna* (Brisman 1915) and later in *Sveriges Riksbank, I* (Brisman 1918), and *Sveriges affärsbanker, Grundläggningstiden* (Brisman 1924a).

Although to a large extent forgotten nowadays, Brisman was an extremely well-known economist especially during the 1910s and 1920s. He had become professor in 'National economy and banking science' at *Handelshögskolan* in Stockholm 1917 and was thus a colleague of Heckscher (he had previously also served as a docent under Heckscher). During the 1910s, his two-volume textbook in economics, *Nationalekonomien* (Brisman 1916), was widely read by students but also reached circles outside the universities. According to Brisman his aim was 'to present a short and easily understood presentation of the most important aspects of economic life' instead of 'endless pages of generalities', and to be as practical as possible (Brisman 1916, part I, p. 1). In the first volume (only sixty-five pages long), he hastily rushed through what he himself defined as 'theoretical economics'. In passing, he spent half a page on the marginal utility principle. In his discussion of price and value there is no reference to either Cassel, Walras or Marshall but to the Frenchman Lenoir and his 'excellent work' 'Etudes sur la formation et le mouvement des prix' (Brisman 1916, part I, p. 6). In the second volume he dealt with 'practical economics' – in a much more thorough manner (the text runs to 268 pages).

However patchy and theoretically underdeveloped Brisman's textbook seems by now, it was nevertheless widely read at the time and sold far more copies than Wicksell's *Lectures in Political Economy* (the first Swedish edition: Wicksell (1901, 1906)). Aiming for a wide public, Brisman was eager to point out in his book the scientific character of professional economics as an objective tool for laying bare the true principles governing economic society. He emphasized in much the same way as Heckscher or Cassel, the role of the professional economist as a useful 'expert' who deals with economic means and leave the ends to the politicians.

This viewpoint is also highlighted in most of his other popularization activities. Although he does not seem to have been so busy in this field as, for example, Cassel and Heckscher, he nevertheless published many articles dealing with popular themes. As a professor in banking economics, he also lectured for *Svenska Bankföreningen* on subsequent occasions (published as Brisman 1921a) while his lecturing activities in the town of Gävle gave rise to several pamphlets published by the local chamber of commerce (*Handelskammaren*). In these lectures, for example, he provided a popular treatment of what he considered to be the modern and scientific economic interpretation regarding such themes as 'the causes of trade cycles', 'the current inflation, its causes and effects', 'Sweden's balance of trade and the current debt situation', etc. (Brisman 1912a,b and 1913).

It is clear that Brisman also presented a view of economics and of the economists that we seem to know well by now. He emphasized the role of the economist as a neutral expert and tutor – both with regard to the popular public as well as to politicians. 'When one follows how important economic questions are treated in the general debate one gets the impression that the official governmental stand-point is that it can do as it pleases and act as if there were no objective economic laws', he writes in a commentary in 1920 criti-cizing the introduction of the 8-hour day during this year. This text contains as usual the following statement: '[From the point of view of scientific economics], the question is rather simple ...' (Brisman 1921b, p. 23). Here, as in so many other contexts, he sets out to make the reader believe that there are objective economic truths which can be detected by the professional economist equipped with a well-defined set of scientific tools and a rigorous methodology. In the same way as Heckscher and Cassel, he separates ends and means from each other and denotes that it is the task of the economists to deal only with the latter. In a small booklet 'The worldview of an economist', which was aimed for a popular public, Brisman (1924b) presents his economic philosophy in the following fashion:

> an economist who carefully reads his daily newspaper often comes upon statements which are completely untrue. However, this is not only so with regard to the press. In fact, he is permanently reminded of this when he studies the programme of the political parties the utterances of statesmen, committee reports and parliamentary decisions which are very often based on viewpoints which are in conflict with the results of his own science. Such differences between the scientific standpoint and the popular view very often have a trivial cause. To a large extent, they extend from mere misapprehensions or from a state of ignorance of the scientific viewpoint regarding the specific matter. ... This difference does not seem to be coincidental but is in fact very common and appears in a systematic fashion. In fact, it seems clear that the subject of economics is currently in the same position as natural science was some two or three centuries ago or to some extent is even today, namely in the sense that it had to confront views which

were proven to be untrue but which were nevertheless retained for non-scientific reasons. Today the situation is exactly the same with regard to economics. It has to confront views which are not logical and take as little consideration of scientific principles as orthodox theology did in the past. Instead it is based upon instincts, passions and interests ...

(Brisman 1924b, p. 3f)

V

It is well-known that Gunnar Myrdal in his *The Political Element in the Development of Economic Theory*, first published in Swedish in 1929, launched a general attack on what he regarded as a naïve optimism on the part of an older generation of economists. He was especially critical of their methodological programme of a value-free and objectively-given science. The publication of this text at this moment must without doubt be seen in relation to the intense, popularizing efforts of the Swedish economists – especially after the First World War. While Myrdal attacked a general phenomenon common to most economics at that time, many of the traits he criticized were especially pertinent among several of the earlier generation of Swedish economists. In this context, Myrdal explicitly mentions both Cassel and Wicksell, as examples of such naïve optimism regarding a value-free economic science (Myrdal 1954, pp. 19, 94, 176f).

As we have seen in this chapter, the message of such a value-free economics and a view of the economist as a neutral expert was undoubtedly communicated to the general public by the popularizing economists during this period. Although Brisman, serving as our witness from the national Economy Club meeting in 1929, was not so explicit on this point, it seems obvious that this type of critique highlighted by Myrdal on this occasion astonished several of the older economists who were present.

It is ironic that the rise of both Myrdal and the Stockholm School relied at least to some extent on the groundwork made by the earlier generation of economists to popularize a view of the scientific process which Myrdal criticized at its root and branch. In this chapter we have seen how an attempt to present the professional economist as a neutral expert equipped with a certain set of scientific theories and a specific methodology was part and parcel of their popularization programme. Without doubt this must be regarded as part of a more general professionalization process which also affected many other academic fields during this period. However, the success of such professionalization efforts have been unequally shared between different academic subjects. Probably because of its low 'technical task uncertainty', economics has been the most successful subject within the family of social sciences in terms of maintaining a high degree of craft control. However, such control within the academic community does not immediately lead to success. In order to understand the increasing prestige of economics in Sweden during the post-1914 period, it is essential to comprehend the popularizing role of this first generation of economists – academic economists like Cassel, Heckscher, Brisman and many others – who were able to make plausible the idea that the expertise of the economist was necessary and that it stemmed from his special knowledge of a certain methodology taught in formal courses in economics departments. 'Nothing is as practical as a good theory', Cassel used to say. Clearly there is a double-meaning in that statement.

NOTES

1 Translated by Rolf Henriksson and included in his 1991 publication. Consult also his article on the 'Political Economy Club' in Stockholm (1989).
2 For a recent and brief summary of the debate see Carlsson (1988), p. 369ff. The most important works in this debate have been Landgren (1960); Öhman (1970); Steiger (1971); and Unga (1976).
3 See, however, the material collected in Jonung (1991) and Jonung and Gunnarsson (1991).
4 See, for example, Whitley (1984, p. 4ff; cf. also Bloor (1981); Coats (1985); Stigler (1982); Brannigan (1981); and Knorr-Cetina (1981).
5 For a critique of a semiotic interpretation of 'language' which is also relevant for McCloskey's interpretative scheme, see the works by Anthony Giddens (1985), for example. Such a critique is also implicit in Hodgson (1988), p. 138ff.
6 Lindell's notes from Rabenius's lectures (1827?), B 142 a 2, UUB.
7 P.E. Bergfalk's lecture notes on *National-economie*, part 1–II, B 174 s.t. UUB.
8 This does not at all indicate that, for example, Knut Wicksell was not an important popularizer in the latter (*e*) sense. Although he is very direct in his main theoretical works (1893), (1898) and (1901, 1906), and goes straight to the point; in his more popular writing he tries to be more pedagogic and sometimes also gives brief methodological intro-

ductions. One must not forget that Wicksell, long before taking up economics as a profession, had been intensively engaged in political campaigning and journalism (as a left-wing liberal, stern republican and neo-Malthusian). He continued with these activities even after his appointment in Lund. Although in his popular works he is much less explicit about the advantages of the analytical hard-core structure in possession by the economist (compared for example to Cassel, Heckscher and Brisman) he leaves no reader in doubt about the scientific claims of his statements. See for example Wicksell (1905). For an outline of his methodology, see the introduction to Wicksell (1901). For a discussion of Wicksell's view of the scientific process, Gunnar Myrdal (1958) is still useful.

9 For a recent discussion of Cassel, see Carlsson (1988) and my article in Magnusson (1990). See also Jonung (1979).

10 See the list of Cassel's collected works and articles in Carlsson and Jonung (1987).

11 For a discussion of Cassel as a scientist, see for example Magnusson (1990) and Benny Carlsson's contribution to this volume (Chapter 10).

12 To what extent such an independent position of ends and means is possible has been discussed by Elster (1983). However, during the 1920s and 1930s such non-interference between ends and means was the gospel of scientific economics – not least that preached by Cassel. Cf. also Hodgson (1988), p. 93ff.

13 Not so much is written about Heckscher. See, however, the articles by Henriksson (1979, 1990). See also Carlsson (1988) who provides a fairly extensive treatment of Heckscher's political and economic activities, as do Flam's and Carlsson's contributions to this volume.

14 Brisman's articles in *Ekonomisk Tidskrift* up to the Second World War were: 'Arbetslönens problem' (1919); 'Räntan vid direkt inflation' (1922); 'Konjunkturväxlingarnas orsaker' (1923); 'Prisnivån som självständig faktor i bytesekvationen' (1925); 'Penningvärde och tullskydd' (1925); and 'Våra sedlars omloppshastighet under världskriget' (1926).

15 To my knowledge, no scholarly work has dealt with Brisman's activities as an economist. Regarding Brisman's career in general, see the article on him in *Svenskt Biografiskt Lexikon*.

16 For a critical attitude of Brisman as a bank historian see Nilsson (1981).

REFERENCES

Bergfalk, P.-E. (1853a) *Bidrag till de under sista hundrade åren inträffade handelskrisers historia*, Uppsala: Nordisk Universitetstidskrift.

—— (1853b) *Skall guldåldern komma*, Uppsala: Inbjudningsskrift, Uppsala Universitet.

Bloor, D. (1981) 'The Strengths of the Strong Program', *Philosophy of the Social Sciences*, vol. 2.

Brannigan, A. (1981) *The Social Basis of Scientific Discoveries*, Cambridge: Cambridge University Press.

Brems, H. (1989) 'The Founding Fathers of the Swedish School: Wicksell and Cassel, in D. Walker (ed.), *Perspectives on the History of Economic Thought*, vol. I, Aldershot: Edward Elgar.

Brisman, S. (1912a) 'Konjunkturväxlingarna och deras orsaker', *Handelskammarens i Gävle småskrifter*, no. 9, Gävle.

—— (1912b) 'Den nuvarande prisstegringen, dess orsaker och dess betydelse', *Handelskammaren i Gävle småskrifter*, no. 10, Gävle.

—— (1913) 'Sveriges handelsbalans och utländska skuldsättning', *Handelskammaren i Gävle smaskrifter*, no. 11, Jönköping.

—— (1915) *De moderna affärsbankerna*, Stockholm: Handelshögskolans skrifter.

—— (1916) *Nationalekonomi, I–II*, Stockholm: P.A. Norstedt & Söner.

—— (1918) *Sveriges Riksbank, I*, Stockholm: P.A. Norstedt & Söner.

—— (1921a) *Den ekonomiska krisens orsaker och sannolika förlopp*, Stockholm: Svenska Bankföreningen, skrifter 28.

—— (1921b) 'Åttatimmarsdagen. Några kritiska synpunkter', *Nationalekonomiska studier tillägnade Knut Wicksell. Ekonomisk Tidskrift* vol. 12.

—— (1924a) *Hur en nationalekonom betraktar världen*, Stockholm: Albert Bonniers förlag.

—— (1924b) *Sveriges affärsbanker. Grundläggningstiden*, Stockholm: Svenska Bankföreningen.

—— (1926) 'Gustav Cassel som ekonomisk folkuppfostrare', *Sunt förnuft*, November.

—— (1930) 'De unga nationalekonomernas revolt', *Göteborgs Handels-och sjöfartstidning*, 5.12.

Carlson, B. (1988) *Staten som monster*, Lund: Ekonomisk-historiska föreningen.

Carlson, B. and Jonung, L. (1987) 'Gustav Cassels artiklar i Svenska Dagbladet', *Meddelande från Ekonomisk-historiska institutionen vid Lunds universitet*, no. 62.

Cassel, G. (1908) *Riksbanken under krisen 1907–1908*, Stockholm: Hugo Gebers förlag.

—— (1917) *Dyrtid och sedelöverflöd*, Stockholm: P.A. Norstedt & Söner.

—— (1935a) *Theory of Social Economics, I–II*, London: Macmillan.

—— (1935b) *On Quantitative Thinking in Economics*, Oxford: Oxford University Press.

—— (1940–1) *I förnuftets tjänst, I–II*, Stockholm: P.A. Norstedt & Söner.

Coats, A.W. (1985) 'The Sociology of Knowledge and the History of Economics' in W. Samuels (ed.), *Research in the History of Economic Thought and Methodology*, Boston: Kluwer Publishers.

Deane, P. (1981) 'The Scope and Method of Economic Science', *Economic Journal*, vol. 93.

Elster, J. (1983) *Sour Grapes. Studies in the Subversion of Rationality*, Cambridge: Cambridge University Press.

Giddens, A. (1985) *The Constitution of Society*, Cambridge: Polity Press.

Hansson, B. (1982) *The Stockholm School and the Development of Dynamic Method*, London: Croom Helm.

Heckscher, E.F. (1910) *Nationalekonomins grundvalar*, Stockholm: Handelshögskolan.

—— (1912) 'De allmänna ekonomiska förutsättningarna för en utveckling af den svenska järnindustriens afsättningsförhållanden', *Jernkontorets Annaler.*

—— (1913) *Varpå beror det att några människor äro rika och andra fattiga,* Stockholm: Albert Bonniers förlag.

—— (1919) 'Utrikeshandels verkan på inkomstfördelningen', *Nationalekonomiska studier tillägnade professor David Davidson. Ekonomisk Tidskrift,* vol. 21, part II.

—— (1921) *Gammal och ny liberalism,* Stockholm: P.A. Norstedt & Söner.

—— (1931) *Merkantilismen, I–II,* Stockholm: P.A. Norstedt & Söner.

—— (1936–49) *Bidrag till Sveriges ekonomiska och sociala historia under och efter världskriget,* Stockholm: P.A. Norstedt & Söner.

—— (1953) 'A Survey of Economic Thought in Sweden, 1875–1950', *Scandinavian Economic History Review,* vol. I, 1.

Henriksson, R. (1979) 'Eli Heckscher och svensk nationalekonomi', *Ekonomisk Debatt,* no. 8.

—— (1989) 'The Institutional Base of the Stockholm School: The Political Economy Club 1917–51', *History of Economics Society Bulletin,* vol. 11, spring.

—— (1990) 'Eli Heckscher', in B. Sandelin (ed.), *A History of Swedish Economic Thought,* London: Routledge.

—— (1991), 'The Political Economy Club and the Stockholm School, 1917–51', In L. Jonung (ed.), *The Stockholm School of Economics Revisited,* Cambridge: Cambridge University Press.

Hodgson, G. (1988) *Economics and Institutions,* Cambridge: Polity Press.

Jonung, L. (1979) 'Cassel, Davidson and Heckscher on Swedish Monetary Policy. A Confidential Report to the Riksbank in 1931', *Economy and History,* vol. 2.

—— (ed.) (1991) *The Stockholm School of Economics Revisited,* Cambridge: Cambridge University Press.

Jonung, L., assisted by Gunnarsson, E. (1991) 'Economics the Swedish Way 1889–1989', *Research Report,* Stockholm: Handelshögskolan.

Klammer, A. (1984) 'Levels of Discourse in New Classical Economics', *History of Political Economy,* vol. 16, 2.

Knorr-Cetina, K. (1981) *The Manufacture of Knowledge: An Essay on the Constructivist and the Contextual Nature of Science,* Oxford: Oxford University Press.

Landgren, K.-G. (1960) *Den nya ekonomien i Sverige,* Stockholm: Göteborgs Universitets Nationalekonomiska institution. Ekonomiska studier, 3.

McCloskey, D. (1985) *The Rhetorics of Economics,* Madison: University of Wisconsin Press.

Magnusson, L. (1990) 'Gustav Cassel', in B. Sandelin (ed.) *History of Swedish Economic Thought,* London: Routledge.

Myrdal, G. (1954) *The Political Element in the Development of Economic Theory,* Cambridge, Mass.: Harvard University Press.

Nationalekonomiska föreningen (1927) *Nationalekomiska föreningen 1877–1927. Minnesskrift,* Stockholm: P.A. Norstedt & Söner.

Nilsson, G.B. (1981) *Banker i brytningstid,* Stockholm: Institutet för ekonomisk-historisk forskning vid Handelshögskolan i Stockholm.

Öhman, B. (1970) *Svensk arbetsmarknadspolitik 1900–1947*, Halmstad: Prisma.
Rabenius, L.G. (1829) *Lärobok i nationalekonomin*, Uppsala.
Schumpeter, J. (1972) *A History of Economic Analysis*, New York: Allen & Unwin.
Seligman, B. (1962) *Main Currents in Modern Economics*, New York: The Free Press of Glencoe.
Steiger, O. (1971) *Studien zur Entstehung der Neuen Wirtschaftslehre in Schweden. Eine Anti-kritik*, Berlin: Duncker & Humblot.
Stigler, G. (1982) *The Economist as Preacher*, Oxford: Oxford University Press.
Thomas, B. (1936) *Monetary Policy and Crises. The Study of Swedish Experience*, London: George Routledge & Sons.
Tribe, K. (1988) *Governing Economy. The Reformation of German Economic Discourse 1750–1840*, Cambridge: Cambridge University Press.
Unga, N. (1976) *Socialdemokratin och arbetslöshetsfrågan*, Kristianstad: Arkivs förlag.
Whitley, R. (1984) *The Intellectual and Social Organization of the Sciences*, Oxford: Oxford University Press.
Wicksell, K. (1893) *Uber Wert, Kapital und Rente*, Jena: Verlag von Gustav Fischer.
—— (1898) *Geldzins und Güterpreise*, Jena: Verlag von Gustav Fischer.
—— (1901, 1906) *Föreläsningar i Nationalekonomi, I–II*, Lund: Gleerups förlag.
—— (1905) *Socialiststaten och nutidssamhället*, Verdandi småskrifter, no. 124, Stockholm.

7

GÖSTA BAGGE: AN ENTREPRENEUR IN SWEDISH ECONOMICS

Eskil Wadensjö

Many economists active in Sweden during the interwar period are still famous today, others forgotten. They can be grouped into three generations. Gustav Cassel, David Davidson and Knut Wicksell belong to the older generation. The members of the Stockholm School of Economics, among whom Erik Lindahl, Gunnar Myrdal and Bertil Ohlin are the most well-known, belong to the younger generation. Of those belonging to the middle generation, Eli Heckscher is the only one well-known to present-day economists. Other economists of that generation who at the time were among the leaders in their field are now almost forgotten, as for example Gösta Bagge.

The ignorance today of Gösta Bagge's contribution to economics stands in glaring contrast to his strong position in the interwar period. In order to demonstrate this, let us go back to 1931.

In 1931 Gösta Bagge held a professorship at *Stockholms Högskola* (now Stockholm University) and was director of the Stockholm School of Social Work and Public Administration, which he had founded. Although officially the joint director of the Stockholm Institute for Social Sciences together with Gustav Cassel, in reality he was independent. This institute, which employed many economists, was mainly financed out of funds received from the Rockefeller Foundation for a project that was based on and which would hopefully expand some of the themes from Bagge's much praised doctoral dissertation on the regulation of wages. In April 1931 new funds were granted by the Rockefeller Foundation both to the project and to a new building for the School of Social Work and Public Administration and the Social Science Institute. The building was already completed by the next year.

Bagge was the only economist among the members of the Committee on Unemployment, a committee which published the major works of the Stockholm School of Economics. Its first major report was published in 1931, a report largely based on Gösta Bagge's ideas and also on his supplement to the report on the causes of unemployment (Bagge 1931). All of the economists whom we now consider as members of the Stockholm School were engaged by the Committee on Unemployment and/or Bagge's project at the Social Science Institute (Wadensjö 1991).

Gösta Bagge was one of the great entrepreneurs in Swedish economic research. Thus, there is ample reason to recall his contributions and to ask why they have largely fallen into obscurity.

EMPIRICAL RESEARCH BASED ON THEORY

Gösta Bagge's main scientific work is his PhD dissertation *Arbetslönens reglering genom sammanslutningar (The Regulation of Wages by Organizations)* which he defended at *Stockholms Högskola* in 1917. It deals with the effects on wages of collective bargaining and state intervention.

His interest in the effects of trade unions can be traced back to his stay at Johns Hopkins University in Baltimore. After completing his undergraduate studies in Uppsala in 1904, he left for Johns Hopkins for the academic year of 1904–5.[1] Gösta Bagge was the first Swedish economist to study in the United States and the only one of his generation. The first and second generation of modern Swedish economists studied for shorter or extended periods in Europe, especially in Germany. It was not until the third generation, the Stockholm School generation, that it became common to go to the United States. In several cases, stays were initiated by Gösta Bagge.

A major research project had started at Johns Hopkins in 1902 aimed at a comprehensive study of the US trade union movement. The research approach was strictly inductive. The method was to collect all forms of information on the trade unions. Bagge took part in the project and his first published paper, 'The Boot and Shoeworkers' Union Stamp', was printed in the Johns Hopkins University Circular.

Back in Sweden, Bagge started to study the Swedish trade union movement. His first work in that field, conducted for the National Board of Trade, was in the institutionalist tradition (Bagge 1909, 1910). The second of these studies, a careful examination of collective agreements in Sweden, was accepted as a licentiate thesis, a step on the way to a PhD at *Stockholms Högskola*. Based on this thesis, he planned to write his PhD dissertation around a detailed description of collective agreements in Sweden leading to conclusions relevant for the formation of an economic theory of unions and their effects.

Bagge changed his mind, however. The dissertation became a theoretical analysis of the effects of collective agreements in comparison to a state without such agreements. The impressive empirical material was used only to illustrate and exemplify the theoretical results. The dissertation was published in 1917, decades before the breakthrough of econometrics.

Bagge's conversion from an inductive to a deductive method is clearly seen in a review article in *Ekonomisk Tidskrift* published in 1914 (Bagge 1914). In this article he critically examines eleven volumes from the Johns Hopkins project, his own starting point. He denounces the method used in the project – the books are dull, filled with uninteresting details and lack contact with mainstream theoretical economics. Instead of the inductive method used in the Johns Hopkins project, he proposes a combination of deductive and inductive methods.

THE DISSERTATION

The starting point for the dissertation *Arbetslönens reglering genom sammanslutningar* is to introduce an exogenous change of the wage rate caused by collective agreements or legislation (minimum wage laws) into a general equilibrium model for a market economy. The new equilibrium is compared to the old one by the use of comparative statics and the transition between the two states of equilibrium is analysed.

The effects of collective agreements on income distribution, labour demand, demand for other factors of production, distribution of labour on industries, unemployment and economic growth are analysed in different chapter of the book. Special attention is given to the case of changing relative wage rates. Bagge deals with several factors complicating the analysis such as monopoly, increasing returns to scale and the existence of non-profit maximizing employers (the governmental sector). One of the few issues he abstains from dealing with is labour supply: 'the relationship between remuneration for work and labour supply is of a complicated and irregular nature' (Bagge 1917, p. 11).

The most impressive aspect of his study is Bagge's incisive treatment of the many cases he actually analyses. The foundations for several of the 'new labour market theories' of the last decades can be found in non-technical versions in Bagge's dissertation. I shall give some examples here.

In recent decades, costs of information (in search theory), risk aversion (in contract theory) and the relation between wage and efficiency (in efficiency wage theory) have become central parts of the development of labour market theory. These issues are all extensively treated in Bagge's study. He analyses, for example, how risk aversion may lead to rigid wages (irrespective of whether there are unions or not):

> But in addition the lowering of the wage rate is much more evident than unemployment as a consequence of wage rigidity; even if the disadvantages of keeping the wage rate above the market rate are taken into account, these are counterbalanced by a higher stability in income and living standard in bad times.
>
> (Bagge 1917, p. 374)

Bagge also analyses under what conditions a wage rate above the market wage leads to an increase in the total wage sum. This is an important issue in current research on the economics of trade unions. There are several other issues considered in Bagge's dissertation. Some examples are:

1 The solidaristic wage policy compared to a policy based on the firm's ability to pay (according to Bagge, in practice a profit-sharing system).
2 The effect of collective agreements with unequal pay for equal work. According to Bagge, the result would instead be an equalization of expected income (wage rate times expected employment rate), where a person's expected employment rate depends on how the jobs are distributed (seniority, lottery, quota system, etc.).
3 Equal pay for unequal work and how it may influence the employment of youth and women. Equal pay for unequal work was used by some (male-dominated) trade unions to exclude women from the workforce.

Gösta Bagge's dissertation was very well received. Gustaf Cassel, for example, was very positive. Even in later years, opinions have been favourable.[2] Karl-Gustav Landgren writes in his survey of Swedish economic research that it 'was undoubtedly one of the foremost doctoral treatises in economics to appear in Sweden' (Landgren 1957, p. 9). For the present-day reader, it is the wealth of ideas and the combination of theoretical structure and detailed empirical knowledge which are most outstanding. In a present-day perspective, econometric methods and a more formal and less partial treatment of the many cases would have been recommended.

For Gösta Bagge, the dissertation was only the first step in his study of this field of research. In 1925, a few years after his appointment to the professorship in economics and social policy at *Stockholms Högskola*, he started a project which combined empirical and theoretical research on wage formation, funded by the Laura Spellman Rockefeller Memorial. It is probably the largest Swedish research project ever in the field of economics. The subject of the project was wage formation and a very extensive collection of data was planned. We shall return to that project below. Here we shall deal only with Bagge's own research for the project which was ultimately much less than he had intended. An important part ought to have been a further development of his dissertation, translated into English. It was never completed.

Many books were published from the project in a special series, *Stockholm Economic Studies*. Bagge is the co-author of two volumes concerning wage development in Sweden – see Bagge, Lundberg and Svennilson (1933, 1935) – two careful statistical studies of long-run wage developments in Sweden. He is also the author of a separate volume in Swedish on the wages of workers in local government (Bagge 1933). He also surveyed wage movements and their consequences for unemployment in a few articles.

PERMANENT UNEMPLOYMENT

Bagge's only major study in labour economics after his dissertation is his supplement to the Committee on Unemployment (Bagge 1931). It was published in 1931 at the same time as the first main report of the Committee but was already presented for the Committee in 1928 in a version very much like the published one.

The starting point for the Committee, when it was established in 1927 and also for Bagge's supplement, was the unemployment of the late 1920s. Those years witnessed a period of prosperity but at the same time unemployment was still high. This unemployment during periods of prosperity was called 'permanent unemployment' and the first task of the Committee was to explain what caused it.

For this study, Bagge used the same methodology as in his dissertation, i.e. comparative statics. The major part of the study is an analysis of the factors which influence size and structure of labour demand. Bagge did not analyse the factors which influence the total labour supply, but instead examined in detail the factors which determine the distribution of labour supply by region and industry. The main conclusion is that wage rigidity and incomplete occupational and geographical mobility in combination with changes in the labour demand result in unemployment.

In the final part of his study, the effects of wage increases on unemployment are analysed. Bagge's analysis and conclusions are very close to those of his dissertation. (Real) wage increases may lead to unemployment.[3]

Bagge's study is a contribution to the theory of equilibrium unemployment – classical unemployment (disequilibrium only in the labour market), structural unemployment (changes in the demand of labour) and frictional unemployment (slow adjustment of labour supply in spite of the existence of vacancies).[4] Bagge is cautious in his conclusions:

> This analysis may thus not be utilized to give a definite answer to the question of the causes of unemployment. It is not possible to present a generally valid 'unemployment theory', nor can any more comprehensive conclusions be drawn here. Not until empirical studies of the size and character of the unemployment and their relation to other phenomena in Sweden in that period have been made, can a plausible picture of the that development appear.
>
> (Bagge 1931, p. 127)

It is important to underline that Bagge's study did not deal with the unemployment of the depression of the 1930s, nor with the actual unemployment of the 1920s. Bagge analyses a number of purely theoretical forms of unemployment at equilibrium under certain restrictive assumptions regarding the operation of the labour market. The empirical application was left to later work by the committee and by other researchers.

SOCIAL INSURANCE AND LOCAL PUBLIC ADMINISTRATION

The major part of Gösta Bagge's publications in economics besides labour economics consist of surveys and shorter contributions to the public debate. Together with Eli Heckscher, he founded and edited the *Svensk Tidskrift*, a conservative political journal. He contributed regularly to that journal up to the beginning of the 1930s. From 1936 until his death in January 1951, the main part of his publications were collections of political speeches. However, in two areas, social insurance and tariffs within public utilities, Bagge wrote a number of more elaborate studies.

In several articles and also in a speech at the Swedish Economic Association *(Nationalekonomiska föreningen)*, he dealt with the national old-age and disability pension scheme decided by the Riksdag in 1913.[5] It was a combination of a premium reserve system and a pay-as-you-go system. The latter, called the supplementary pension, would secure a minimum standard for those granted a disability pension. The supplementary pension was means-tested.

Bagge consistently opposed this combination of two principles and wanted to separate the two systems. The pay-as-you-go part, according to him, was only social welfare in disguise and he believed that pensioners would also consider it as such. He stressed that means-testing would influence incentives to work and save. The work incentive in particular would be affected by the income-testing while saving would be influenced by the means-testing of wealth. Bagge's view on social insurance is developed in great detail in *Socialpolitik (Social Policy)*, a 300-page manuscript used as course literature at the School for Social Work and Public Administration (Bagge 1935). Bagge planned to publish it but never found the opportunity. Other tasks took more and more time.

Bagge shows a streak of insensitivity in the debate on the pension scheme. He does not see the change of name from poverty assistance *(fattigvård)* to old age or disability pension *(folkpension)* and the introduction of fixed rates of support in spite of the remaining means-testing meant an important change of policy. It became for many a very popular policy.

Bagge was very familiar with the tariffs for public utilities. As early as the 1910s, he became a member of the Stockholm local council and took active part in the formation of local policy as a member of the conservative party. In two papers he presents a general analysis of the tariffs for public utilities. The analysis has a welfare economic foundation. His main recommendation is that the activities of local government should be financed by tariffs (prices) and not by taxes. Exceptions were made for 'collective goods' and 'merit wants' (Bagge of course does not use these denominations from later decades). A modified marginal cost price system would be used, according to Bagge. Decreasing marginal costs (when there are high fixed costs) and peak-load pricing were mentioned as cases when the principle would need to be modified. These 'modern' pricing methods are realistically discussed with regard to distributional effects and the costs for the various price systems themselves.

THE ACADEMIC ENTREPRENEUR

Gösta Bagge's scientific publications are also of interest for researchers today, especially his study of the effects of trade unions on wage formation. There were, however, several Swedish economists who were his contemporaries who made more outstanding scientific contributions. As a research entrepreneur, Bagge is the most important. It is difficult to find a counterpart in the history of economic science in Sweden.

Bagge defended his dissertation in 1917 at the age of 35. He had already published several other studies. He was a very strong candidate for a professorship and was one of two applicants for a position in Uppsala in 1920. He gave a trial lecture (later published in *Ekonomisk Tidskrift*) and was the most likely to be appointed. However, he withdrew his application. Bagge wanted to become professor in Stockholm and not in Uppsala.[6] He worked diligently towards that goal. Together with Otto Järte he wrote for the Central Organization for Social Work (CSA) a programme for an institute at university level for the training of civil servants for local government. According to the proposal, the director of the institute would be a professor in economics with social policy. The Stockholm Municipal Council (with Bagge as a member) supported the proposal after the approval of the Central Board of the Administration of the Municipality (Bagge was also a member of that board). The CSA collected funds for the professorship which was to be placed at *Stockholms Högskola* and combined with the directorship of the new School of Social Work and Public Administration. The professorship was established and Bagge was appointed without having to make an application.

Besides the directorship for the School of Social Work and Public Administration, Bagge was also appointed to share the directorship of the Social Science Institute with Gustaf Cassel. At the time of his appointment, the institute consisted of only a small library and an assistant in addition to the two directors. Bagge had higher ambitions than that for the institute.

Bagge visited the United States and Canada for an extended period in 1924 and on that occasion met representatives of the Laura Spellman Rockefeller Memorial Foundation, later a part of the Rockefeller Foundation.[7] Contacts developed and in 1925 a first grant of $US75,000 was made to the Social Science Institute for a research programme based on Bagge's dissertation. The size of the grant was impressive considering prices and wages at that time. In 1931 an additional $US300,000 was granted, of which $US100,000 went to a new building for both the School of Social Work and Public Administration and the Social Science Institute. Later a grant to a library was given.

The main results were to be published in a new series, *Stockholm Economic Studies*. As already mentioned, the original plans to follow up Bagge's doctoral dissertation were only partially fulfilled. Other parts of the project became more important, such as Erik Lindahl's study of national income and Erik Lundberg's doctoral dissertation, *Studies in the Theory of Economic Expansion*.

The majority of the studies were careful, empirical investigations of the long-term economic development in Sweden. Most of the economists whom we now consider as members of the Stockholm School of Economics were engaged in the Rockefeller project: Alf Johansson, Karin Kock, Erik Lindahl, Erik Lundberg, Gunnar Myrdal and Ingvar Svennilson. There is, however, no direct connection between this project and the founding of the Stockholm School tradition, but rather an indirect one – the establishment of a setting for research.

Such a relation is much more obvious for another of Bagge's 'projects'.[8] Bagge was the only economist among the members of the Committee on Unemployment, which started its work in 1927. Gunnar Huss, who was much involved when Bagge got his professorship and the School of Social Work and Public Administration was established, was chairman of the committee.

The committee on Unemployment engaged several members of Bagge's staff at the Social Science Institute, among them Alf Johansson, Karin Kock, Erik Lindahl, Gunnar Myrdal and Ingvar

Svennilson. Other economists engaged by the committee were Dag Hammarskjöld and Bertil Ohlin. The initiative to engage Ohlin (a relative of Bagge) was taken by Bagge.

Among the studies made for the committee, the four supplements to the second report written by Hammarskjöld, Johansson, Myrdal and Ohlin should be mentioned. These four studies are major works in the early Stockholm School tradition.

The studies originated by Bagge, led in practice to the undermining of Bagge's own position in the academic community. Bagge has been associated, especially by a later generation, not with the Stockholm School but with the active opponents to the ideas of the school and of Keynes, such as Cassel and Heckscher. A more correct classification is that Bagge did not take part in the academic debate from the mid-1930s. He had become a full-time politician.

Bagge was well aware that his most important part was as entrepreneur in economics. His awareness of that is evident in a letter to Eli Heckscher:

> I sent you and some other friends the account in question [on the programme of the School of Social Work and Public Administration], so that you could see that I wasn't idling away my time, even though I haven't achieved a lot scientifically, but also because I am quite frankly pleased with it and a little bit vain about what I have accomplished. Actually, it is the only thing I am satisfied with in my work – if I allow myself to be sentimental – and I'm not going to allow it to slip away.
>
> (Letter from Gösta Bagge to Eli Heckscher, 8 December 1931,
> KB (Royal Library, Stockholm))

THE POLITICIAN

Gösta Bagge was involved in practical political work most of his life. Already at the beginning of this century, he started the first club modelled after the British settlement movement. For several years he was responsible for a journal published by *Klubben*, as the association and the journal of the association were called. The settlement-movement, in Sweden called *Hemgårdsrörelsen*, with activities mainly for working-class youth, may be classified as socially conservative.[9]

Gösta Bagge combined research and political activities for many years. He was of the opinion that it was possible to do this successfully. In his inaugural lecture he emphasized that:

If a careful distinction is made between the scientific investigation and what belongs to the practical and political area, the conflicts within economic science will actually disappear.

(*Dagens Nyheter* 1921)

Bagge became more directly involved in political activities when he, together with Eli Heckscher, started the conservative journal *Svensk Tidskrift* in 1911. Especially in the first decade of the new journal Bagge wrote numerous articles. He wrote 60 articles between 1911 and 1920, including editorials, and 21 articles between 1921 and 1930. His main area was social policy but he also wrote many articles on foreign policy, and on military defence.

In 1913 Bagge became a member of the Stockholm City Council. He took an active part in the activities and wrote, for example, part of a report on free school lunches for the council (*Betänkande* 1915). In the 1920s, he gradually withdrew from the political scene. In 1926 he left the Stockholm City Council and in 1930 resigned as editor of *Svensk Tidskrift*. In an interview in November 1931, he answered the question if he intended to be active in political life again in the following way:

'No, no! I don't have the time for it. I have so many other obligations. But, one can be politically active without being a member of Parliament or writing in the newspapers or making speeches', he concluded with an expression of relief like a student who has successfully completed an examination.

(*Nya Dagligt Allehanda*, 8 November 1931)

By the following year, 1932, Gösta Bagge had already become a member of Parliament, and in 1935 he became the leader of the Conservative Party. In so doing, Gösta Bagge by and large gave up research and also his position at the *Stockholms Högskola*. When the coalition government was formed during the Second World War he tried to avoid being a member, but was compelled to become a minister and was appointed Minister of Educational Affairs. He remained in that position until he resigned as leader of the Conservative Party in December 1944.

WHY IS BAGGE FORGOTTEN?

Gösta Bagge was one of the leading Swedish economists in the beginning of the 1930s. He was an important entrepreneur who started the School of Social Work and Public Administration and remoulded the Social Science Institute into a large and active scientific environment. By its research, financed by the Rockefeller Foundation and based on Bagge's dissertation and the studies he initiated in the Committee of Unemployment, Bagge contributed strongly to the establishment of the Stockholm School of Economics.

One and a half decades later, Bagge was back at the *Stockholms Högskola* and the School of Social Work and Public Administration, but now without any form of influence on economic research in Sweden. What explains this total change in his situation?

One explanation may be that for ten years Gösta Bagge totally abandoned scientific research for the political arena. This, however, is not sufficient as an explanation. Bertil Ohlin made a corresponding career in the Liberal Party (*Folkpartiet*) but was not forgotten in the same way.

One important reason may be that Bagge's political career was less successful than that of Bertil Ohlin's. The Conservative Party lost ground during his years as a party leader and several commentators are critical of his achievements in the government. Two typical examples:

> Bagge, ... was an anxious and rather indecisive person.
> (Boheman 1964, p. 35)

and

> Gösta Bagge is mainly remembered for having coined the phrase 'the Swedish hedgehog' [in Sweden this means approximately having a defence in all directions]. Otherwise, he was a crashing bore and nothing special as professor in economics.
> (Björk 1986, p. 231)

The negative evaluation of his contribution as a politician may also have coloured the opinion of his achievements as a researcher and research entrepreneur.

There is up to now no study of Bagge as a politician.[10] It is, however, evident that he did not manage to make a new start as a researcher following his decade in the centre of Sweden's political life. He wrote only a few articles in the years after his return to *Stock-*

holms Högskola prior to his death in 1951. Erik Lundberg (1951) captures this:

> Life had made Gösta Bagge very tired. By the time he returned to his professorship and old place of work for a few years at *Stockholms Högskola* after the end of the Second World War he was mentally tired. He could no longer maintain continuity with the great traditions he had created during the 1920s.

To some extent ignorance of Bagge's contributions may depend on his area of research. Bagge's main contributions are to be found in the economic analysis of trade unions and on unemployment at equilibrium, i.e. other forms of unemployment than the cyclical one. The great depression of the 1930s caused his research area to attract only peripheral interest. Both fields have returned to the centre of economic theory, but only in recent decades: equilibrium unemployment with the search theory in the 1960s and the economic analysis of trade unions in the 1980s.

The methodology used by Bagge may also have contributed to the ignorance of Bagge. The very detailed description of various cases (variation of the variables one by one) was long-winded and not very efficient. His dissertation was published in Swedish which means that very few people outside Sweden have read it.

One further reason why Bagge has fallen into oblivion may be that he came into conflict with most of the leading economists in the 1930s, one after the other.[11] It was the case with Erik Lindahl, Gunnar Myrdal, Eli Heckscher and Bertil Ohlin, persons who had all previously been close friends of Gösta Bagge. The reasons for the animosity differ but common to all of these cases is Bagge's combination of over-sensitivity and moral rigidity.[12] Many of Bagge's students became politically active but not in the same party as Bagge. Instead they became his political opponents.

From a modern perspective, the dissertation is Bagge's major contribution. Many of his ideas and empirical observations are now common knowledge but there is more to find in his voluminous book. The long-term consequences of his entrepreneurship are still important.

NOTES

1 See Carlsson (1991) for an account of Bagge's stay in the United States.
2 Sven Brisman was Bagge's official opponent in the oral defence of his dissertation appointed by the university. He also wrote a positive review article in the *Ekonomisk Tidskrift* and together with Gustaf Cassel and Emil Sommarin formed the committee of experts who reviewed the applicants when Bagge was subsequently appointed professor.
3 Bagge's analysis consistently assumes stable prices. See, for example, Bagge (1931, p. 115).
4 Landgren (1961) wrote a long, critical examination of Bagge's supplement to the Committee on Unemployment in his study of the Stockholm School of Economics.
5 See Bagge (1913a,b, 1923a, 1924).
6 A lively account of the lobbying which took place to arrange the professorship to Bagge is given by Andreen and Boalt (1987).
7 Bagge's contacts with the Rockefeller Foundation, and the work (and conflicts) with the project are described in Andreen and Boalt (1987), Carlsson (1982) and Craver (1991).
8 See Wadensjö (1987, 1991).
9. Those who have written on the development of the settlement movement in Sweden, Olson (1982) and Olsson (1990), have not observed this first club.
10 The only two short accounts are to be found in the memoirs of Gjöres (1967) and Wigforss (1954). Both stress that Bagge was uncomfortable in his position as minister in the coalition government and had difficulty in making decisions.
11 The development of the conflicts can be traced in Bagge's collection of letters at *Riksarkivet* and in the corresponding collections of Heckscher (KB – Royal Library, Stockholm), Myrdal (*Arbetarrörelsens arkiv*) and Ohlin (KB).
12 The origin of Bagge's conflict with Lindahl was a combination of work-related and personal reasons. Lindahl was slow to complete his study on national accounting but more important was probably Bagge's dislike of Lindahl's marital separation and divorce (Craver 1991). Relations between Bagge and Heckscher broke down after sharp criticism by Heckscher that Bagge was not as eager to read Heckscher's manuscripts as Heckscher was to read Bagge's. The conflict between Gunnar Myrdal and Bagge had its origin in that Alva Myrdal in a public debate on 'the problem of population' labelled those who were against contraception and limiting their families to two children or less as hypocrites. The tragedy of Bagge's life was that he and his wife had only one child and became very upset not only with Alva but also with Gunnar Myrdal. The conflict between Bagge and Ohlin started with a letter in which Bagge criticized Ohlin for contributing to the pro-German *Stockholmstidningen*. Ohlin responded with an angry letter breaking the friendship.

REFERENCES

Andreen, P.G. and Boalt, G. (1987) 'Bagge får tacka Rockefeller', Stockholms universitet – Socialhögskolan. *Rapport i socialt arbete* no. 30.

Bagge, G. (1905) 'The Boot and Shoeworkers' Union Stamp', *The Johns Hopkins University Circular*, no. 6, The Economic Seminary 1904–5, pp. 32–7.

—— (1909) 'Organisationsväsendet och aftalen inom tryckeriindustrien', in Kommerskollegium, *Arbetsstatistik* A:7 Stockholm: Norstedt & Söner, pp. 165–203.

—— (1910) 'Kollektivaftal angående arbets-och löneförhållanden i Sverige', Kommerskollegium, *Arbetsstatistik* A:5, Norstedt & Söner, Stockholm.

—— (1913a) 'Folkförsäkringen', *Svensk tidskrift*, pp. 1–9.

—— (1913b) 'Riksdagens viktigaste fråga' (penionsförsäkringen), *Svensk tidskrift*, pp. 155–70.

—— (1914) 'Amerikanska fackföreningsstudier', *Ekonomisk tidskrift*, vol. 16, pp. 63–8.

—— (1917) *Arbetslönens reglering genom sammanslutningar* (doctoral dissertation), AB Nordiska Bokhandeln, Stockholm.

—— (1922) 'De kommunala affärsverkens tariffer', *Svenska stadsförbundets tidskrift*, pp. 7–15, 67–79.

—— (1923a) 'Den svenska socialförsäkringen', *Svensk tidskrift*, pp. 303–21.

—— (1923b) 'Anförande vid förhandlingarna vid den skandinaviska kommunalkonferensen', *Stadskollegiet Utlåtanden och Memorial*, Bihang no. 44.

—— (1924) 'Pensionsförsäkringen', *Nationalekonomiska föreningens förhandlingar*, pp. 1–15, 39–44.

—— (1931) *Orsaker till arbetslöshet*, Supplement 1 to Arbetslöshetsutredningens betänkande. SOU 1931:21.

—— (1933) *Kommunalarbetarnas löner i Sverige 1865–1930*, Norstedt & Söner, Stockholm.

—— (1935) *Socialpolitik*, Anteckningar efter professor Gösta Bagges föreläsningar 1930–1931. Socialinstitutet, Stockholm.

Bagge, G., Lundberg, E. and Svennilson, I. (1933) 'Wages in Sweden 1860–1930', Part I, *Stockholm Economic Studies* 3a, P.S. King & Son, London.

—— (1935) 'Wages in Sweden 1860–1930' Part II, *Stockholm Economic Studies* 3b, P.S. King & Son, London.

'Betänkande angående ordnande av barnbespisningen vid Stockholms folkskolor' (1915) Bihang nr 90 till Beredningsutskottets utlåtanden och memorial för år 1915.

Björk, K. (1986) *Ett krig*, Tidens förlag, Stockholm.

Boheman, E. (1964) *På vakt. Kanslisekreterare under andra världskriget*. Norstedt & Söner, Stockholm.

Brisman, S. (1919) 'Arbetslönens problem', *Ekonomisk tidskrift*, vol. 21, pp. 1–14.

Carlson, B. (1982) 'Bagge, Lindahl och nationalinkomsten. Om "National Income of Sweden 1861–1930"', *Meddelande från Ekonomisk – historiska institutionen*, Lunds universitet no. 27.

―――― (1991) 'Gösta Bagge's American Lessons', *Scandinavian Economic History Review*, vol. 39, no. 2.

Craver, E. (1991) 'Gösta Bagge, The Rockefeller Foundation, and Empirical Social Science Research in Sweden, 1924–1940', in L. Jonung (ed.), *The Stockholm School of Economics Revisited*, Cambridge University Press, Cambridge.

Dagens Nyheter (1921) 'Prof. G. Bagge installerad i sitt ämbete', 22 April.

Gjöres, A. (1967) *Vreda vindar*, Norsted & Söner, Stockholm.

Landgren, K.-G. (1957) *Economics in Modern Sweden*, Library of Congress, Washington.

―――― (1961) *Den 'nya ekonomien' i Sverige. J.M. Keynes, E. Wigforss, B. Ohlin och utvecklingen 1927–39*, Almqvist & Wiksell, Stockholm.

Lundberg, E. (1951) 'Gösta Bagge död', *Dagens Nyheter*, 4 January.

Olson, H.-E. (1982) *Från Hemgård till Ungdomsgård*, RSFH's förlag, Stockholm.

Olsson, S. (1990) *Social Policy and Welfare State in Sweden*, Arkiv förlag, Stockholm.

Wadensjö, E. (1987) 'Före Stockholmsskolan – arbetslöshetsutredningen, Ernst Wigforss och Gösta Bagge', *Ekonomisk Debatt*, vol. 15, no. 4.

―――― (1991) 'The Committee on Unemployment and the Stockholm School' in L. Jonung (ed.) *The Stockholm School of Economics Revisited*, Cambridge University Press, Cambridge.

Wigforss, E. (1954) *Minnen III, 1932–1949*, Tidens förlag, Stockholm.

8

ERIK LINDAHL'S NORM FOR MONETARY POLICY

Klas Fregert

INTRODUCTION

In 1924 Erik Lindahl published a book entitled *Penningpolitikens mål* (*The Aims of Monetary Policy*), hereafter *Aims*, and in 1930 a sequel *Penningpolitikens medel* (*The Means of Monetary Policy*), hereafter *Means*.[1] The two books were conceived together and form a programme for monetary policy to which Lindahl would adhere throughout his life. The topic was not new in Sweden, with theoretical contributions having been made principally by Wicksell and Cassel long before the First World War. The monetary upheavals during and after the First World War incited a lively discussion in Sweden among leading economists such as Cassel, Wicksell, Heckscher and Davidson. Perhaps surprisingly, there is almost no reference to these events in either of the books though they must have inspired him. On the other hand, the treatment was in the form of a theoretical treatise.

The purpose of this essay is to review Lindahl's remarkably systematic and, in many ways, modern framework for monetary policy. I also discuss his reasoning regarding the specific norm he advocates: prices should move in inverse proportion to productivity, a suggestion akin to present-day proposals for stabilizing nominal GNP. I will not deal specifically with his macroeconomic theory which is intimately connected with his development of dynamic theory and sequence analysis associated with the Stockholm School.[2]

The essay is organized around the following questions, which were suggested by Alesina (1988) to determine which is the 'best' monetary regime:

- Are monetary rules better than discretionary policies?
- How can policy rules be enforced?
- Which is the best rule?

Lindahl addressed all three questions. With the renewed interest in monetary regimes and emphasis on rules, Lindahl has closer links to contemporary economists than to those during the intervening 'macroeconomic era' with its emphasis on discretionary policy actions and neglect of expectations.[3] Arguably, few writers today attempt the level of generality achieved by Lindahl. The essay ends with a short account of the failed adoption of the rule in Sweden after the Second World War.

LINDAHL ON RULES AND ENFORCEMENT

Lindahl states right at the beginning of *Aims*, that monetary policy should follow a rule. This requirement has priority over which specific rule is chosen and is motivated separately. Lindahl calls it the 'first basic principle of a rational monetary policy' (*Aims*, p. 4).

> The main thing is, *that*, a definite aim is set for monetary policy in every country and is clearly presented and motivated, and that the programme thus established is carried out using all possible means under all circumstances.
>
> (Lindahl's italics; *Aims*, p. 4)

The goal is to reduce risks in economic life:

> A clear goal should be stated for monetary policy and be guaranteed by the constitution: otherwise the public will have no firm basis for their opinions of the future value of money and must engage in guesses about the future course of monetary policy [*valutapolitik*], whereby all commitments for paying or receiving a certain sum of money will be based on uncertain ground, and thus increase the risks in economic life hindering a sound economic development.
>
> (*Aims*, p. 4)

The motivation, or even more basic principle, is to reduce business cycle fluctuations:

> Apart from changes in the distribution, disturbances within production easily arise. An unforeseen price fall is generally accompanied by depression and unemployment, price

increases by excessive optimism and misguided speculations, whereby society as a whole suffers.

(Aims, p. 8)

Lindahl attributes the successful establishment of a norm to the credibility the norm holds among the public at its inception. For the norm to be credible, it must be: (1) widely publicized, (2) clearly justified, and (3) credibly enforced. Enforcement should rely on a constitutional guarantee and on an independent board of governors of the central bank. His assessment of the importance of enforcement is prescient (and presumably based on history): 'In general, the solution of the given problem accounts for the largest practical difficulty in carrying out the programme' *(Means*, p. 30). An interesting side observation on a weak board of governors is that it should not publish its justifications since they may give rise to discussion and thereby jeopardize credibility in the programme. Once the norm is established, credibility can only be preserved through actions to validate it:

> Further, the established goal must be realized with the utmost consistency: if the state fails to uphold commitments which it made in this regard, it would amount to a violation of the legal content of economic contracts, which is regrettable in itself but also because it reduces credibility in the established programme.

(Aims, p. 4)

Lindahl stresses that publicity can be used to influence expectations about future price levels. These expectations in turn affect the current price level. For publicity to have an effect, expectations must be forward-looking; hence Lindahl comes close to the rational expectations school, as opposed to simpler expectations mechanisms such as adaptive expectations. The link between the actual price level and the expected will tend to make credible rules self-fulfilling and thereby improve the actual functioning of the rule. The idea can be supported by an arbitrage argument. A price level lower than the norm prescribes would induce an expected inflation, making it profitable to shift purchases to the present and thereby increase demand and prices today. Barro (1986, p. 34) makes a similar argument in favour of a stable price rule; an expected inflation decreases the demand for money and thereby increases aggregate demand and prices today.[4] Lindahl states:

As a general rule it can be stated that the greater the publicity, the greater the effectiveness of monetary policy actions. Publicity is a means of psychological influence on the public in a price-stabilizing direction. ... Because of the great impact of the beliefs about the future as a determining factor for price changes, the central bank must at any moment adjust its actions to current beliefs. To uphold a constant price level requires therefore a different interest-rate policy than if the public believes that current prices will continue into the future than if they believe in an increasing or falling price level. If the public in this respect cannot base their beliefs on a firm declaration of the programme from the central bank but must engage in uncertain guesses about the future, these beliefs may change considerably from time to time and since it is very difficult for the central bank to evaluate these changes and adjust their actions accordingly, mistakes cannot be avoided. ... In reality it is easier to realize a programme that the public believes in than another programme. A belief in a certain price-level movement will in itself contribute to its realization.

(*Means*, pp. 27–8)

Lindahl's case for rules is the same as that made by proponents of the rational expectations school of the 1970s; a stable rule minimizes uncertainty and confusion.[5] This is, however, not the same as in the modern game theoretic literature on rules versus discretion. In these models there is generally no uncertainty regarding the inflation rate, no matter the type of regime. The case against discretion is instead based on the higher inflation rate that occurs under discretion because the monetary authority may have an incentive to induce higher employment through surprise inflation. The public will realize this and the result of the game between the monetary authority and the public will only be higher inflation without higher employment. In a much later pamphlet, with the telling title *Spelet om penningvärdet* (1957) (*The Game over the Value of Money*), Lindahl reaches a similar conclusion:

A precondition for a programme of mild and beneficial inflation is that it is secret and that the public is convinced that the inflation is only temporary and will not be repeated. Only if the inflation comes as a surprise will it have the stimulating effects intended. Such a fooling of the public could possibly only be defended by those who think that the public interest demands that the public is deceived. ...Apart from the morally questionable in such a philosophy, it could not be applied with any success in a democratic society with a free political debate. The mild and pleasant inflation one would like to see, would soon become an inflation of the disadvantageous kind.

(p. 20)[6]

LINDAHL'S CHOICE OF RULE: THE PRICE LEVEL SHOULD MOVE IN INVERSE PROPORTION TO PRODUCTIVITY[7]

Lindahl's 'second principle for a rational monetary policy' runs:

To the degree that the choice is free, the norm should be preferred that probably gives a *minimum of deviations* between the planned and the real content of money contracts in force.
(Lindahl's italics; *Aims*, p. 8)

The principle is rather a corollary of the first principle; having established that a rule leads to less uncertainty than no rule, the choice is now for the rule that produces the least uncertainty.

The focus on contracts is implicitly motivated by the specific choice of contract, namely debt contracts between entrepreneurs and investors. According to Lindahl such contracts play a significant role in business cycle fluctuations. In *Means* though, he does not mention contracts explicitly. Instead he states more generally that the rule should: '*reduce the risks that not fully expected events imply for economic activities* and thereby minimize the amount of dislocation in economic life' (Lindahl's italics; *Means*, p. 7). But he refers to *Aims* as the normative basis for his choice of rule which is to be studied in *Means* from a positive point of view. Lindahl focuses on nominal-debt contracts with the argument that

with respect to the dominant role of capital formation and capital use in modern economic life, it must be considered as one of the most important roles of monetary policy to create a useful balance between the interest of lenders and borrowers through such a stabilization of the price level, that their mutual agreements maintain their original content as far as possible.

(*Aims*, p. 25)

Lindahl arrives at a 'useful balance' by considering the 'individual dispositions that lead to the conclusion of debt agreements'. His result is that the planned (or expected) outcome should be fulfilled for the entrepreneur, and the unavoidable losses or gains due to unanticipated shocks should be borne by the saver/investor. Entrepreneurs should be protected from risk; neither going bankrupt as a result of negative shocks nor gaining from positive shocks. Monetary policy can, of course, only reduce aggregate risk from common shocks, i.e. systematic risk. The argument is that savings are inelastic with respect to risk, whereas entrepreneurs may be adversely affected by risk which may aggravate the business cycle. Lindahl has in mind losses to society as a whole due to business cycle fluctuations caused by unanticipated gains and losses to entrepreneurs. The reason is *not* that savers are risk-neutral and entrepreneurs are risk-averse. The effect on the welfare of entrepreneurs is uncertain:

> If this result [reduced entrepreneurial risks] is an advantage to the entrepreneurial class is not easy to say. However, it will benefit society as a whole, which is protected from far-reaching and detrimental effects of dislocations in the economy.
>
> (*Aims*, p. 29)

Lindahl's preferred rule should shift systematic risk from the entrepreneurs to the debt holders, effectively transforming debt into equity. If all investment were equity financed there would be no need to protect entrepreneurs against unforeseen shocks since capitalists would bear the whole burden. In this way, Lindahl assumes a market failure, the absence of an equity market. His choice of rule, that the general price level should move in inverse proportion to general productivity changes, turns out – in his model – to neutralize the effects of productivity changes on the nominal incomes of entrepreneurs. A general productivity increase, for example an energy-saving invention or cheaper energy, would be enjoyed by the debt holders through a reduced price level while entrepreneurs would be compensated for the price fall through larger output with given inputs. By transforming debts to contingent claims through the feedback from productivity to prices, the government creates the missing equity market.

Lindahl's derivation of the optimal rule in terms of an implicit loss function with losses due to unforeseen shocks has a modern flavour, although the formulation of losses as discrepancies between planned and actual outcomes is somewhat peculiar. Modern analyses formulate the loss function as deviations between the actual and some hypothetical optimal value, not the expected. Due to some assumed 'distortion', the optimum is not reached. For New Keynesians, the optimum is the outcome which would have occurred had there not been some contract precluding agents from reaching that level. For the New Classicals (1970s), the optimum is the outcome that occurs when all agents have full knowledge of shocks and prices. One interpretation of 'minimizing the deviation between planned and real content' is that had there been a market for contingent claims, all the risk would have been borne by the investors. Thus preserving the intentions of the entrepreneurs replicates the optimum of an economy with fully contingent markets. The implicit distortion argument gives a Keynesian flavour to Lindahl.

It is strange that Lindahl does not even mention the equity market or give reasons why it may be too small. Typical explanations point to limited access to risk capital of smaller entrepreneurs due to moral hazard and limited collateral. One explicit inspiration is Irving Fisher (1911) whom he quotes with a statement analogous to Lindahl's second principle for monetary policy. Later Fisher (1933) presented his 'debt-deflation theory', where he attributed the Great Depression to entrepreneurs being wiped out or denied access to new capital through bankruptcy or reduced net worth. The deflation in Sweden during the early 1920s (prices fell by more than 30 per cent in 1920–22) led to heavy increases in the debt burden that presumably also influenced Lindahl's thinking. Recent work has also analysed inefficiencies in the credit market that could have macroeconomic repercussions.[8]

The choice of rule is studied in *Aims* by comparing the effects of different shocks on the relation between the planned and actual content of contracts under different rules. A final assessment is then based on the feasibility of such a rule with the instruments available to the central bank. This is the investigation carried out in *Means*. The style of analysis accords with modern policy evaluation which stresses 'the operating characteristics of the economy under different rules' evaluated by a loss function in terms of fluctuations attributed to unanticipated shocks. Three rules are investigated: (1) stable prices, (2) prices in inverse relation to productivity, and (3) stable exchange rates. Lindahl's shock taxonomy in *Aims* is summarized in Table 8.1. With roughly eight types of shocks and three rules we get

Table 8.1 Shock taxonomy according to *Aims*, chapter 3 (factor supply shocks) and chapter 4 (productivity shocks)

Shocks	Examples	Forecastability
Factor supply:		
labour	demographic change	high
	emigration	low
	change in length of workday	low
capital	international capital movements	low
	normal capital growth	high
Productivity:		
permanent	climate, inventions	low
	socio-political, world trade	low
temporary	strikes	low
	harvests	low
	trade changes	low

24 cases. Lindahl also considers the effects on other types of contracts. With four types of contracts we would get 96 cases. Needless to say Lindahl does not analyse every case, but nevertheless covers a considerable number. Table 8.2 tabulates the contracts considered. The analysis shows how the ability to pay back loans changes relative to the nominal debt commitment. For the borrower – the entrepreneur – to be able to repay the loan the capitalized value of his returns must at least suffice to repay the loan:

$$E \sum_{i=1}^{N} \frac{P_{t+i} \cdot MPK_{t+i} \cdot K_{t+i}}{1 + r_{t+i}} \geq \text{debt incurred}$$

where E stands for expected value of, P the output price, MPK the marginal product of capital, K the capital stock, and r the interest rate. If the interest rate on the loan is flexible, the entrepreneur and the investor must make an assessment of future interest rates. The condition is verbally stated on page 27 in *Aims*. A marginal investment is just equal to the debt (a zero net present value). The left-hand side can also be thought of as the price of the capital good. If it becomes less than the debt incurred, the entrepreneur makes a loss and if he has no equity, he goes bankrupt. The left-hand side may change during the lifetime of the capital good and hence the ability to pay back. The strategy is then to determine how the components of the left-hand side change in response to

Table 8.2 Type of contracts according to *Aims*, chapter 5

Type of contract	Effect of inverse p-rule
Firm debt	
flexible r	good
fixed r	bad
Consumption loans	good
Mortgages on land and houses:	
flexible r	bad
fixed r	good
Wage contracts:	
fixed	good
indexed	bad
Fixed land rentals	good
Fix price goods[a]	reasonable

[a]Exemplified by tariffs on railways, postal services and electrical energy.

various shocks and how these may be counteracted by monetary policy. Only supply shocks are considered as Lindahl assumes a pure credit economy; in a money economy, the considered rules would in addition neutralize demand (velocity) shocks.

Two basic types of shocks are analysed: (*a*) a proportional change in all factors of production (*Aims*, chapter 3), and (*b*) a proportional change in the marginal productivities of all factors; in contemporary terminology Hicks' neutral technical change (*Aims*, chapter 4). In neither case is there any effect on the interest rate, as it is assumed to be determined according to the Böhm-Bawerk/Wicksell theory of interest as 'the marginal productivity of waiting, that is the relation between the marginal productivity of a capital good of a certain age and (the lesser) marginal productivity of the nearest younger vintage' (*Aims*, p. 32). This is the natural rate which is thus assumed to always be equal to the market rate. When factor supplies change in the same proportion, there is no effect on marginal productivities as 'the economic situation is, so to speak, reproduced on a larger or smaller scale' (*Aims*, p. 31), thus assuming linearly homogeneous production functions. As neither the numerator nor the denominator is affected, the ability to service existing nominal debt is unaffected with a fixed price level. In contrast, changes in productivity (marginal and average at all vintages) must be countered by an opposite proportional change in the price level to make it possible for the entrepreneurs to pay back their loans on existing capital

133

equipment. Hence the norm that the price level should move in inverse proportion to productivity. Various cases of disproportionate changes in factor supplies and productivities are then considered but are not found to cause discrepancies sufficiently large as to modify the norm.

The final chapter in *Aims* is entitled: 'Stable exchange rate or stable price level?' Since the proposed norm assumes autonomous control of the price level it must be combined with floating exchange rates. Lindahl discusses the effects of exchange-rate risks, but considers that they are not large enough to warrant fixed exchange rates. One argument is that many risks may be reduced by use of the forward market in foreign exchange. (He refers to Keynes (1924) on this point.)

Although *Aims* contains analyses of the working of the economy, it does not contain a complete macroeconomic model. *Means* presents an intertemporal two-sector model with consumption and investment goods. For a modern economist, the model is a difficult construct as it relies on the Wicksellian assumption of a pure credit economy. The price level and its development over time is studied in an economy without money. The analysis starts from the observation that under perfect foresight, any price path is possible as 'expected price level changes are without economic significance as they neither change relative prices of the factors of production and consumption goods nor the size or direction of production (*Means*, p. 16). Much of the book then analyses changes in the price level that would occur as a result of unforeseen disturbances and necessary countermeasures from the central bank to achieve a certain norm. The analysis is made in terms of changes in total monetary demand and supply of consumption goods and the implied effect on the price level – a construct used earlier by Wicksell. The chief conclusion is the following:

> keeping the price level stable requires fairly large interest-rate movements, determined on the basis of a profound knowledge of the situation, whereas a regulation of the price level in inverse proportion to productivity can be achieved with rather moderate changes in the interest rate. Dislocations in the economy will therefore become considerably smaller with the latter norm than the former.
>
> (*Means*, p. 98)

Thus, the norm suggested on normative grounds in *Aims* is also supported from a practical point of view.

THE INVERSE PRODUCTIVITY RULE, NOMINAL INCOME STABILIZATION AND WAGE STABILIZATION

Lindahl's norm is akin to present-day suggestions of nominal income stabilization.[9] When supply shocks arrive in the form of neutral technical change, the inverse productivity norm amounts to holding nominal national income constant as well as factor incomes. With neutral technical change, output changes in the same proportion as productivity when factor supplies are given. Thus, nominal income – being the product of output and price – is constant when these change in inverse proportion. With non-neutral technical changes, individual factor incomes may change as relative factor rewards change. When factor supplies increase, nominal income grows by the same amount. This feature was stressed in *Means*:

> If everybody could more or less correctly foresee the future price level that arises as a consequence of this norm for monetary policy, the total nominal income of the society would not in fact be affected by changes in productivity. The norm in question implies that productivity fluctuations would be neutralized.
>
> (*Means* p. 91)

Nominal income targeting neutralizes velocity shocks and allows negative supply shocks to raise prices and reduce real output (and vice versa for positive supply shocks). In textbook parlance, the nominal income rule creates a unitary elastic aggregate demand curve that is fixed in the price/income plane. Along the curve, nominal national income is constant and supply shocks will move the economy along the fixed aggregate demand curve. A difference between nominal income stabilization and the inverse productivity rule is that changes in factor supplies are treated analogously to productivity disturbances with nominal income targeting. *Ceteris paribus*, a nominal income target of zero change implies a fall in the price level when factor supplies grow and nominal incomes per unit of factor supply would decrease, whereas the inverse productivity rule implies that nominal income would grow in proportion to factor supplies. In practice, this may not make a big difference if nominal income target growth is set equal to the average growth in factor supplies.

One way to rationalize a nominal income rule is that it tends to stabilize nominal wages. If sticky wages is a propagation mechanism in business cycles, a stabilization of nominal wages also stabilizes the business cycle.[10] Lindahl made this observation when he examined the rule from the point of view of wage contracts. The same conclusion has been reached in the literature on supply shocks and whether they should be accommodated. Phelps (1978) and Fischer (1985) analysed the short-run response to supply shocks when nominal wages are fixed. They concluded that full employment is assured if real wages change equi-proportionately to the marginal product of labour with Hicks' neutral technical change and a fixed labour supply. This can be achieved with unchanged nominal wages if the price level moves in inverse proportion to the productivity shock, which it will with a unitary elastic aggregate demand curve.[11] Lindahl argues analogously fifty years earlier:

> The employers base their offers on an estimate of the value of labour, in money terms, for the period when the work is done. For the agreements to have an unchanged content, a regulation of prices is required sufficient to maintain the nominal value of work carried out during the period in question. If the marginal product of labour, in real terms, is unchanged, the price level should stay constant; if labour's marginal product is decreasing, the price level should change in inverse proportion, so that the workers at increased productivity through the lowering of the price level achieve higher real wages, in spite of money wages being constant, and vice versa at decreased productivity.
>
> (*Aims*, p. 63)

Lindahl states that the advantage of the rule is that it reduces the discrepancy between the contractual and 'the economically motivated wage' (*Aims*, p. 64) instead of the planned outcome. In this case, both parties are interested in the new equilibrium value of the real wage, not the planned or expected. The inverse productivity rule replicates the outcome of a missing spot market for labour that does not exist because of wage contracts.

He also considers the effect of changes in the supply of factors. He considers these to be of little consequence for cyclical fluctuations as they probably change slowly and are easy to forecast and include in contractual terms. In contrast, he believes productivity disturbances to be of greater importance for short-term fluctuations as they are more difficult to forecast. Lindahl points out a specific welfare gain of having to revise nominal wages less frequently (longer contracts) by referring to labour unrest in connection with wage revisions. He thus predicts that the length of wage contracts will be longer under his rule; a prediction made in models on endogenous wage contracts. The rule is especially favourable to white-collar workers who tend to have longer periods between wage revisions. He also mentions the possibility of indexed wage contracts but presumes that these will only appear during very volatile periods.[12]

EPILOGUE: ADOPTION OF THE NORM IN SWEDEN IN 1944

The following motion was put to the Swedish parliament in 1944:

A stabilization of money should be attempted, within the limits of fluctuations in the provision of goods that derive from changes in productivity or the exchange relations with foreign countries. Accordingly, an improvement in the provision of goods after the war should imply a corresponding improvement in the value of money. Money incomes should neither be raised nor reduced.

(Quoted from Hammarskjöld 1944, p. 48)

The motion was accepted unanimously and thus Lindahl's and Davidson's norm was adopted as the official policy.[13] Similar announcements had been made previously during the war to defend the inflation on the basis of decreased production. It was also claimed that this was in accordance with the norm of price stabilization adopted during the 1930s.[14] Even if the Riksbank never wholeheartedly embraced price stabilization and allowed movements in the price level, the alleged continuity of the norm with the old was far-fetched.

The peace did not bring price reductions but produced stable prices for a while; inflation in 1945 and 1946 was less than 1 per cent. The Riksbank did stem inflationary impulses from abroad in 1946 by a 17 per cent appreciation of the krona against the dollar which temporarily stopped inflation. In 1947 inflation started to rise (2.5 per cent) and rose to 8 per cent in 1948. As the norm failed, belief in it as well as announcements to that effect gradually disappeared. Lindahl (1943) had advocated a 15 per cent deflation, in itself less than the rise in the price level. As the norm had not been declared before the inflation, a sudden adoption retroactively by the full amount of the war inflation would have caused losses to borrowers who took up loans during the war and might have triggered a depression (like in 1921–2). The failure to uphold the norm did not deter Lindahl from continuing to advocate the rule as he did in *Spelet om penningvärdet* (1957).

The following two quotations reflect opinions on the experiment. A less than favourable review was given in a policy document a few years later by the national trade union organization (LO):

> An idea in the economic literature is that the nominal wage level should be kept constant and that productivity improvements should instead be expressed as price reductions and thereby increase incomes for wage earners and others. The practical impossibility of this idea under full employment and preserved freedom of action for the trade union movement in relation to the government, ought to be understood without further thought.
>
> (*Fackföreningsrörelsen och den fulla sysselsättningen* 1951, p. 141)

A more generous judgement of the episode is given by Lundberg (1957, p. 285):[15]

> However utopian the aims of monetary policy may have been in the postwar years, there was still a great deal of theoretical sense in their motivation. It can be justifiably claimed from the point of view of the theories of Davidson and Lindahl that it was the very failure to bring down prices during the transitional period immediately following the end of the war that created the basis of the subsequent inflation.

CONCLUSION

Lindahl's conclusions as well as his style of reasoning accord well with modern analyses of monetary rules. He belongs to economists who believe fluctuations are exacerbated by some 'distortion' in the economy, rather than viewing the government as the (only) distortion. He focused on the relation between entrepreneurs and investors though he also investigated the norm from other points of view. I have argued that his basic argument rests on an implicit assumption of a missing capital market that precludes efficient risk-sharing between investors and entrepreneurs. Finding an optimal policy rule in this tradition amounts to identifying the distortion and designing a policy rule to alleviate the distortion. In this sense, Lindahl can be seen as an activist, but in his insistence on a norm, a moderate one. Present macroeconomic models of the distortion type typically focus on one market – labour, goods or the credit market – and we still seem far away from a 'general theory'. Lindahl treated a number of aspects in his two-part treatise. Perhaps the scope was too grand but if we are to make recommendations, we ought to put together our insights – however imperfect – into one framework.

If our theoretical understanding of monetary norms has not advanced much since Lindahl – as there is no general agreement regarding whether there are distortions and of what type – we may ask how much our empirical knowledge of various norms has advanced. Lindahl was optimistic about the eventual rational management of the value of money, but took a long view on the accumulation of factual knowledge:

> Even if we have not yet found the rational principles for this management (for which, perhaps, further experimentation during *a century or more* may be necessary), we can hardly return to the old method of more or less 'automatic' regulation of the currencies.
>
> (My italics; Lindahl 1934, p. 169)

NOTES

1 *Penningpolitikens mål* was first published in 1924 under the title *Penning-politikens mål och medel. Första delen* (part 1), and then in a second edition in 1929 under the title *Penningpolitikens mål*, in conjunction with the publication of *Penningpolitikens medel*. As the publication of part 2, *Penningpolitikens medel*, was delayed, Lindahl separated the work into two volumes with separate titles. A major part of the latter book is translated in *Studies in the Theory of Money and Capital* (1939). Translations from the Swedish original by the author.

2 See Hansson (1983), Petersson (1987), Steiger (1987), and Jonung (1991). Steiger also contains a biography and a bibliography of Lindahl.

3 This statement accords with Leijonhufvud's (1991, p. 464) judgement of Lindahl's contribution in the context of an evaluation of the Stockholm School. To quote: 'Lindahl's work was there for us to read ten, twenty, thirty or forty years ago – before Lucas and Sargent – and could have

been read with great profit by anyone wise enough to look for the alternative futures at the time.'

4 Lindahl seems to have in mind both the actual working of a rule and the establishment of the rule. Regarding the establishment of the rule, standard theory, including game theoretic treatments, has little to say since they study equilibria where expectations are fulfilled. Announced rules are either credible or not. Backus and Drifil (1985) study a change of regime where a new rule is announced and neither part is certain of the others' intentions and expectations. Lindahl believes that the mutual uncertainty and distrust can be alleviated through clear motivations. In the game theoretic literature such announcements, referred to as 'cheap talk', are usually considered to be of little value.

5 A more elaborate defence for rules along the same lines is given by Leijonhufvud (1983). Under non-rule regimes, expectations may be ill-behaved and incoherent (across individuals) with resulting confusion. A rule makes expectations well behaved (or rational) and improves the functioning of the economy.

6 The main mechanism through which surprise inflation leads to higher activity goes via higher profits caused by the redistribution from lenders to borrowers. Higher profits in turn increase capital formation and employment (Lindahl 1957, pp. 10–12). Hansen (1979) claims that Lindahl in this book was the first to clearly express the accelerationist idea a decade before Friedman and Phelps and suggests that the pamphlet should be translated. But the idea is at least implicit in *Aims* and explicit in *Means*; see below. Cf. also Wicksell (1906, p. 144).

7 The norm had been suggested earlier by David Davidson and it is sometimes referred to in Sweden as the Davidson norm. Davidson justified the rule in terms of fairness: lenders should also enjoy increased productivity which they would experience through falling price levels. Cf. Uhr (1975) and Hammaskjöld (1944). The norm has also been advocated internationally by, for example, Marshall, Edgeworth, Pigou, Robertson, Hayek, Haberler and Machlup according to Selgin (no date). Lindahl, however, makes no reference to these.

8 See Bernanke and Gertler (1989).

9 See Taylor (1985) for an exposition and discussion of nominal income targeting.

10 Keynes (1936, chapter 19) advocated wage stabilization on these grounds. Myrdal (1939, pp. 200–2) argued that the choice between price and wage stabilization hinges on which are the most sticky. He also found that wage stabilization is roughly consistent with the inverse productivity norm.

11 The question asked by Phelps and Fischer was whether this would entail an expansive or contractionary policy which will depend on the elasticity of the aggregate demand curve with a given monetary and fiscal policy stance.

12 See Gray (1978) who predicts that reduced uncertainty about supply and demand shocks increases the length of contracts and that increased nominal uncertainty increases the incidence and degree of inflation

indexation. An investigation of contract characteristics in Sweden between 1908 and 1988 is done by Fregert (1991).

13 For a more extensive account see Lundberg (1957, pp. 127–31) and Bentzel (1956). The Social Democrats put it as their first point in their *Postwar Programme of Swedish Labour* ('The 27-point programme'): 'Price rises must be prevented; in times of plentiful supply prices should fall. But the price level must never be allowed to fall so low as to induce economic depression' (p. 6).

14 See Lundberg (1957, p. 130). See Jonung (1979) on the adoption and implementation of Wicksell's rule of price stabilization in Sweden in the 1930s.

15 The previous comment is also quoted by Lundberg (1953, p. 284) who juxtaposes it with the acceptance made earlier by the labour movement.

REFERENCES

Alesina, Alberto (1988) 'Alternative Monetary Regimes', *Journal of Monetary Economics*, 21, 175–83.

Backus, David and John Drifill (1985) 'Rational Expectations and Policy Credibility following a Change in Regime', *Review of Economic Studies*, 52, 211–21.

Barro, Robert J. (1986) 'Recent Developments in the Theory of Rules versus Discretion', *Economic Journal*, 96 Conference papers, 23–37.

Bentzel, Ragnar (1956) 'Produktivitetsproblem i den penning- och löne-politiska diskussionen i vårt land', *Ekonomisk Tidskrift*, 58, 219–36.

Bernanke, Ben and Mark Gertler (1989) 'Agency Costs, Net Worth, and Business Cycle Fluctuations', *American Economic Review*, 79, 14–31.

Fackföreningsrörelsen och den fulla sysselsättningen (1951) (*The Trade Union Movement and Full Employment*), Stockholm: Landsorganisationen.

Fischer, Stanley (1985) 'Supply Shocks, Wage Stickiness, and Accommodation', *Journal of Money, Credit and Banking*, 17, 1–15.

Fisher, Irving (1911) *The Purchasing Power of Money*, New York: Macmillan.

Fisher, Irving (1933) 'The Debt-deflation Theory of Great Depressions', *Econometrica*, 1, October, 337–57.

Fregert, Klas (1992) *A Contractual History of Sweden 1908–1988. A Study in Macro-economics and Collective Agreements*, Lund: forthcoming.

Gray, Jo Anna (1978) 'On Indexation and Contract Length', *Journal of Political Economy*, 86, 1–18.

Hammarskjöld, Dag (1944) 'Den svenska diskussionen om penning-politikens mål' ('The Swedish discussion of the aims of monetary policy'). In *Studier i ekonomi och historia*, Uppsala: Almqvist & Wiksell, pp. 47–59.

Hansen, Bent (1979) Review of E. Lundberg (ed.), *Inflation Theory and Anti-inflation Policy* (1977), *Scandinavian Journal of Economics*, 81, 119–25.

Hansson, Björn A. (1983) *The Stockholm School and the Development of Dynamic Method*, London: Croom Helm.

Jonung, Lars (1979) 'Knut Wicksell's Norm for Price Stabilization and

Swedish Monetary Policy in the 1930s', *Journal of Monetary Economics*, 5, 459–96.

—— (ed.) (1991) *The Stockholm School of Economics Revisited*, Cambridge: Cambridge University Press.

Keynes, John M. (1924) *A Tract on Monetary Reform*, London: Macmillan.

—— (1936) *The General Theory of Employment, Interest, and Money*, London: Macmillan.

Leijonhufvud, Axel (1983) 'Keynesianism, Monetarism, and Rational Expectations: Some Reflections and Conjectures', In Frydman and Phelps (eds) *Individual Forecasting and Aggregate Outcomes*, Cambridge: Cambridge University Press, pp. 203–23.

—— (1991) 'Roundtable discussion', in Jonung (ed.) *The Stockholm School of Economics Revisited*, pp. 461–4.

Lindahl, Erik (1924) *Penningpolitikens mål och medel (Aims)* Första delen, Malmö: Förlagsaktiebolaget. Second edition in 1929 under the title *Penningpolitikens mål.*

—— (1930) *Penningpolitikens medel (Means)*, Lund: Gleerup.

—— (1934) 'Sweden's Monetary Program: The Experiment in Operation; its Results and Lessons', *Economic Forum*, 2, 169–81.

—— (1939) *Studies in the Theory of Money and Capital*, London: Allen & Unwin.

—— (1943) 'Sveriges penning- och prispolitik efter kriget. Några synpunkter' ('Sweden's monetary and price policy after the war'), *Ekonomisk Tidskrift*, 45, 91–105.

—— (1957) *Spelet om penningvärdet (The Game over the Value of Money)*, Stockholm: Kooperativa förbundets förlag.

Lundberg, Erik (1953) *Konjunkturer och ekonomisk politik*, Stockholm: Studieförbundet näringsliv och samhälle.

—— (1957) *Business Cycles and Economic Policy*. Translation of Lundberg (1953), London: Allen & Unwin.

Myrdal, Gunnar (1939) *Monetary Equilibrium*, London: Hodge & Co.

Petersson, Jan (1987) *Erik Lindahl och Stockholmsskolans dynamiska metod*, Lund: Lund Economic Studies.

Phelps, Edmund (1978) 'Commodity Supply Shock and Full-Employment Monetary Policy', *Journal of Money, Credit and Banking*, 10, 206–21.

The Postwar Programme of Swedish Labour. Summary in 27 Points (1946) Stockholm. Translation of the Swedish 1944 edition.

Selgin, George A. (no date) 'Monetary Equilibrium and the "Productivity Norm" of Price-level Policy', mimeo. University of Georgia.

Steiger, Otto (1987) 'Lindahl, Erik', in Eatwell, Milgate and Newman (eds) *The New Palgrave: A Dictionary of Economics*, London: Macmillan.

Taylor, John B. (1985) 'What would Nominal GNP Targeting do to the Business Cycle?' *Carnegie–Rochester Conference Series on Public Policy*, 22, 61–84.

Uhr, Carl G. (1975) *Economic Doctrines of David Davidson*. Studia oeconomica Upsaliensia 3. Uppsala: Almqvist & Wiksell.

Wicksell, Knut (1906) *Föreläsningar i nationalekonomi II (Lectures II)* Lund: Gleerup.

9

BERTIL OHLIN'S CONTRIBUTIONS TO INTERNATIONAL ECONOMICS[1]

Harry Flam

INTRODUCTION

The Royal Swedish Academy of Science awarded the Nobel Prize to Bertil Ohlin in 1977 – jointly with James Meade – for a 'path-breaking contribution to the theory of international trade and international capital movements'.[2] Ohlin's contributions to international economics have been surveyed and evaluated by Caves (1978) on the occasion of the award, and by Samuelson (1982) in a commemorative paper on the occasion of Ohlin's death in 1979. Caves's and especially Samuelson's claims that Ohlin made original contributions on par with Eli F. Heckscher to the Heckscher–Ohlin theory can be disputed. I will argue that Ohlin received the fundamental ideas from Heckscher and that Ohlin's contribution to international trade theory was to recognize the revolutionary character of these ideas, integrate them with general equilibrium, neo-classical price theory, and to increase our understanding of Heckscher's model by making it more general and by applying it to a large number of cases of empirical relevance. This was no lesser achievement. The original part of Ohlin's contributions is the analysis of international capital movements, in particular of balance of payments adjustment, where he integrated real and monetary aspects and used his own concept of buying-power as a powerful tool.

To many economists, including Ohlin himself, the academy's motivation must have looked deficient for not making more of Ohlin's contributions to macroeconomic theory, particularly to stabilization theory. Ohlin's reputation as an academic economist in

143

Sweden rests not so much on his contributions to international economics as on his role as one of the principal figures in the development of the 'Stockholm School' in the 1930s. This chapter focuses on Ohlin's contributions to international economics, and ignores Ohlin's macroeconomics and the Stockholm School.[3]

THE INFLUENCE OF OHLIN'S TEACHERS

Bertil Ohlin received his first academic training in statistics, mathematics and economics at the University of Lund, where he enrolled in 1915 at the age of 16, and graduated in 1917 with the degree of a candidate of philosophy. His two years in Lund seem not to have influenced his thinking in any particular direction, despite the fact that he was lectured to by Knut Wicksell. According to his memoirs, Ohlin (1972) was more impressed by Wicksell's physical apparition and modesty than by his teaching.

From Lund, he went on to *Handelshögskolan* (Stockholm School of Economics), where he immediately signed up for Heckscher's seminar for second-year students. Heckscher reluctantly admitted him, but his reservations were quickly dispelled. What seems to have impressed Heckscher in particular was Ohlin's resolution of the problem of the optimal rotation period in forestry economics, something that had occupied Heckscher for years. Heckscher had maintained in heated argument with Swedish forestry economists that a tree should be cut when its declining rate of growth equalled the rate of interest. Ohlin observed that forest land normally has a positive value in other uses, and that this opportunity cost should be added to the rate of interest. Actually, Ohlin had independently derived a result that the German forester and forestry economist Martin Faustmann had already shown in 1849.[4]

Heckscher published his paper on international trade theory, 'The Effect of Foreign Trade on the Distribution of Income', in *Ekonomisk Tidskrift* in 1919.[5] This must also be the time when Ohlin was first exposed to Heckscher's path-breaking ideas, because the paper had been inspired by Wicksell's review of a collection of Heckscher's papers the same year.

Ohlin soon became not only a respected but also a favourite student of Heckscher. He was made a member in 1918 of 'The Economics Club', which frequently met in Heckscher's home. The club had been formed in 1917 as a forum for discussion between leading academic and practising economists in Stockholm, and also to provide Wicksell with an academic environment upon his retirement from the University of Lund and subsequent move to Stockholm. The informal exchange with older colleagues and fellow students at the club and elsewhere were more important for Ohlin's development as an economist than formal education, of which there was quite little.

Gustav Cassel presented his grand synthesis *Theoretische Sozialökonomie* to the club at the time of its publication in 1918. This work contained a formal general equilibrium model in the tradition of Walras (without mention of Walras in the first and many subsequent editions) and introduced Ohlin to general equilibrium analysis. Ohlin had more reason to familiarize himself with this kind of analysis when he became Cassel's graduate student at *Stockholms Högskola* (Stockholm College, now Stockholm University) in 1920. He stayed with Cassel and *Stockholms Högskola* until the end of 1924, when he received his doctorate and moved to the University of Copenhagen and a chair in economics.

Ohlin spent the academic year 1922–3 at Harvard, where he took courses in international trade and finance (with John Williams), the history of economic doctrine, economic theory (with Frank Taussig) and agricultural economics. His taking this last course (and the term paper he wrote for it on the pricing of Michigan onions) was the result of his desire to study with Thomas Nixon Carver, whose books on income distribution he had read and whom he admired for his 'unremitting logic'.

Of major importance during his stay at Harvard was his contact with Taussig's students in international economics, especially John Williams and Jacob Viner. Viner let Ohlin read the manuscript of his *Canada's Balance of International Indebtedness, 1900–1913* (Viner 1924), parts of which are recounted in Ohlin's thesis. Williams and Ohlin spent much time together criticizing classical trade theory. According to Ohlin, Williams was exercised primarily over the lack of dynamics but was not clear as to what elements of the classical theory need to be changed, and how. Ohlin's thesis contains much of the analysis Williams (1929) pleads for, particularly dynamics, and domestic and international factor mobility.

A comparison of *International and Interregional Trade*, Ohlin's English-language monograph published in 1933 that came to revolutionize international trade theory, and Ohlin's thesis published in Swedish in 1924 as *Handelns teori*, reveals that the former is essentially an expanded version of the latter. It was

Heckscher and Cassel, and to some extent a few teachers and colleagues at Harvard, who provided the major influence behind Ohlin's work in international economics. Ohlin dates the plan for the thesis and the later monograph to a day in 1920, when he was taking a stroll on the popular promenade *Unter den Linden* in Berlin. No new ideas seem to have been conceived during his five years in Copenhagen, from where he returned to Stockholm at the beginning of 1930 to take up Heckscher's chair at *Handelshögskolan*.

At about this point in his career, he started to take a stronger research interest in stabilization theory and policy. He had always been interested in macroeconomic issues, however. As early as 1919 he published a 48-page critical discussion of monetary theory (Ohlin 1919), which deeply impressed his Swedish contemporaries and established his reputation. When in Copenhagen he frequently commented on current economic events in daily newspapers, a habit he kept up until he died in 1979. He wrote a total of about 1,200 newspaper articles.[6] His strong interest in real-world problems was also manifest in a political career that started in 1934, when he was elected leader of the youth wing of the liberal party, and ended in 1967 when he resigned as party leader. He was the leading politician on the non-socialist side of Swedish politics from the end of the Second World War until his resignation.

HECKSCHER'S CONTRIBUTION

Heckscher's 1919 paper is, in the words of Samuelson (1982), 'a work of genius'. It starts by discussing why comparative costs differ between countries. Ricardo, who showed in 1817 that gains from trade were due to comparative cost differences, assumes that they are the result of differences in production efficiency. Heckscher's answer is very different. He explicitly assumes identical technology between countries in the same activity and assigns differences in comparative costs to differences in factor endowments: 'A difference in the relative scarcity of the factors of production between one country and another is thus a necessary condition for a difference in comparative costs and consequently for international trade.'

From this he goes on to derive the two central results of what is known today as the Heckscher–Ohlin theory of international trade. Since comparative costs will be low for those commodities that are intensive in a country's abundant factors' each country tends to export commodities using relatively large amounts of its abundant factors ...'. This is the *Heckscher–Ohlin theorem*. Heckscher goes on to say that such trade 'must continue to expand until an *equalization of the relative scarcity of the factors of production among countries* has occurred'.[7] 'With fixed supplies of the factors of production and the same techniques of production in all countries – the final effect of international trade ... is the equalization of the *relative* prices of the factors of production.' And with 'the same prices of products, the absolute returns to the factors of production must also be equalized'. This is the *factor-price equalization theorem*.[8]

Heckscher is explicit about most of the necessary conditions for factor-price equalization. The condition of identical technology is stated in the quotation. He mentions various trade barriers, and deals at length with the condition that the fixed factor supplies be sufficiently similar to allow for non-specialization: 'each country must have enough of its most scarce factor so that the proportions of factors in each branch of production can be the same as the corresponding proportions in other countries'. Land/labour ratios in the United States and Europe in the nineteenth century are taken as an example of a situation where labour was too scarce in the United States to allow for factor-prize equalization, which in turn induced labour to migrate from Europe.

OHLIN'S CONTRIBUTION IN RELATION TO HECKSCHER'S

Taking the central propositions of modern Heckscher–Ohlin theory as the yardstick, it is clear that Ohlin did not add anything to what Heckscher had already done.

In fact, in his dissertation (1924, 1991) and in *Interregional and International Trade* (1933) Ohlin allocates considerable space to *contest* factor-price equilization on both theoretical and empirical grounds. Chapter III of the former and Appendix I of the latter work present a two-country version of Cassel's formal general equilibrium model, which is then used to prove factor-price *non*-equalization. Ohlin's argument runs as follows: in isolation, both countries produce the same set of goods, using the same factors and technology. They have different factor endowments, therefore different factor and commodity prices. When the possibility to trade arises, a comparison of commodity prices at any exchange rate will show that some commodities are cheaper to produce in one of the countries and the rest in the other country *at the old factor combinations and factor prices.* From this Ohlin concludes that the countries will specialize accordingly, and that factor prices cannot be equalized. He overlooks the fact that if countries are to change their respective commodity mix and if commodities use factors in different combinations, there will be excess demand of some and excess supply of other factors. This in turn will lead to changes in factor prices and factor combinations, making it possible to produce the same set of commodities in both countries (provided factor endowments are not too different).

Ohlin's mistake in the formal analysis, repeated in the second edition of *Interregional and International Trade* (1967), is hard to understand in view of the fact that the verbal analysis is full of examples where the crucial element is changes in factor prices and factor combinations. Consider the following quotation from *The Theory of Trade*, the translation into English of Ohlin's dissertation (1991):

> If there is increased demand for a commodity that requires much land, for example wheat, and decreased demand for a commodity requiring much capital, such as fine cloth, the rise in the production of the former and the decline in output of the latter lead to an increase in land rents and a decrease in the rental on capital. It then becomes profitable to use more capital and less land in all production, including that of totally different products. This will free some land which can be transferred to wheat production.

Ohlin's contribution was to recognize the importance and originality of Heckscher's model, to demonstrate its workings in great detail, using many real-world examples, to generalize it by introducing factor mobility and financial capital flows in conjunction with real flows of commodities, capital and labour, and to investigate the implications of the model's assumptions and of his own generalizations. Ohlin was motivated by what he saw as the unrealism of many of Hecksher's assumptions and conclusions. Fixed and internationally immobile factors were prime targets among the assumptions, and factor-price equalization among the conclusions.

The title *Interregional and International Trade* tells the reader that this is a general model of spatial exchange. In the *Theory of Trade* Ohlin declares:

The geographical distribution of factors of production would become completely arbitrary under perfect factor mobility. The inter-local exchange that would take place, and which would be due to the limited divisibility of factors of production, i.e. the advantages of large-scale production, would be of no interest. ... [I]t is the limited mobility of the factors of production which necessitates an extension of general price theory with respect to the geographical dimensions of the exchange.

From this observation Ohlin goes on to consider partial mobility of factors and of commodities in great detail; about half of *The Theory of Trade* is devoted to its implications.

Not much new is learned from the many pages of somewhat tedious and repetitive verbal analysis. The original parts are, first, the analysis of the role of non-traded commodities in the adjustment to some exogenous disturbance, and, second, the analysis of international capital flows and its integration of monetary and real elements, which primarily is a contribution to the theory of balance-of-payments adjustment and is discussed later.

Ohlin would argue that the detailed descriptions of the adjustment to various exogenous shocks are tantamount to *trade dynamics*. In other words, his ambition was to develop a dynamic theory of spatial exchange and price determination. In a letter written not long before his death he exclaims: 'you insist on regarding my theory as an equilibrium analysis, while I regard it as a comparison of different positions with essential comments on the forces of transition from the one to the others. The equation system and equilibrium serve only as an introduction!'[9,10]

OHLIN'S CONTRIBUTION IN RELATION TO CASSEL'S

The formal and verbal general equilibrium, neo-classical nature of Ohlin's analysis was seen by him, as well as by Heckscher and Cassel, as at least as important a contribution as the explanations of comparative costs in terms of factor endowments and factor proportions. This is evident by Ohlin's foreword to his thesis and his monograph and by Heckscher's 'Prefatory Note' to the 1949 English version of Heckscher's paper. Cassel was delighted with a preliminary version of the thesis to which his only objection was that

Ohlin had made use of Heckscher's paper (!). In a letter to Ohlin in 1926, quoted by Ohlin in his memoirs, Cassel writes: 'Since Heckscher's treatment is totally and fundamentally wrong, it would be of little use to you to refer to him.'

All of them failed to see that Heckscher's paper was as much general equilibrium in nature as Ohlin's analysis. The reason is that at the time – and well into the 1950s – general equilibrium analysis was synonymous with working with a system of many equations à la Walras. This should not be interpreted as a depreciation of Ohlin. When Ohlin wrote his thesis, it was indeed a major achievement to integrate the factor proportions theory of Heckscher with the neo-classical general equilibrium price theory that had emerged from the writings of Walras and others.

To Ohlin's credit we should also mention, as a minor point, that he made the technical coefficients (input–output coefficients) endogeneous in contrast to Cassel, who assumed fixed coefficients (as did Walras initially), and that he endogenized the determination of aggregate income.[11]

OHLIN'S CONTRIBUTION TO THE THEORY OF CAPITAL MOVEMENTS

As mentioned, Ohlin devoted much attention to factor mobility. His most original contribution to international economics lies here, in his integration of real and monetary capital flows; not in the integration itself, because that is what balance-of-payments theory is about and Ohlin was certainly not first to enter the area, but in his use of the new, neo-classical factor proportions trade theory in conjunction with his original concept of *buying power*, a variable that determines aggregate spending.

The Taussig school[12] that Ohlin came into contact with at Harvard must have influenced him in his analysis of balance-of-payments adjustment, although it is difficult to pinpoint any particular element that he incorporated. Rather, their influence can probably be seen by the share of balance-of-payments analysis in *The Theory of Trade* and *Interregional and International Trade*. Ohlin uses material from Viner's *Canada's Balance of International Indebtedness, 1900–1913*, published in 1924, and from Williams's *Argentine International Trade under Inconvertible Paper Money 1880–1900*, published in 1920, already in his thesis.

Two types of capital movement are considered by Ohlin. The

first comes about as a result of an exogeneous shock, such as a harvest failure that leads to borrowing to smooth consumption over time. The second type is when capital moves in response to differences in rates of return, as in the case of Canadian and Argentine capital imports at the turn of the century. Ohlin recognizes that the initial flow of financial capital influences buying power and therefore spending in both the borrowing and the lending country. In particular, an increase in buying power of the capital importing country will result in an increase in demand for commodities produced by the capital exporting country. The mechanism is described in detail; there is an elaborate account of how financial capital travels between countries through a financial intermediary country, and between the accounts of different agents in the capital-importing country, and of how the importation of financial capital results in spending on commodities, some of which are produced by the lending country. The central question is if the surplus in the capital account will be fully offset by a resulting deficit in the current account.

This is precisely the issue in Ohlin's famous interchange about the effects of German reparations with Keynes in the *Economic Journal* in 1929 (Ohlin 1929a,b; Keynes 1929a,b,c). Keynes argued that to be able to make a financial transfer to England, Germany would have to create a trade surplus of equal size by depressing domestic demand, and this must lead to a worsening of its terms of trade, an additional burden to the transfer itself. Ohlin begins his argument with the observation that the transfer would serve to shift buying power and hence spending from Germany to England. This would reduce Germany's demand for its own commodities and increase English demand for German commodities. In other word, the transfer would create the necessary trade surplus. If the marginal propensities to demand German commodities were the same in Germany and England, no change in the terms of trade need take place.

The effects of a transfer had been discussed in the literature long before the interchange between Keynes and Ohlin. It was Ohlin's concept of buying power, his matching of aggregate supply and demand, and his profound understanding of general equilibrium that allowed him to see the problem clearly.[13]

CONCLUDING COMMENT

It is an irony of fate that Ohlin always regretted the fact that his work on stabilization policy in the early 1930s, in particular his *Monetary Policy, Public Works, Subsidies and Tariffs as Remedies for Unemployment* (1934) had not been published in English at the time. He was convinced that this would have given him – and his colleagues in the Stockholm School – a much more prominent place in the development of macroeconomic theory and policy.[14] The irony is that had Heckscher's paper been published in English in 1919, it is less likely that Ohlin would have been associated with the Heckscher–Ohlin theory by name, though he made the theory known to the world and played an important role in developing it.

NOTES

1 Parts of this article follows closely M. June Flanders's and my introduction to our edition and translation of Eli Heckscher's pathbreaking paper 'The Effect of Foreign Trade on the Distribution of Income' and Bertil Ohlin's dissertation *The Theory of Trade*, all of which can be found in Heckscher and Ohlin (1991). I am grateful for comments from Don Patinkin.

2 The official name of the prize is 'The Prize in Economic Sciences in Memory of Alfred Nobel'. It was set up in the late 1960s and endowed by a gift from the Bank of Sweden.

3 A comparison of the relative importance of the two areas of Ohlin's work is made by Lars Werin (1991). Werin argues, apparently as did the academy, that the contributions to international economics are much more important.

4 The history of the optimal rotation rule in forestry economics is discussed by Johansson and Löfgren (1985) and by Samuelson (1976). See also Löfgren's contribution to this volume (Chapter 12).

5 *Ekonomisk Tidskrift (Economic Journal)*, the predecessor of *The Scandinavian Journal of Economics*, was the vehicle of most of the exchanges and debates among Swedish economists, most notably Cassel, Heckscher and Wicksell. A somewhat shortened version of Heckscher's paper first appeared in English in 1949 (Heckscher 1949).

6 According to the bibliography in Caves (1978) that was put together by Ohlin himself. Ohlin told Lars Jonung that he had surpassed Cassel's total of 1,507. The number 1,200 probably refers to articles dealing with economic issues. In addition to these Ohlin wrote on many other issues, especially during his time as leader of the Liberal Party.

7 The italics in this and following quotations are from the original.

8 Both Caves (1978) and Chipman (1966) state that the roots of the Heckscher paper are to be found in the writings of Wicksell, based on Heckscher's 'Prefatory Note' to the English version of his paper.

Heckscher wrote that, 'the article owes its origin to Knut Wicksell's criticism of an earlier book of mine'. The relevant passage in Wicksell's review (Wicksell 1919) of Heckscher's *Svenska produktions problem* (*Swedish Production Problems*) is quoted in the Swedish version of Heckscher's path-breaking paper but not in the 1949 English version. The passage reads:

> Assume that the price of iron-ore and lumber rose so high relative to the price of manufactured goods and foodstuffs, that it became profitable for our mine- and landowners to export only iron-ore and unfinished or slightly finished wood products, even allowing trees to grow on all fields and pastures. As long as such a tendency is weak, as it is at present, it can still – albeit under the pressure of falling wages! – be offset by more intensive use of the best agricultural land and some still-surviving industries. If it becomes stronger, then, under competitive conditions, the majority of the population must emigrate or decline in number by some other means. For the *world economy* as a whole this would be highly advantageous; from the point of view of the world economy nothing is more beneficial than that those parts of the earth best suited to the production of raw materials be devoted to that purpose, even if their population is thereby rendered *sparse*; for the Swedish people, as a nation, it is a different matter [italics in original].

Wicksell described the situation of Sweden in the late nineteenth century as one where prices on iron-ore and lumber had served to depress wages and thereby force a substantial portion of the population to emigrate to the United States. It is clear that Wicksell here provides Heckscher with the building blocks of Heckscher–Ohlin theory, namely differences in factor combinations and factor endowments. It was left to Heckscher to use them to derive a new explanation of comparative costs and factor-price equalization.

9 In a letter to Professor Peter Gray. Professor Don Patinkin made the comment in conversation that Ohlin used to stress that the macro theory of the Stockholm School is dynamic in nature.

10 Actually, Heckscher had listed lack of dynamics as one of the limitations of his analysis, others being the absence of international factor mobility and of factor-supply responses. Heckscher's list thus served as 'suggestions for future research' to Ohlin.

11 Aggregate income was endogenized formally in Appendix I of *Interregional and International Trade*. The model in Chapter III of *The Theory of Trade* lacks a formal determination of aggregate income.

12 The reader is referred to Flanders (1989) for a detailed account. Flanders dubs Taussig and his famous students (Angell, Viner, White and Williams) 'The Late Classicals', which is more informative about their place in the history of doctrine.

13 Ohlin describes in his memoirs how he, having read Keynes's first article in the *Economic Journal*, immediately sat down to write a reply.

This only took him five or six hours, since the problem was already familiar to him. See also the translation of parts of Ohlin's memoirs in Jonung (ed.) (1990).

14 Ohlin used part of his Nobel Prize money to set up a foundation (*Bertil Ohlin's Fond*) to finance research and *translation* of works by Swedish economists into English. See Ohlin's comment in the translated parts of his memoirs in Jonung (ed.) (1990).

REFERENCES

Cassel, Gustav (1926) *Theoretische Sozialökonomie*, Leipzig: C.F. Winter. (Translated from German into English as *Theory of Social Economy*, London: T.F. Unwin, 1923.)

Caves, Richard E, (1978) 'Bertil Ohlin's Contribution to Economics', *The Scandinavian Journal of Economics*, 80, 86–99.

Chipman, John (1966) 'A Survey of the Theory of International Trade: Part 2, The Neo-classical Theory', *Econometrica*, 33, 685–760.

Ellis, Howard S. and Lloyd A. Metzler (eds) (1949) *Readings in the Theory of International Trade*, Philadelphia: Blakiston for the American Economic Association.

Flam, Harry and M. June Flanders (1991) 'Introduction', in Eli F. Heckscher and Bertil Ohlin *Heckscher–Ohlin Trade Theory*, Cambridge, Mass.: MIT Press.

Flanders, M. June (1989) *International Monetary Economics, 1870–1960: Between the Classical and the New Classical*, New York: Cambridge University Press.

Heckscher, Eli (1919) 'Utrikeshandelns verkan på inkomstfördelningen. Några teoretiska grundlinjer', *Ekonomisk Tidskrift*, 21, 497–512.

―――― (1949) 'The Effect of Foreign Trade on the Distribution of Income,' in Howard S. Ellis and Lloyd A. Metzler (eds) (1949).

―――― (1991) 'The Effect of Foreign Trade on the Distribution of Income', in Eli F. Heckscher and Bertil Ohlin, *Heckscher–Ohlin Trade Theory*, Cambridge, Mass.: MIT Press. Unabridged and corrected translation of Heckscher (1919).

Johansson, Per-Olov and Karl-Gustaf Löfgren (1985) *The Economics of Forestry and Natural Resources*, Oxford: Blackwell.

Jonung, Lars (ed.) (1990) *The Stockholm of Economics Remembered*, in preparation.

―――― (1991) *The Stockholm School of Economics Revisited*, Cambridge: Cambridge University Press.

Keynes, John Maynard (1929a) 'The German Transfer Problem', *Economic Journal*, 39, 1–7, reprinted in Howard S. Ellis and Lloyd A. Metzler (eds) (1949).

―――― (1929b) 'A Rejoinder to "The Reparation Problem: A Discussion", by Professor B. Ohlin', *Economic Journal*, 39, 179–82.

―――― (1929c) 'A Reply to a Criticism on "Mr. Keynes' Views on the Transfer Problem" by J. Rueff', *Economic Journal*, 39, 404–8.

Löfgren, Karl-Gustaf (1991) 'Economics and Mathematics in Forest Economics: Some Swedish Contributions', in this volume.

Ohlin, Bertil (1919) 'Kvantitetsteorien i den svenska litteraturen' ('The Quantity Theory in the Swedish Literature') *Ekonomisk Tidskrift*, 21, 1–48.

——— (1921) 'Till frågan om skogarnas omloppstid' ('On the Question of the Rotation Period of Forests'), *Ekonomisk Tidskrift*, 23, 89–114. (In the issue of this volume that is the *Festschrift* to Knut Wicksell.)

——— (1924) *Handelns teori*, Stockholm: AB Nordiska Bokhandeln.

——— (1929a) 'The Reparation Problem: A Discussion', *Economic Journal*, 39, 172–8. Reprinted in Howard S. Ellis and Lloyd A. Metzler (eds) (1949).

——— (1929b) 'A Reply to a Criticism on "Mr. Keynes' views on the Transfer Problem", by J. Rueff; A Rejoinder from Professor Ohlin', *Economic Journal*, 39, 400–4.

——— (1933) *Interregional and International Trade*, Harvard Economic Studies Volume XXXIX, Cambridge, Mass.: Harvard University Press.

——— (1934) *Penningpolitik, offentliga arbeten, subventioner och tullar som medel mot arbetslöshet* (*Monetary Policy, Public Works, Subsidies and Tariffs as Remedies for Unemployment*), Stockholm: Statens Offentliga Utredningar 1934:12.

——— (1967) *Interregional and International Trade*, revised edition, Harvard Economic Studies Volume XXXIX, Cambridge, Mass.: Harvard University Press.

——— (1972) *Bertil Ohlins memoarer. Ung man blir politiker* (*Bertil Ohlin's Memoirs. Young Man Turns Politician*), Stockholm: Bonniers.

——— (1991) 'The Theory of Trade', in Eli F. Heckscher and Bertil Ohlin *Heckscher–Ohlin Trade Theory*, Cambridge, Mass.: MIT Press.

Samuelson, Paul A. (1976) 'Economics of Forestry in Evolving Society', *Economic Inquiry*, 14, 466–92.

——— (1982) 'Bertil Ohlin: 1889–1979', *Journal of International Economics*, 12 (supplement), 33–49.

Viner, Jacob (1924) *Canada's Balance of International Indebtedness 1900–1913*, Cambridge, Mass.: Harvard University Press.

Werin, Lars (1991) 'There were Two Stockholm Schools', chapter 6 in Lars Jonung (ed.) (1991).

Wicksell, Knut (1919) 'Svenska produktionsproblem' ('Swedish Production Problems'), *Forum*, no. 2.

Williams, John H. (1920) *Argentine International Trade under Inconvertible Paper Money 1880–1900*, Cambridge, Mass.: Harvard University Press.

——— (1929) 'The Theory of International Trade Reconsidered', *Economic Journal*, 39, 195–209. Reprinted in Howard S. Ellis and Lloyd A. Metzler (eds) (1949).

10

THE LONG RETREAT: GUSTAV CASSEL AND ELI HECKSCHER ON THE 'NEW ECONOMICS' OF THE 1930s[1]

Benny Carlson

INTRODUCTION

It was not by chance that Gustav Cassel's and Eli F. Heckscher's stars stood at their zenith in the 1920s. This was the decade of economic liberalism's gala performance, and Cassel and Heckscher were the dominant figures on the Swedish scene. Immediately after the middle of the 1920s, however, certain dissonances began to be heard behind the harmonies; dissonances which resonated in permanent high unemployment, deepened in step with the world crisis, and in time set the tone of the entire score.

For Cassel and Heckscher this change of scene, marked by the onward march of the New Economics (i.e. the new economic theory and policy), meant that they were forced to shift from the offensive to retreat. The story of this long retreat, extending over a period of about twenty years, has never before been told as far as I am aware. Some authors have discussed Cassel's and Heckscher's reactions to Keynes's *General Theory* (e.g. Hansson (1988) and Landgren (1960)). Others have formulated summary assessments of their reactions to the New Economics – not least Bertil Ohlin and Erik Lundberg, both of them advocates of the New Economics in Sweden.

Arthur Montgomery's (1947, p. 540) picture of Cassel shows him as a helpless dogmatist: 'He was not able to do much more than reiterate his old theoretical opinions with scarcely any significant change.' Lundberg (*SvD*, 16 April 1973) writes of Cassel that he 'rejected with emphasis and contempt all theories that smelt of primitive ideas about inadequate purchasing power or excessive saving', and that 'Cassel flatly rejected Keynes's' new gospel and

156

looked with the greatest suspicion upon the politico-economic conclusions with respect to an active budget policy that was drawn from the theories of the Stockholm School. Regarding Heckscher, Lundberg (*DN*, 23 December 1952 – cf. Lundberg (1984, p. 181)) writes that he was 'strongly critical of expensive governmental economic policies as a method of curing the depression of the thirties, not because he did not see that modern Keynesian theories could be right within a limited framework but because he feared the danger of a permanent advance of state power positions'. Ohlin (1972, p. 270) observes that Heckscher 'resisted with great energy the countercyclical policy which the younger generation of economists ardently recommended', and goes on:

> Eventually, of course, he realized that as far as theory was concerned he had landed himself in an untenable position. He shifted more and more towards a more practical political argument in defence of his negative attitude. The consequences of this countercyclical policy would be a multiplication of state intervention and thus a heavy bureaucratization of society.

TRADE-CYCLE AND CRISIS

Before we plunge headlong into the story, let us summarize very briefly first Cassel's and Heckscher's attitudes to trade-cycle theory, then their views on the character and causes of the crisis.

As time went on, both Cassel and Heckscher became increasingly sceptical of contemporary trade-cycle research. For Cassel it was the trend, long-term growth, that formed the centre of interest. Nevertheless he did analyse the economic fluctuations of the period 1870–1914 in the spirit of Tugan-Baranovsky and Spiethoff. He found that the trade cycle was in substance a wave-motion in the production of fixed real capital – a wave-motion arising from the interaction between entrepreneurs' investment plans on the one hand, and interest, prices of materials and wages on the other. Slumps had nothing to do with overproduction: they occurred because when entrepreneurs were making their plans, they overestimated the supply of savings. By the early 1920s, Cassel was giving vent from time to time to his distaste for all mathematical 'curve analysis', which reflected a determinism most reminiscent of 'Babylonian astrology'. (See especially 1904, 1918, 1933b, 1942 and articles in *SvD*, 15 November 1921, 1 November 1923 and 11 April 1928.)

Heckscher's explanation of the trade cycle followed Wicksellian paths, finding its starting-point in differences between interest on loans and the yield on capital. The remedy, consequently, lay in a skilful interest-rate policy. The trade-cycle discussions of the 1930s wore out his patience. He declared that precisely nothing was known about cyclical fluctuations, that they were 'figments of the brain', and that he was 'a confirmed unbeliever' with regard to the theories in that field. (See especially *Stockholms Dagblad*, 5 January 1921, 1926; *DN*, 28 July 1931; and two contributions to the debates at the Swedish Economic Society, 12 October 1931 and 23 March 1936, pp. 44–5.)

In Cassel's view, the 1930s slump was a deflationary crisis, the origins of which were to be found in war debts, demands for preparations and demands for payment in gold instead of goods, and which took an increasingly severe turn as attempts were made to avert the perils of deflation by continual new doses of deflation (see especially 1932a, 1933c, 1937a, 1942 and 1944b).

As far as Heckscher was concerned, the 1930s slump was of the same type that had struck the industrial economy several times before and was caused by structural changes, primarily the changed role of Europe in the world economy. He explained the acuteness of the crisis in terms of political factors, chiefly the political uncertainty following the war and the Versailles settlement, and of the fact that several sectors were hit sumultaneously (see especially 1932 and 1936).

CENTRAL ISSUES

Let us also, as a final preliminary to the narrative itself, take note of some of the issues which were central to the debate in the 1920s and 1930s, questions to which we shall direct attention and which concerns the attitude towards:

1 the possibility of insufficient demand, i.e. the possibility of asymmetry between total demand and total supply, i.e. the question of the validity of Say's law, which says that supply creates its own demand;
2 the possibility of unutilized saving, i.e. saving which does not lead to investment and thereby causes demand to fall short of supply;

3   lower factor prices as a remedy for unemployment, i.e.
   (a) the question of whether wage cuts will lead via reduced
       costs to higher sales/profits and thus to increased pro-
       duction and employment, or else via reduced purchasing
       power to a diminution of demand and thus to decreased
       production and employment;
   (b) the question of the effectiveness of lower interest rates in
       raising the level of investment;
4   public works as a remedy for unemployment and then especially:
   (a) the question whether the state will trespass upon saving
       which would otherwise be utilized by private enterprise (the
       treasury view) or activate saving which would not otherwise
       have been utilized;
   (b) the question of the existence of the multiplier effect.

WHEN THE CENTURY WAS YOUNG

Our narrative can now begin. It begins in fact as far back as the turn
of the century. If Knut Wicksell is sometimes regarded as a fore-
runner in the field of the new economic theory, then the proposals
for redistributive works to combat cyclical unemployment which
were proposed during the early decades of the twentieth century are
usually held to have been precursors in the field of economic policy.
These proposals emanated principally from German and English
sources. As early as 1902, in his book *Socialpolitik (Social Policy)*
(p. 104), Cassel made such a proposal for 'a deliberate policy aimed
at forestalling unemployment as far as possible':

> We must so arrange that in every public enterprise we take
> account of the market situation and act in conformity there-
> with as far as possible. In this way the public organs of society
> could achieve not a little by way of levelling out the market
> and thus forestalling unemployment.

We can only speculate about where Cassel got hold of this idea. The
sources were probably Gustav Schmoller in Germany or the Webbs
in England, since Cassel had contacts in both quarters.
   Heckscher put forward the same proposals when unemployment
came under discussion at the so-called poor relief congress of 1906
(p. 235):

When there is a good boom period one should abstain from major public undertakings, which require the labour of a number of people and serve to force up the prices of all necessaries. On the other hand, when it is seen that prices beginning to fall or are remaining stationary, this is the time to intervene with large-scale undertakings.

In 1909 the Swedish Social Democrats, possibly influenced by the Webbs' 'Minority Report', proposed a motion for public works to counteract unemployment. During 1910–12 the Social Democrats made new appeals for redistributive works, and in 1912 measures against 'more permanent unemployment' were also demanded. Otto Steiger (1971a, p. 115; 1971b, p. 20; 1973, pp. 71–3) has interpreted this as a demand for expansionist works and argued that the 'ideas of 1912' served as models for the Social Democratic crisis policy of the 1930s.

Cassel (*SvD*, 14 February) gave lukewarm support to the Social Democratic appeal of 1912 for redistributive works. He considered that they were not to be relied on as a way of levelling out economic fluctuations – but that much would still be gained if public enterprise could be prevented from aggravating the irregularities of private enterprise. And with regard to the demand for measures against more permanent unemployment, Cassel (*SvD*, 15 February) thought at first that the proposers of the Social Democratic motion were on the right track. But on the same day that the Riksdag was to consider the motion, he (*SvD*, 11 May) published a recommendation that the demand should be rejected:

It is an extremely dubious enterprise for the state to initiate productive activity *for the purpose* of creating new job opportunities. For the state as for private individuals, the goal is to be found in the outcome of production, and the *less* labour has to be employed for a given result, the better.

It seems as if Cassel's writings had some influence on the outcome in the Riksdag. When the First Chamber committee recommended rejection of measures against permanent unemployment, the Social Democratic proposer of the motion took the floor to say he did not hesitate 'to point to Professor Cassel as the committee's oracle (*Första kammarens protokoll,* 1912: 40, p. 9).

During the 1910s and 1920s, ideas from the beginning of the century occasionally cropped up in the debate. This was not thought to be particularly remarkable. As the problem of unemployment had still not become a subject for profound theoretical and ideological contention, even Heckscher was able to let slip one or two unorthodox pronouncements. Thus, when he (1918a, p. 34) was surveying the postwar European scene he ventured to speculate on the possibilities of overproduction. Soon all the soldiers would return from the front and be set to work, and 'this will probably bring about a feverish rise in production and exports, which will make the supply of goods too large in relation to the available purchasing power'.

The view of unemployment which Heckscher represented along with Gösta Bagge, the expert in that field, and which became dominant in the 1920s, suggested two explanations: insufficient mobility of labour and insufficient 'flexibility' of wages. The natural remedies, accordingly, were labour exchanges and more flexible wages. Attempts to 'create job opportunities' might attract those already in employment as well as the unemployed, and 'may increase unemployment at least as easily as it may reduce it'. (Heckscher, 1918b, pp. 80–2, 92). In his book *Gammal och ny ekonomisk liberalism* (*Old and New Economic Liberalism*) (1921, pp. 61–2), Heckscher nailed up the theses on unemployment policy that he was to be guided by during the 1920s and 1930s: wages in excess of the equilibrium position lead to rationalization and unemployment. Relief works and unemployment benefit involve a risk of freezing this situation and must therefore be adjusted – by means of sufficiently low wages/benefit – in order not to hinder a return to normal. Cassel (see, e.g. 1928, pp. 130, 138, 188) reasoned along the same lines.

SIGNALS FROM ENGLAND

Immediately after the middle of the 1920s, new signals began to emerge from various quarters: an early indication, but one typical of its time, was the title of Keynes's book of 1926, *The End of Laissez Faire*.

In April 1926, Cassel (1926, p. 19) began to argue against the view that there is such a thing as unutilized capital. New capital – i.e. saving – must be tied up immediately in real capital, and the existing capital was thus 'continuously in use':

It should also then be obvious that it is not possible by any money grants to create new capital for the relief of unemployment. For the grant entails the withdrawal of an equivalent amount of new capital from other uses and thereby gives rise to new unemployment, which possibly may be less, but may also be on a larger scale than that which has been relieved.

During 1927 new signs of unease were to be detected in the economists' ranks. Ohlin, for example, in 'Saet Produktionen i Gang' ('Let's start up production again') came up with certain intimations about the multiplier effect of loan-financed public works. Cassel launched an attack on the concept of 'inadequate purchasing power' in a couple of articles (e.g., SvD, 20 June) and his memorandum to the Geneva conference (1927a, pp. 13–16) during the spring and early summer. The concept, he argued, was a product of superstition and childish fantasies probably deriving from the observation that an individual producer must be careful not to produce more than is demanded: 'this elementary wisdom in private business is simply applied to social economics'.

It is, of course, correct to say that at any given moment the purchasing power for a certain product is limited. But the total sale of the entire production of a community can never be limited to any lack of purchasing power in the community as a whole. The notion of an abstract purchasing power in the community, determined independently of production, must be relegated to the region of economic mysticism. The entire purchasing power of the community is in reality nothing but the total value of its production. This is self-evident if we consider that a purchase is not, and never can be, anything but a form for the exchange of goods and services. From this point of view, it is manifest that the purchasing power of the community is always sufficient to purchase the entire production. All that is necessary is to find such a level of prices and thus also such an adjustment of production to the desires of the consumer, that the entire production can find a market.
(Cassel, 1927b, p. 21)

The English Liberals' report on *Britain's Industrial Future* ('The Yellow Book') was published in February 1928. In the trade-union movement, criticism of traditional unemployment policy was growing, and in May 1928 LO (*Landsorganisationen*, the Swedish Trade Union Confederation) proposed in a letter to the government that the system should be overhauled and public works at market wages introduced. In December, the Social Democrat Ernst Wigforss, in an article on 'The saver, the spendthrift and the unemployed', contended that it was possible for saving to lie idle instead of going into investment, and put forward the argument that if state action robbed private firms of capital, then private firms robbed each other of capital.

In March 1929, 'The Yellow Book' was followed by *We can Conquer Unemployment*, and a couple of months later came Keynes and Henderson's *Can Lloyd George do it?*. Heckscher (*DN*, 26 March) wrote an article taking up the English Liberals' diagnosis of unemployment and the medicine they proposed against it. If the diagnosis – that the savings flowing into the banks remain lying there, so that the quantity of money decreases, prices fall and unemployment rises – was correct, then would not the obvious remedy be to stimulate the demand for credit by lowering interest rates? If one tried to cure unemployment by means of vast public works, would this not result in a relapse once the cure was over? Heckscher did not on the whole believe that Lloyd George would be any more successful in fulfilling his election pledge to abolish unemployment than he had been ten years earlier in redeeming his similar promise to hang the Kaiser.

Ohlin declared in his memoirs (1972, p. 167) that the Liberals' written programme gave his thinking a push in expansionist directions. In an article in *Stockholms-Tidningen* in 1929 (18 April) he voiced the question, as had Wigforss before him, why public initiative could not reduce unemployment just as well as private. This article has been singled out by Steiger (1976, pp. 349–50, 364) as having been especially important in Ohlin's development of the 'aggregate demand approach': Ohlin describes how loan-financed public works can increase total purchasing power in relation to total production, thereby bringing about an expansion of production and employment.

Heckscher took up this article for discussion in a letter (21 April 1929) to Ohlin:

I have read your article on Lloyd George's unemployment programme with great interest, which is undiminished by the fact that it is presumably aimed primarily at mine. I still do not know whether I have correctly grasped the position which you represent and which perhaps coincides with the Keynes–Henderson line; but at all events I do understand what the Englishmen mean better than I did before; for previously it had seemed to me as though they had got the wrong end of the stick in fundamental matters, and this I will not now assert.

As Heckscher saw it, the positions were as follows: he himself thought that capital must be utilized for less capital-intensive tasks in order to be able to employ more labour. Ohlin and Keynes were more of the opinion that the amount of capital within the country ought to be increased by preventing its export. This could only be effected through the requisitioning by the state of capital judged by the market to be incapable of being utilized profitably, Heckscher admitted that 'this line of reasoning makes sense in itself', but how would it be implemented in practice?

> The programme ... ought to require the state to pay a rate of interest on its new borrowings that would be higher than the market rate and would thereby absorb the capital which now goes to other countries. Such a device would perhaps not be impossible, although mightily complicated.

Cassel's reaction to the writings of the Liberals came in a couple of articles in April and May. In the first of these (*SvD*, 10 April) he began by praising Lloyd George's election programme for its 'positive character' and did not doubt that it would inspire imitation throughout the rest of the world. He did not wholly reject the notion that the state might have a counter-cyclical role to play:

> If ... the state neglected its own tasks for long periods, then it would be reasonable to say that a period of unemployment is particularly suitable for making good the deficiency and for making exceptional exertions to bring the state's economic activities up to full effectiveness.

He did doubt, however, whether by intervening in the economy, the state would be able to improve the business outlook. The acquisition of capital was the crux of the matter. If the state withdrew it from the private sector of the economy, employment would be reduced there. There was always a shortage of capital and an economic upturn must itself create the capital it needed for its own development. 'If there is a shortage of capital, therefore, it is necessary to secure a rise in people's incomes and saving sufficient to enable the need for new capital to be satisfied.' How this was to come about, however, Cassel did not explain.

In the second article (*SvD*, 26 May), Cassel addressed the key issue of the English election campaign, on which the Treasury's views and those of Lloyd George were at odds. This was the question of whether there could exist any unutilized saving which the state could requisition. Keynes and his followers held that there was significant scope for increased bank credit before any inflation need arise. Cassel believed that this was to involve the central bank in electioneering and to give nourishment to 'those tendencies which strive, in the name of democracy, to bring the central bank under state control'. The sole duty of the central bank ought to be the maintenance of a stable price level, and if the bank accomplished this task 'a constant conformity between society's net saving and its production of real capital is guaranteed'. The doctrine that unutilized savings would still exist was one that required eradicating root and branch.

In July 1929, Cassel (1929, pp. 37–40) renewed his attack upon the notion that excessive saving would reduce purchasing power: 'In times of depression we hear people say that money is being amassed in large repositories, where it is kept pending an opportunity for some good investment', he bantered. But such 'idle money' did not exist. Saving could not diminish the capacity of society's income to purchase society's production, since it was utilized for buying real capital. Minor adjustments between consumption and saving were regulated by means of variations in stocks, long-term adjustments through the medium of changes in the production process. It was no more remarkable than the fact that the production of different goods adjusted itself to changes in demand. All income was invested in real capital from the outset and must remain so until it was consumed – all saving was thus tied up immediately in real capital. Furthermore, if money lay in reserve for future use, this was tantamount to an excess of supply of capital over demand, and in that case there ought not to be any interest on capital.

A couple of months after the New York stock exchange crash, Cassel (*SvD*, 31 December 1929) aired his aversion to Hoover's programme of public works. The programme assumed that there was an over-abundance of savings. Cassel believed the American problem to be the opposite. Saving had proved inadequate to sustain the vigorous production of real capital. At that time, the most menacing element was the Federal Reserve's tight monetary policy. Its justification had been an attempt to damp down speculation on the stock exchange, but in Cassel's view it involved 'an unwarrantable transgression of the boundaries of a central bank's natural duties'. This monetary policy had led to a fall in prices, and to continue along this road 'must drag all the rest of the world along with it and so precipitate a depression'. Cassel had in fact warned as early as the spring of 1928 that the Federal Reserve's squeeze on credit would provoke a depression, both in a lecture delivered to the American House of Representatives' banking committee and in a newspaper article (*SvD*, 5 March). His emphasis upon the significance of the tight American monetary policy in the Great Depression clearly anticipates Milton Friedman's explanation of the crisis.

CRISIS POLICY IN THE MELTING-POT

In 1930 the concrete groundwork of future Swedish crisis policy was laid in a Social Democratic motion proposing that relief works should be abolished and 20 million kronor appropriated instead for a programme of productive public works at market wages.

Cassel (*SvD*, 19 February) was taken aback by the 'utterly preposterous' demand for the proposed works to be paid for at market wages. The motion actually spoke of 'agreed wages', which made it clear that these works were intended for trade-union members, rather than for unorganized workers in agriculture. Cassel's objections to the proposals were three:

1   The brake on trade unions' wage demands would be removed when they were not themselves forced to pay for the unemployment consequent upon excessive wage claims but were able to shift the costs onto the state.
2   The brake on the state's expenditure would be removed since it would seem meaningless to knock off a million here and there on the supply estimates for government-owned public utilities when it was in any case intended to add millions to the budget in order to increase government works.
3   The money would presumably be raised, in accordance with socialist custom, by taxing the rich and thus reducing saving,

with a transfer of capital from the private sector to state-owned establishments as the sole result.

On the theoretical plane, Erik Lindahl's *Penningpolitikens medel* (*The Means of Monetary Policy*) was the big event of 1930. Subsequent assessments of it are divided, however. Karl-Gustav Landgren (1960, pp. 124–34, 226) and Don Patinkin (1982, pp. 44–5) have played down its significance; Steiger (1971a, pp. 165, 170) and Ohlin, on the contrary, have emphasized its significance for the development of the Stockholm School – it 'started the ball rolling', in Ohlin's (1981, pp. 200, 221) words. However, it is apparent from a letter to Gösta Bagge of 15 October 1930 that Heckscher, at any rate, did not pounce upon Lindahl's book. In this letter he stated that he had no knowledge of the book.

Cassel emphasized several times in late 1930 and early 1931, the responsibility of central banks for putting a stop to falling prices by increasing the quantity of money. 'It is unreasonable to put a brake on the progress of the entire world economy simply because we cannot produce a corresponding supply of money' (Cassel, 1931a, p. 5). He denied that a more liberal credit policy would lose in effectiveness by virtue of the means of payment being left unutilized, and declared his faith in the ability of central banks to increase activity in the economy by lowering interest rates.

In 1931 the Social Democrats again raised their demand for 20 million kronor for relief works, and the Liberal government proposed – and received assent for – three million kronor's worth of such works on a trial basis. Cassel (*SvD*, 1 May) endeavoured to get the Liberals to stand their ground against the Social Democratic pressure, citing unemployment policy in England and Germany as cautionary examples of what might happen to the government's finances.

At the Nordic economic congress in Stockholm in June, Ohlin gave a lecture which he himself cited afterwards (1972, p. 163; 1981, pp. 192, 229) as proof of his early commitment to public initiatives against unemployment. Heckscher (1931a, pp. 117–8) also appeared at the congress with a contribution in which he categorically rejected general overproduction as a possibility, 'As long as there is production, purchasing power corresponding to it is also created ... aggregate purchasing power is equal to the value of society's aggregate production.' The argument that higher benefit for the unemployed would create more purchasing power made Heckscher (p. 118) see red:

Is this not a *deductio in absurdum*, however? It means that if only a society pours out enough in benefit payments, all our trade-cycle problems will disappear.... Much of what Professor Ohlin said ... on which I did not agree with him at all, bore precisely this stamp, namely that if only we use more and more money, everything will come right.

Cassel expressed himself in equally categorical terms at this time (*SvD*, 17 June): 'In the economy, there can never be any question of general overproduction but only of an incorrect alignment of productive power in various fields.'

The first major report from the 1927 commission on unemployment was issued in the summer of 1931. The shock-waves produced by the world slump made the autumn a period of intense activity in terms of the development of the New Economics: Ohlin brought out a report for the League of Nations, Gunnar Myrdal published his book *Sveriges väg genom penningkrisen* (*Sweden's Way through the Monetary Crisis*) and Wigforss produced his on *Den ekonomiska krisen* (*The Economic Crisis*). All of this work emphasized the link between saving, demand and employment, and the effect of wage cuts on both costs and purchasing power. Certain multiplier arguments were also presented.

A SUDDEN RETREAT

In the autumn of 1931, Heckscher took an almost feverish part in the debate on the causes and cure of unemployment. He drew attention in a newspaper article (*DN*, 20 September) to the paradoxical fact that unemployment existed alongside so many unfulfilled needs. This must result from an organizational failure 'of the same sort as when we button our waistcoat wrongly and get a buttonhole too many at the top and a button too many at the bottom, or vice versa'. All the indications were that rising wages underlay the rising unemployment, said Heckscher, refuting the argument that wage cuts would do harm by decreasing purchasing power:

What is meant is that wage cuts would result in some form of overproduction because there will be no customers for the goods when the workers do not have sufficient means to buy them. However, unless one foresees some general fall in prices, it is obvious that the income which the workers relinquish through reduced wages accrues to other members of society and that the latter thus receive an increment of purchasing power equal to the amount which the workers lose.

Only a couple of days later, Heckscher (*DN*, 22 September) returned to the question of whether reduced wages would improve the business outlook by increasing profits or worsen it by decreasing demand. And now, remarkably enough, he laid stress on the latter effect on the grounds that businessmen's expectations regarding prices and market conditions are of crucial significance.

In a lecture in October, Heckscher (1931b, p. 99) urged calm in face of the crisis and expressed particular disapproval of the frenzied calls for saving:

> For unless there is a simultaneous growth in the demand for capital, this will cause less money to be in circulation, which thus has the effect of lowering price and helping to deepen the depression.

Heckscher also inaugurated the debate on 'Unemployment and its treatment', held at the Swedish Economic Society (12 October) on the occasion of the unemployment commission's report. Heckscher declared that he proposed to ignore cyclical unemployment, expounded the thesis that the exceptional Swedish wage trend after 1913 had led, via the rationalization of industry, to high unemployment, and drew the conclusion that it was 'distinctly probable that a fall in real wages would bring about a reduction of unemployment' (pp. 93–8).

Both Myrdal (p. 108) and Wigforss (p. 121) raised objections to Heckscher's having applied the results of an equilibrium analysis (wages above the equilibrium point) to the current crisis. Heckscher acknowledged without equivocation that this was a mistake (p. 126).

In an article some weeks later (*DN*, 3 November) Heckscher agreed unreservedly that saving could subtract from purchasing power. He reasoned as follows: if saving means to abstain from buying goods, this must have a depressing effect on the economy. Now saving does not mean abstention from buying but expenditure upon means of production instead of consumer goods. But 'in order that saving should be able to function in this way, the increased deposits made at the banks by savers must be reflected in an equally increased volume of lending to industry by the banks'. As long as the 'buying strike' goes on, however, industry will not dare to borrow from the banks and 'under such conditions it is therefore in fact true that saving can subtract from purchasing power and deepen the depression further'. Heckscher concluded his article accordingly:

> Perhaps what is most dangerous is a specially high level of frugality at the present juncture in so far as public works under the control of central and local government are concerned; nothing could be better calculated to create an insoluble problem on the labour market than if the public sector helped to increase unemployment at a time when private firms are to quite a large extent being forced to do so.

In a review of Wigforss's *Den ekonomiska krisen* (*The Economic Crisis*) (*DN*, 11 December), Heckscher again discussed the possibility of general overproduction. He rejected the argument that lower wages could lead to overproduction by referring to experience – the depression would in that case hit consumer goods industries hardest, whereas in fact it primarily affected the means of production. But consistent with his November article, he did admit the possibility that saving might not be utilized for investment: 'As far as I understand, however, this forms the only possibility of so-called general overproduction, i.e. a general price-fall ...'. This was the only case in which it would be explained where the purchasing power leftover had gone – e.g. that money had accumulated in the banks because lending failed to keep in step with saving.

INFLATION AS A CURE

In 1932 the Social Democrats proposed a motion for measures against unemployment costing 93 million kronor, and Wigforss instructed 'the sceptical Riksdag members' in multiplier theory (Lewin, 1967, p. 94).

In the autumn of 1932, Cassel (*SvD*, 14 October) declared that the idea that there was idle capital which the state could borrow in order to put works in hand might be justifiable in other countries, but not in Sweden, where government borrowing would only draw money away from private enterprise. On the other hand, new purchasing power could be placed at the disposal of the state by means of inflation if the Riksbank printed paper money. An isolated action of that kind on the part of Sweden, however, would be 'rather unfortunate'. The only chance of employing more labour through the medium of public works would be by cutting wages in those works. The objection that this reduced the working class's purchasing power lost its significance 'if one succeeds in increasing the numbers of employed workers to such an extent that the total sum paid out in wages remains unchanged or, preferentially, increases'. If monopolistic trade unions succeed in driving up wages beyond what the market situation permitted, and the state pays similar 'agreed wages' in its public works projects, then the unemployment policy will establish much too high a level of wages and thus permanent unemployment.

Somewhat later on, Cassel published an article under the Hamlet-parodying title of 'To save or not to save' (*SvD*, 27 October). The immediate occasion for the article was a statement in *The Times* by a number of leading economists, including Keynes, to the effect that no one should save more than he was forced to, since saving was not necessarily followed by an equivalent investment but might cease to function as purchasing power. Cassel confessed that the statement 'by no means lacked a theoretically correct basis':

> For it is possible to destroy a saving if savings are utilized for repaying sight loans to the banks and ultimately for reducing the banks' indebtedness to the central bank. Then the saving really does have the consequence that the amount of bank means of payment and thus active purchasing power is reduced and the level of prices is pressed down. In point of fact this amounts to a deflationary process.

Cassel again (1932b, pp. 321–2) dismissed the idea that there could be any unutilized savings – they could not very well exist in the air, could they? However, he did remark that savings could 'become inactive to the extent that they were placed in stocks piled up in warehouses for lack of a market', but added that capital which is tied up in stocks would not be reduced to any appreciable degree by launching public works. Since no savings stood at the state's disposal there was only one way out: to print notes. Inflation, however, was a perilous road for a single country to tread. But international collaboration on those lines would be the right way out of the crisis. If resort had to be made to public works, then the conditions were that they must 'do the most possible good' and that the money must stretch further than it would if utilized in the private sector, i.e. the wages must be lower than the market level.

At the same time as well, Cassel, writing in the *International Labour Review* (1932c, p. 647), advocated a more liberal credit policy.

171

Here we find him indeed busily discussing an increase in purchasing power: 'If state enterprise is found necessary, it is important to remember that it can further real recovery only by increasing active purchase power.' Public works should therefore be financed not by loans or taxes but by increased bank credit. The primary goal must be to bring about a previously-determined raising of the price level.

PRACTICAL POLITICAL ARGUMENTS

Lindahl's lecture to the Swedish Economic Society (25 November) on 'Public works in times of depression' is usually regarded as momentous; according to Landgren (1960, p. 157) it marked 'the emergence of public works as a politico-economic tool among the group of economists who were to make recruits for the "new" economic theory in Sweden', and it 'crystallized public opinion and support for a positive recovery programme', according to Carl G. Uhr (1977, p. 97). When Heckscher began to speak, he took issue mainly with a contribution from Ohlin. The latter had contended that increased public activity would not displace private activity provided there was idle productive capacity available. More people at work signified increased demand and thus increased production in the private sector. From the Swedish standpoint, the only cost involved in the increased activity would be that associated with an increase in imports. Heckscher objected (p. 154):

After what I have heard this evening, I am less convinced than before that the new and increasingly popular theory is the right one. If it means what Professor Ohlin has said, namely, that no productive powers other than those brought in from abroad cost anything, then I find myself somewhere in between the Ohlin and Cassel standpoints. I believe that the relationships are considerably more complex than that, in as much as productive powers existing at all stages between cost-free and full cost enter into production.

Heckscher now argued (pp. 154–5) that the dissension over public works did not have so much to do with differing theoretical opinions: 'The crucial error in the view which I am now contesting on principle seems to me ... to be, not that it reasons wrongly from given premises, but rather that these premises have very little connection with practical reality.' Since no one could predict economic conditions, economic policy could not be adapted to them but only to people's opinions about them:

> All the probabilities suggest that if we embark upon public works which are to be liquidated by a decision to be taken at the beginning of the boom, people will deny that the boom has started. They will demand that it should be regarded as a slump for as long as any difficulties are present in the economy, and there are always difficulties in the economy.

Therefore, Heckscher (pp. 156–8) demanded, there must always be constitutional guarantees that works projects would be broken off in boom periods, e.g. when unemployment fell to a previously-defined level. Otherwise there was a risk that public works would not function counter-cyclically but would simply mushroom in the long term. It was best to stick chiefly to relief works and not experiment with public works at market wages. The advantage of relief works was that they were self-liquidating: the low wages meant that workers took themselves off them as soon as they could find a job on free market terms.

TO SAVE OR NOT TO SAVE

At the beginning of 1933, Cassel brought out a short paper on his theme 'To save or not to save' (1933a). In it he discussed the role of saving in normal times and crisis times respectively. During normal times, savings could never lay inactive. However, he said, there was 'a whole school' which claimed that in a time of slump, savings were not put to productive use but instead merely meant that purchasing power was destroyed, a school which obviously could not be casually waved aside. Cassel wrote (pp. 14–15):

> It is a customary conception that the public use their savings to amass paper money, which they hide in safes, desk-drawers or wallets. In certain countries, this has indeed happened. If as a result, the supply of the active means of payment in the nation has been reduced, then the prices of goods must be forced down, and this price-fall cripples enterprises, resulting in a worsening of business conditions and unemployment. In such a case, savings have undoubtedly been harmful. It can also be imagined that entrepreneurs may utilize their savings for repaying, in notes, their debts to the banks.

In this way, the notes flow back in the end to the central bank which issued them. Then the nation's overall note issue is diminished, and the consequence, as in the previous case, will be a fall in prices and a worsening of conditions in the economy.

The first point about these contingencies was that they could be neutralized if the central bank issued more notes, and the second was that they had not arisen in Sweden. Swedish problems derived from the world slump, characterized by falling prices in countries on the gold standard, along with protectionism, which hampered Swedish exports and thereby reduced domestic purchasing power. If economic great powers such as Great Britain and the United States increased the quantity of notes and set a general price-rise going, 'the business outlook would be changed immediately'. Sweden would be able to travel the same road on its own, but then the price-rise would have to be kept within narrow limits (pp. 15, 17–19, 57–9).

What, then, could be achieved by public works? The consequence could be reduced stocks in the private sector, Cassel argued (pp. 46, 51), and 'in that case, certain saved monies might of course be liberated'. Moreover, a fall in unemployment might be brought about if relief works were carried out with a shorter working week or else at lower wages than prevailed on the free market.

BATTLE OVER CRISIS POLICY

The year 1933 opened with the new social Democratic government's budget proposals, containing the main features of its crisis programme. Cassel's first reaction to the budget, as Wigforss (1954, p. 21), now minister of finance, wrote, was almost respectful.

Cassel (*SvD*, 12 January) began by praising the budget proposals for presenting 'such a clear view of the economic situation'. But if the state were to mobilize such sums as were here in question, the consequence must be that 'the private sector's supply of capital will dry up or at least be curtailed to the highest conceivable degree'. However, that was not the end of it as far as Cassel was concerned:

Whether the state can stimulate the private sector of the economy by doling out large sums of money for public works, of course, depends to a certain degree on how the money is procured. If it can be obtained through an expansion of credit

174

by the banks, and especially by the Riksbank, then of course the private sector's capital supply need not be curtailed to the same degree as the state's is augmented. Undoubtedly there is at present a certain amount of room in the Swedish economy for such an expansion of credit.

There was leeway, Cassel argued, for a price rise of a few per cent. There was also the possibility, via excise taxes and tariff increases, of increasing the scope for credit without getting into the danger zone.

Up to this point, then, Cassel's comments were constructive and not far from the position he had criticized Keynes for taking in 1929. In a second article (*SvD*, 13 January) the tone was more negative. The demand for agreed wages in public works would make them permanent – the end would come only when the state's finances had been ruined.

Heckscher (*DN*, 14 January) was highly critical of the proposal. The new works which were proposed (*beredskapsarbeten*) paid higher wages and required more capital compared with the old relief works (*reservarbeten*). In other words 'higher wages per worker and at the same time, a smaller share of the total amount available for wages'. This was the same as saying that only a small proportion of the unemployed could get work. What was to happen to the others? 'There can only be one answer: they will receive cash benefit.' Which would result in 'benefit payments, the like of which have not been witnessed in our country'. If the aim was that increased public borrowing should offset falling prices and 'cash being stuffed into money-boxes', then it was crucial that borrowing should materialize, not that relief works should be replaced by public works on the open market.

In March, the government presented its crisis programme, which included measures costing 160 million kronor. Keynes published his articles on 'The means to prosperity' in the same month. In April, Ohlin's article 'Till frågan om penningteoriens uppläggning' ('On the formulation of monetary theory') was published, in which, according to Landgren (1950, p. 166), Ohlin succeeded in developing 'a preliminary Keynesian theory before Keynes himself'; since then the article has been the subject of a wide-ranging debate. (See chiefly the Ohlin symposium in the *History of Political Economy*, 1978, no. 3.)

In April, Wigforss called in twelve 'prominent men', including Cassel and Heckscher, as currency experts. His ulterior motive was 'to be able to soften up resistance to the government's crisis policy by eliciting some tolerably united statement concerning monetary policy' (1954, pp. 52–3). The twelve came out with a statement in May to the effect that the first aim should be to achieve an international agreement on raising price levels and that the objective of an independent Swedish monetary policy should be a moderate price rise.

This was in line with the view which Cassel came to adopt under the pressure of rising unemployment in the winter of 1932–3 and of which we have already caught a couple of glimpses. He (1933c, p. 23) wrote out the following prescription for the crisis in April:

In such abnormal conditions as at present positive action with intent to increase the purchasing power will be necessary. The measure to that end which immediately suggests itself is that the central bank should buy bonds and thus force means of payment out upon the market. Had such a policy been adopted in time, and with the predetermined purpose of raising the level of commodity prices up to a certain limit, it would no doubt have been successful. Under present conditions, however, it may be necessary to bolster up such a policy by the direct issue of central bank notes to meet the expenditure on such public works as are considered to be absolutely necessary in order to relieve unemployment. In such a case it is of vital importance that the normal budget should be balanced, so that the state will not find itself constrained to create means of payment to meet its current expenditure. Should the state be compelled to take such steps, there is no limit to the inflation which may ensue. It is essential that the new supply of means of payment should have the definite aim of bringing about a predetermined rise in the level of commodity prices.

Cassel thus had every reason to be pleased with the experts' suggestions and the currency policy proposals to which they led (see Cassel, SvD, 28 May; 1933d). Heckscher was more sceptical. He pointed out (DN, 21 April and 28 May) that Swedish economic trends were entirely dependent upon international conditions, and warned that a combination of business boom and increased money supply might trigger off rampant inflation.

Heckscher opened the Swedish Economic Society's 1933 debate (28 April) on 'Unemployment policy', singling out the three novel features of the government's proposals for public works; namely, agreed wages, the influencing of business conditions and deficit financing. He considered (pp. 83–8, 119) that a policy which did not allow wage adjustments was dangerous. As long as there were monopoly wages on the open market, the state could not be permitted to pay market wages. Moreover, for any given sum of money, fewer workers could be found employment in *beredskapsarbeten* than in *reservarbeten*, since wages were higher in the former. He stressed Sweden's heavy dependence upon international economic conditions and doubted that public works could do anything about it. He realized that deficit financing was unavoidable, since increased taxes would aggravate the slump, but he argued that it would be better to borrow for *reservarbeten* than for *beredskapsarbeten*. However, in one respect he had drawn nearer to Ohlin's standpoint in the debate of 1932. Since 'there is an unprecedented amount of productive powers standing idle', said Heckscher (p. 89):

> this means that the new activities must be fitted into as many as possible of the immense gaps which the present level of unemployment is creating in our productive equipment. If this should succeed, then on the whole no demands would be made on new powers and strictly speaking no costs would be involved ...

If success was achieved in bringing 'intermittently idle productive powers' into use in this way – there was a link here with the theory which Heckscher had elaborated in the 1920s – no price rise need occur either. The trick was to ensure that the financing did not make the procurement of capital more difficult for private firms. Increased note-issue was one solution which for the moment would not lead to inflation but which 'creates an element of disquiet whose ultimate effects are very difficult to foresee' – it might lead to stock exchange speculation for example (pp. 89–91).

In May, agreement on the crisis was reached between the Social Democrats and the Farmers' Party; the measures to be taken would cost 180 million kronor, of which 100 million kronor was represented by public works. A group of Liberals accepted the agreement as well. Autumn brought the publication of Dag Hammarskjöld's *Konjunkturspridningen* (*The Transmission of Economic Fluctuations*), the first in a series of appendices to the report of the unemployment commission. Likewise during the autumn (*SvD*, 6 September), Cassel attempted to prove with the aid of statistics that there was no increased or excess saving in Sweden.

The 1934 budget proposals announced the continuation of the crisis policy. In the budget debate, the claim that the crisis policy had contributed to the improvement of the economic climate was called into question by Gösta Bagge in the first instance. The flow of unemployment commission appendices continued: Myrdal's *Finanspolitikens ekonomiska verkningar* (*Economic Effects of Fiscal Policy*), Alf Johansson's *Löneutvecklingen och arbetslösheten* (*Wage trends and unemployment*) and Ohlin's *Penningpolitik, offentliga arbeten, subventioner och tullar som medel mot arbetslöshet* (*Monetary Policy, Public Works, Subsidies and Tariffs as Remedies for Unemployment*). Unemployment problems were considered in the Riksdag in June and the wing of the Liberal Party which had stood aloof from the crisis agreement in 1933 now accepted the new policy. After that the debate gave 'the impression that the Conservatives were somewhat isolated from the other parties over these matters' (Nyman, 1947, p. 216). The Social Democrats Ernst Wigforss and Gustav Möller both brought up in their writings the idea of abolishing permanent unemployment.

In articles published in the autumn of 1934 (*SvD*, 8 and 16 September) Cassel denied the crisis policy any credit for the economic recovery which had taken place. The net result of the crisis programme could be 'reckoned at nil'. The recovery had come through improved conditions for exports, improved terms of trade and a rational monetary policy.

In the debate on 'Economic planning' at the Swedish Economic Society (20 November) in 1934, Heckscher invoked empirical material in an attempt to show that government intervention in various countries in the early 1930s had been ineffective or harmful. He cited production indices, indicating how activity first rose and then fell back after the various cures had been adopted. He concluded (p. 160):

> The interventions bear the same characteristics as the kind of medical treatment which used to be applied by market horse-traders with old nags for sale. They gave them half a stoup of aquavit to make them pirouette as they had done in the springtime of their youth, only to revert, of course, to their former sloth once the intoxication wore off.

As far as Sweden was concerned, he maintained (p. 162) that the upturn had started 'before any Swedish programme for dealing with

178

trade-cycle fluctuations had even been formulated'. The upturn had started in the middle of 1932, the programme was adopted in 1933, and its central feature, the building programme, could not come into operation until the beginning of 1934 because of the strike in the construction industry. When Heckscher published his economic planning lecture in expanded form, he explained the recovery of the Swedish economy in terms first of increased foreign demand for Swedish goods, and second of foreign exchange policy. The policy of stimulating the business climate had done no good at all. It was the same all over the world: 'The admittedly rather rough-and-ready observations which it has been possible to make point in exactly the opposite direction: the greater the recovery, the milder have been the interventions' (Heckscher 1934, pp. 47, 60–1).

In the budget proposals of 1935, Wigforss declared that the state must intervene with measures to stimulate purchasing power even when the economic trend was upward. Lindahl too, in 'Arbetslöshet och finanspolitik' ('Unemployment and fiscal policy') (the first volume of *Ekonomisk Tidskrift* for that year) advocated measures for increasing the demand for labour even in boom conditions.

LAME RESISTANCE

In the spring of 1935 Cassel (1935a, pp. 29–32) is again to be found dissecting the concept of inadequate purchasing power. He affirms that the phenomenon cannot occur when the money supply is normal. However, an insufficiency of money can lead to marketing difficulties, falling prices and production cutbacks. Cassel reflects on the following sequence of events: if saving increases and the banks do not react quickly enough by cutting interest rates, money will flow into the banks, which leads to a shortage of means of payment, which leads to falling prices, which leads to increased saving as people postpone their consumption in the expectation of further price falls. In this way a cumulative deflationary process sets in.

It follows from the above that what is called shortage of purchasing power invariably is a *monetary* phenomenon, connected with a process of deflation. There is nothing in the purely *economic* mechanism of society that can give rise to a lack of purchasing power. The realization of this fact is of extreme political value. The consequence will, of course, be that the evil which is popularly designated as a 'shortage of purchasing power' will have to be conquered by monetary measures. A shortage in the supply of means of payment can be overcome only by positive action on the part of the banks with intent to increase that supply. On the other hand, to attempt to remedy 'shortage of purchasing power' with measures of a purely economic character must be regarded as an error. The remedies nowadays so much recommended, of diminishing saving, or of cutting down the profits of companies, or curtailing the reservation of profits, must be regarded as falling wide of the mark, just because they address themselves to economic phenomena, whereas what is really wanted is a remedy for the deflation, which is a *monetary disease.*

In the summer of 1935, Cassel (1935b, pp. 51–2) continued to reason about saving and public works. He expressed misgivings about investment being regarded as a separate concept, distinct from saving. It was calculated to give the public the idea that some saving could be left over uninvested and thus 'be doomed to lead a mysterious existence out in the blue, rather like a disembodied spirit'. Cassel argued further: the characteristic feature of the depression is that the production of capital is falling more than consumption. Efforts must therefore be directed towards raising the production of capital. Thus, the argument in simplified form should read: don't reduce saving, increase investment!

Cassel's opposition to public works in principle was now broken (p. 53):

So long as private enterprise is insufficient for the necessary increase in economic activity a reduction of unemployment by the aid of public works seems to be a natural way out. This enables a more complete use of the productive powers available, and what is thus produced is obtained, from the point of view of the social economy, without sacrificing any other satisfaction of wants.

The objections to public works were now somewhat lame. They might perhaps lead to 'further crippling of private enterprise' through the latter's 'finding itself at a disadvantage'. Neither would they offer any lasting solution to the problem, at least as long as it was a matter of giving full employment to all productive powers in the private sector of the economy.

In an article of January 1936, Cassel (1936, pp. 2–4) repeated the thesis that there could be no such thing as 'unused' money. On the other hand, the economy could suffer from 'retarded turnover'. If the central bank made money available for public works 'the nominal purchasing power will undoubtedly be increased and it may be expected that the stimulus thus imparted to trade and industry will accelerate the turnover and result in a better utilization of the productive apparatus'. However, Cassel was dubious about the state's ability to accomplish a levelling-out of the trade cycle in good time. The sluggishness of the state machinery would make it impossible to set public works in motion in time to relieve the depression. Conversely, they would be broken off too late and would reinforce the subsequent boom.

In 1936, when the Swedish Economic Society (23 March) had 'Government expenditure and economic activity' on the agenda, Heckscher conceded (pp. 44–5) that the unemployed must be found jobs, that there must therefore be public works, that these works must be financed by loans, and that the budget must therefore go into deficit in times of depression. Works projects must provide 'very extensive employment' and also avoid drawing capital away from private firms. The crucial point in Sweden concerned whether they were to be *reservarbeten* or *beredskapsarbeten* – in other words, what sort of wage policy was to be followed in the projects. On the one hand, low wages were an encouragement to private firms: on the other, high wages generated more demand. Heckscher had difficulty in deciding which line was best – but personally he preferred the former.

In a lecture in the same year, Heckscher (1936, pp. 4, 16–17) declared that economic science was 'in the melting-pot', so that the search for a new theory was 'decidedly justified'. The character of economic life had to a large extent changed 'in a direction which was at odds with the assumptions of the previous theory'. Unemployment was a manifestation of this change. The trouble lay primarily in the 'increased significance of intermittently free utilities'.

In 1936, finance minister Wigforss appointed a committee, of which Cassel, Myrdal, Lindahl, Ohlin and others were members, to consider the problem of balancing the national budget over the period of a trade cycle. The committee proposed that the budget for individual years could show a deficit or surplus, to be balanced via a 'budget-balancing fund', and the 1937 Riksdag approved a bill along these lines. Cassel (1938, p. 53) was somewhat dubious about the new arrangement despite his own participation: 'And, if the way is left open for the underbalancing of the budget in years of depression, the deficits are liable to swell to such proportions that the prospects of being able to cover them in a future boom will be very small.'

CASSEL ON *GENERAL THEORY*

During the course of 1937, Cassel presented his views on Keynes's *General Theory*. Our account here will be based on four articles in *Sunt Förnuft, Quarterly Report, Svenska Dagbladet* and *International Labour Review*. Cassel's general reaction was one of repugnance: 'Among the numerous products of the slump with which we are still afflicted, Keynes's attempt at a complete revolution in economic science occupies a position of special eminence in terms of its vastly harmful effects' (1937b, p. 137).

Cassel's primary objection to Keynes's theory was that it was not general. It was based on the artificial conditions prevailing in the British economy during the depression and failed to reflect crucial features of a normal economy (1937b, p. 137; *SvD*, 4 August; 1937d, p. 442).

> *One* such feature is undoubtedly *progress*, and even the most elementary picture of society must explain in broad outline how progress comes about. This aspect of the economy disappears in a most disquieting manner in the picture of society which we are now offered. What we are shown instead is a picture of a society falling into hopeless stagnation. However, since this stagnation seems to be mainly the result of temporary government measures, it is impossible to see in it, a necessity conditioned by given economic factors. People with any vestige of the will to live left in them must instinctively rebel against an attempt to establish, as a norm for our perception, a picture of society characterized so onesidedly by sickness, decline and ageing.
>
> (1937b, p. 137)

The new doctrine, Cassel continued, 'is based mainly upon the theory, long cherished by the ignorant, that saving is too large and therefore consumption is too small'. But only by leaving growth out of account was it possible to represent saving as excessive and harmful. In reality, the modern economy was characterized by a never-ending superfluity of investment opportunities. These investments which materialized were always the result of selection of the best opportunities. The demands for capital had to 'wait their turn' for savings. One proof of the matter was interest on capital, which must be regarded as reflecting precisely this scarcity of savings in relation to the demand for them. Cassel considered Keynes's concept of 'liquidity preference' to be 'a most astonishing step backward in the development of the theory of interest'; and neither by theoretical analysis nor by observation of facts could the 'marginal productivity of capital' be demonstrated as tending towards zero. There was no reason why the rate of interest should exhibit any general tendency to fall (1937b, p. 137; 1937c, pp. 41–3; SvD, 4 August; 1937d, pp. 440–1).

Just the same, Cassel continued his line of reasoning by postulating a fall when 'the saving will be permanently kept in the form of notes', a fall when total saving exceeded investment. But this was no problem. If people hoarded notes, the supply of the means of payment would diminish and prices would fall. But of course there was no reason to fix the quantity of money without reference to hoarding. On the contrary, it ought to be regulated with the aim of maintaining a stable price level and thus ought to be increased so as to neutralize the effect of hoarding (1937c, pp. 43–4; 1937d, p. 443).

> Let us suppose that the state printed notes and paid part of its expenditure with them, so that the taxes could be reduced, and that this operation was carried out on a scale just large enough to counterbalance the hoarding of notes. In that case no purchasing power would be lost, nor would there be anything to cause a general fall of prices. On the other hand, there would not be any depreciation of the currency either, seeing that the actual amount of notes in circulation would remain unchanged. The note-hoarders would then be found to be the benefactors of the community, having voluntarily renounced their share in the results of production.
>
> (1937c, p. 44)

Cassel's conclusion from his scrutiny of Keynes, of course, was that there is no defect in the capitalist mechanism that causes permanent unemployment. There is always an equilibrium solution that ensures full employment to all factors of production. Unemployment is caused by temporary disturbances and adjustments. The problem during the 1930s' slump had been inadequate investment, not excessive saving. And it was the consequence of incorrect monetary policy, capricious state intervention and confiscatory taxation (1937c, p. 44; 1937d, p. 444).

Ohlin's celebrated 'Notes' in the *Economic Journal* for 1937 met with Cassel's approval, thanks to their dynamic element. Cassel wrote (15 July) to Ohlin: 'I have read with great interest your articles against Keynes in the *Economic Journal.* Without doubt, it is very valuable, in opposing Keynes, to present, as you do, a well-based dynamic theory.'

At the beginning of 1938, Cassel (*SvD*, 25 January) tried out a new and vague formulation of his view of public works. 'It is possible,' he wrote,

> that the state may be able to raise the tempo of the economy and increase the national income by means of extraordinary works. In order for this to happen, however, conditions must be particularly favourable and the public works in question must be economically well-chosen and prepared.

THE WAR YEARS

If war should break out, Heckscher argued in a debate on 'Sweden's economy in the world situation' held by the Swedish Economic Society (16 May 1939, p. 101), and a scarcity of goods and labour prevails, 'then prewar economic theory will regain its essential validity, for it is a theory of scarcity'. The prophecy is interesting, bearing in mind that the shift from a depressive to a 'manic' phase is often held to have been a cause of the Stockholm School's having died out.

At the same time, Cassel (1939, p. 56), with 'the danger of in-flation' in mind, again raised the question of whether the state could 'create purchasing power' without simultaneously creating inflation, declaring that this was possible provided the new purchasing power stimulated efficiency in the economy:

> It is even conceivable that this stimulus may be so great that the increase in production will completely counterbalance the increase in purchasing power, so that no inflation sets in. Such a result may particularly be expected when industry and commerce have previously been languishing and state inter-vention has been resorted to in order to counteract widespread

unemployment. Such a case would be in line with the theory now in vogue that it is possible by the creation of spending power to relieve unemployment and provide work for the whole population. It cannot be denied that such a consummation is conceivable under particularly favourable conditions. As a general economic theory, however, this new doctrine is very questionable.

Cassel made a special reservation against the idea that increase in production would be able to exceed the input of state purchasing power. The multiplier was 'no constant which can be calculated, even approximately'.

During the years 1943–4, Cassel was again grappling with the problem of unemployment. In an article (1943, p. 12) provoked by an account in the *Economist* of the basic lines of modern unemployment theory, he started off by making a considerable theoretical concession:

> The *Economist* strongly emphasizes that there is a complete consensus of opinion among all serious economists regarding the nature of the problem: a slump sets in when the national community spends less than is required to buy all the community is able to produce. The reason for this is that saving is in excess of investments or, in other words, that the supply of savings exceeds the demand on the capital market. There is undoubtedly some truth in this statement.

However, Cassel (1943, pp. 13–14; 1944a, p. 1) pointed out that saving 'is by far the most stable of these two economic factors'. All attempts to adapt saving to the fluctuations of investment must be combated. The urge to save was the result of 'many thousands of years of education'. 'It must not be supposed that one can simply "turn on" a nation's desire to save, just as one turns on the gas.' The stabilization policy must be based on the assumption of continued growth. Growth would demand ever-increasing amounts of capital. Thus, saving must be sustained and stabilization must have investments in view. Here the old method of regulating the capital market, via interest rates, was to be preferred. The new method, which aimed at 'direct physical control of all investment', would only lead to 'bureaucratic control' over trade and industry, and in the end to 'general petrification'.

In point of fact, however, Cassel's continued campaign came to focus upon exposing weak spots in the argument for a stabilization of investment activity. The argument that the state must either direct private investment or itself be responsible for a major share of total investment was met (*SvD*, 23 April and 19 July 1944) by the counter-argument that experience did not suggest that the state looked after its investments in a more stable manner than private firms, and that it was sometimes the state which created such unfavourable conditions for private firms that their investments declined.

HECKSCHER ON *GENERAL THEORY*

Heckscher's showdown with Keynes did not come until 1946, ten years after *General Theory*, in an article in *Ekonomisk Tidskrift*. The article should be viewed bearing in mind that Heckscher had a bone to pick with Keynes. In his 'Notes on mercantilism' in *General Theory*, Keynes had made use of Heckscher's 'Mercantilism' in attempting to show that in several respects – and not least in the feeble propensity to invest – the mercantilists had had a clearer vision of the economic realities than had their successors, the 'classical economists'. Heckscher seems to have felt, as his colleague Arthur Montgomery (1945, p. 9) expressed it, that Keynes read 'Mercantilism' in the same way as 'the Devil reads the Bible'. Consequently, the article was angled from an economic history standpoint to establish whether Keynes's *General Theory* was really valid in a long-term perspective. To begin with, Heckscher (1946, p. 162) aired his dissatisfaction with Keynes's 'psychological categories' – propensity to consume, to hoard, to save, liquidity preference, inducement to invest – which could not be checked empirically even in the present, 'and to institute psychological tests with families long deceased is also out of the question'. The notion that throughout history, the propensity to save should have exceeded the willingness to invest did not fit in well with the fact that during the longest periods since the sixteenth century, western Europe had been so well furnished with the means of payment that price rises had resulted.

> The only possibility of uniting this assertion with reality seems to be that this is how matters stand in the wholly unchecked psychological sphere, but that despite this, the superfluity of money normally prevailing throughout the centuries has more than ensured that 'liquidity preference' has been satisfied

without detracting from the investment possibilities.

(1946, p. 176)

Far the greater part of the unemployment predominating in the industrial field in former times was frictional unemployment and not the consequence of any lack of 'inducement to invest' (p. 179).

Not unexpectedly, Heckscher (p. 180) drew the conclusion that Keynes's theory was not at all general but, on the contrary, was the fruit first of large-scale fixed capital formation and second of the Great Depression. Large-scale fixed capital formation had for the first time given true meaning to the phenomenon of 'intermittently free utilities', and here Heckscher (p. 181) suggested that there was more to be gained from elaborating a theory based on his own ideas than on Keynes's. Heckscher went on to say of Keynes's *General Theory* that:

> its real impulse has come from the never-ending unemployment of the interwar era, by which he almost seems to have been obsessed. Never before, perhaps, has a work laying claim to universal validity been based to such a degree upon a single point of view.

Finally, Heckscher (p. 182) speculated that Keynes might have come to regret his sins and mend his ways:

> Whether Keynes would have held fast to his design if he had lived must be regarded, perhaps, as an open question. With his quite unique capacity for self-renewal and the admirable courage he showed in not only renouncing former opinions but indeed tearing them to pieces, it is not impossible that he might next have turned against his own admiring disciples.

SUMMARY

Let us now summarize the main stages of the long retreat: Cassel opened the question of redistributive works as an expedient against unemployment as early as 1902 and must be regarded as a pioneer among Swedish economists in the field. Heckscher followed in his footsteps four years later. Consequently Cassel was cautiously favourable to the 'ideas of 1912' as far as redistributive works were concerned, but with regard to measures against 'more permanent unemployment' he took a contrary view.

As early as 1926–7, Cassel was hearing notes that jarred against

187

the harmonies of liberal doctrine. He turned against the idea that there could exist any unutilized saving; thus, the state could not create employment without drawing capital from the private sector and reducing employment there. He turned against the view that there could be a shortage of purchasing power; total purchasing power could always purchase total production. In other words Cassel agreed wholeheartedly with Say's law and what came to be known as the 'treasury view'.

The writings forming the English Liberal programme and their transplanting onto Swedish soil by Wigforss and Ohlin constitute the background to Cassel's and Heckscher's reactions in the spring and summer of 1929. Cassel discussed the 'treasury view' versus Lloyd George and Keynes, denying categorically that any unutilized saving could exist and reduce the capacity of the nation's income to purchase the nation's production. All saving was tied up in real capital. If the supply of capital exceeded the demand, moreover, there ought not to be any interest on capital. Heckscher considered that if saving was really left lying in the banks, the best course would be to lower interest rates. He did not believe in large-scale public works. After the stock exchange crash of 1929, Cassel warned that the Federal Reserve's tight monetary policy would drag the whole world down into a depression.

In face of the Social Democratic motion of 1930 for productive public works at market wages, Cassel rebelled: the brakes would come of both trade-union wage demands and government expenditure, and the consequence would be a transfer of capital from the private sector to the state.

During the course of 1931, the tide of discussion of trade conditions and unemployment surged higher and higher. At the Nordic economic congress in Stockholm in June, Heckscher reacted against Ohlin's proposals that the state should 'pour out' money in order to increase purchasing power and rejected emphatically the possibility that total purchasing power might not be able to buy total production. The autumn of 1931 arrived with new contributions from Ohlin, Myrdal and Wigforss whose message broadly speaking was that saving which does not go into investment signifies a loss of purchasing power, and that in such a situation, public works need not take away resources from other uses, while wage cuts mean further losses of purchasing power. Heckscher participated in the debate with feverish ardour. In September he was still arguing that unemployment must be the result of an organizational failure somewhat akin to buttoning a waistcoat wrongly, and denying that wage cuts would diminish purchasing power. Shortly thereafter, however, he beat a retreat, began to stress the power of saving and wage cuts to reduce demand, and conceded the existence of 'so-called general overproduction'.

During 1932 Lindahl, Myrdal and Ohlin continued to hammer out their arguments. Lindahl's lecture to the Swedish Economic Society in November, especially, is usually considered to have been momentous. In the subsequent discussion, Heckscher objected to Ohlin's contention that public works in a situation with idle productive powers need not displace private enterprise but on the contrary could stimulate it via increased demand. Hence, on this question, he ranged himself 'somewhere between the Ohlin and Cassel positions'. Heckscher's main line of argument now, however, was that the disagreement over public works had nothing to do with conflicting theoretical opinions but with differing views on the possibility of putting theory into practice. Unless public works were hedged about with constitutional guarantees or paid for at wage rates below the open market level, thus becoming 'self-abolishing', they would mushroom in the long term. In line with his view that the world slump was a crisis of deflation, Cassel called for international cooperation with a view to raising prices by means of an expansive monetary policy. If resort had to be made to public works, they must be productive and be paid for at less than market wage rates.

At the beginning of 1933, Cassel accepted the possibility that savings might lie idle in desk-drawers, with the consequence that the quantity of money would decrease, prices and economic activity fall, and unemployment rise. In the first place, however, this sequence of events could be neutralized through the medium of the note issue, and in the second, it had not happened in Sweden. Sweden's troubles lay in diminished exports consequent upon the deflationary and protectionistic world slump. Even so, Sweden, acting alone albeit carefully, could increase the quantity of money in order to raise prices and improve the business climate. Public works could increase production and employment to the extent that they released saving tied up in stocks and were paid for at wages below market rates. Cassel's programme for monetary policy reappears in the recommendation promulgated in the spring of 1933 by the so-called currency experts, among whom Cassel and Heckscher were two of the twelve 'prominent men'.

Both Cassel and Heckscher took a very critical view of the Social Democrats' crisis programme of 1933. As noted, Cassel felt there was scope for increased credit, and that this scope could be enlarged by means of excise taxes and higher customs duties; but he opposed absolutely the calls for agreed wages in public works projects. Heckscher's primary objection was likewise concerned with the calls for market wages. Like Cassel, he stressed Sweden's dependence upon international economic conditions, but he approached Ohlin's standpoint on the question of whether public works would pull resources away from the private sector.

During the years 1934–5, Social Democrats such as Wigforss and Möller along with economists such as Lindahl and Myrdal began to speak of abolishing permanent unemployment and of continuing the crisis policy even during trade-cycle upturns. Cassel considered that the significance of the crisis policy in economic recovery could be 'calculated at zero'; the improvement resulted from international economic conditions and a rational monetary policy. Heckscher devoted himself to demonstrating that crisis programmes in the world generally and Sweden particularly had done more harm than good. Admittedly, Cassel did consider that increased saving and the consequent reduction in the quantity of money would trigger off a cumulative deflationary process. But since the illness was of a monetary character, it ought to be cured by monetary means. Neither should stabilization policy be aimed at saving but at investment. Cassel's theoretically-based resistance to public works, however, was not all but broken. He acknowledged that in a situation with idle productive resources, public works could increase activity in the economy without drawing resources from elsewhere. His objections now, like Heckscher's, were of a more practical nature. The sluggishness of the state machinery would make it difficult to get the timing of trade-cycle policy right, and in balancing the national budget over a complete cycle there was a risk that government expenditure would get out of control in the longer term.

Some years into the 1940s, Cassel conceded that there was 'a certain degree of truth' in the explanation that a depression occurs when demand becomes less than total production because saving exceeds investment. However, he stuck to his view that saving should be left alone and investment regulated through monetary policy.

Cassel's reaction to Keynes's *General Theory* came as early as

1937: Heckscher's was delayed until 1946. Both raised the same principal objection: Keynes's theory was not general but a theory for the (British) depression economy of the interwar period. Cassel contended that a normal economy was a growth economy in which investments must always 'queue up' while awaiting savings. Heckscher pointed out that over a 500-year West European perspective, the propensity to save had by no means exceeded the willingness to invest.

CONCLUSIONS

What sort of concise conclusions can be drawn from this long-winded narrative? Well:

1 The picture of Heckscher's reaction handed down by Ohlin and Lundberg remains. Heckscher put up a theoretical resistance at first, then beat a retreat and switched to resistance on the practical political plane. The theoretical retreat occurred quite suddenly in the autumn of 1931.

2 The uninspiring picture of Cassel previously handed down, showing him firmly locked in old positions, utterly unable to understand the new currents of thought, needs to be revised somewhat. Cassel grasped at an early stage what was brewing; he wrestled with the problems, year out and year in; it is true that unlike Heckscher he did not beat a sudden retreat but went on retiring step by step until his death in 1945. His stubborn resistance appears less barren and his positions less completely overrun from the perspective of the 1970s and 1980s, when economic developments have landed Keynesianism in difficulties and created a seedbed for a monetarist reaction, than they did in the 1940, 1950s and 1960s when Keynesian management seemed to have the situation under control.

NOTE

1 The following abbreviations will be used in the text and references: *DN* = *Dagens Nyheter*; *QR* = *Quarterly Report* from *Skandinaviska Kreditaktiebolaget*, after 1939 Quarterly Review from *Skandinaviska Banken*; *SvD* = *Svenska Dagbladet*. Articles from the daily press are not given in the list of references. Cassel's and Heckscher's collected letters are held in *Kungliga biblioteket* (the Royal Library), Stockholm.

REFERENCES

Gustav Cassel

(1902) *Socialpolitik (Social Policy)*, Stockholm.

(1904) 'Om kriser och dåliga tider', ('On crises and hard times') *Economisk Tidskrift.*

(1918) *Theoretische Sozialökonomie (The Theory of Social Economy)*, Leipzig.

(1926) 'Movements of capital', *QR*, April.

(1927a) *Recent Monopolistic Tendencies in Industry and Trade. Being an Analysis of the Nature and Causes of the Poverty of Nations*, League of Nations, Geneva.

(1927b) 'The dislocation of prices and its consequences', *QR*, April.

(1928) *Socialism eller framåtskridande (Socialism or Progress)*, Stockholm.

(1929) '"Idle" money', *QR*, July.

(1931a) 'The shortage in the supply of money', *QR*, January.

(1931b) 'The influence of bank policy on the level of prices', *QR*, April.

(1932a) 'A contribution to characterization of the crisis', *QR*, October.

(1932b) 'Arbetslöshet och offentliga arbeten', (Unemployment and public works'), *Sunt Förnuft*, November.

(1932c) 'World economic reconstruction: a criticism of the economic resolution adopted by the International Labour Conference', *International Labour Review*, no. 5, November.

(1933a) *Spara eller icke spara. Frågans innebörd (To Save or not to Save. That is the Question)*, Stockholm.

(1933b) 'The problem of business cycles', *QR*, January.

(1933c) 'Monetary reconstruction', *QR*, April.

(1933d) 'Sweden's monetary policy', *QR*, July.

(1935a) 'Fallacies regarding the lack of purchasing power', *QR*, April.

(1935b) 'The activity of economic life', *QR*, July.

(1936) 'The equalization of the Swedish budget', *QR*, January.

(1937a) 'Looking back on the world crisis', *QR*, January.

(1937b) 'En förvänd samhällsbild', ('An absurd picture of society'), *Sunt Förnuft*, May.

(1937c) 'The equilibrium of the capital market', *QR*, July,

(1937d) 'Keynes' "General Theory"', *International Labour Review*, no. 4, October.

(1938) 'Long-run balancing of the budget', *QR*, June.

(1939) 'The danger of inflation', *QR*, July.

(1942) 'The problem of economic fluctuations', *QR*, January.

(1943) 'The problem of full employment', *QR*, January.

(1944a) 'The problem of employment', *QR*, January.

(1944b) 'A retrospect', *QR*, October.

Eli Heckscher

(1906) in *Berättelse öfver förhandlingarna vid kongressen för fattigvård och folkförsäkring i Stockholm den 4, 5 och 6 okt 1906.* Enligt uppdrag utgifven af Erik Palmstierna (*Report on the Proceedings of the Congress on Poor Relief and*

National Insurance in Stockholm, 4, 5 and 5 October 1906. According to information given by Erik Palmstierna), Stockholm.

(1918a) 'Staten och det enskilda initiativet efter kriget'. *Föredrag vid Sveriges industriförbunds* årsmöte den 23 april 1918, Småskrifter nr 15 ('The state and private initiative after the war'. Lecture to the annual general meeting of the Federation of Swedish Industries, 23 April 1918, Publication no. 15), Stockholm.

(1918b) *Svenska produktionsproblem (Swedish Production Problems)*, Stockholm.

(1921) *Gammal och ny ekonomisk liberalism (Old and New Economic Liberalism)*, Stockholm.

(1926) *Nationalekonomiens grundvalar (Foundations of Economics)*, Stockholm.

(1931a) in 'Konjunkturbevaegelser og Arbejdsløshedsforsikring', *Förhandlingar vid nordiska nationalekonomiska mötet i Stockholm 15–17 juni 1931* ('Business cycles and unemployment insurance', *Proceedings of the Nordic Economic Congress in Stockholm, 15–17 June 1931*), Stockholm.

(1931b) 'Sveriges näringsliv under depressionen', Föredrag hållet vid Mercuri-Schartauanernas föredragsafton den 8 okt 1931, ('Sweden's economy during the depression', Lecture given at Mercuri-Schartauanernas lecture evening, 8 October 1931), *Mercuri-Bladet*, no. 10.

(1932) 'Den ekonomiska krisen och dess orsaker', ('The economic crisis and its causes'), *Kristen Gemenskap*.

(1934) *Tvångshushållning och 'planhushållning'. (Forced Economy and 'Planned Economy')*, Stockholm.

(1936) 'Det privata näringslivet i tvångshushållningens tid', *Föredrag hållna inför svenska ekonomföreningen*, nr 1, 1936. ('The private sector in times of forced economy', *Lecture given to the Swedish Economist's Society*, no. 1, 1936), Stockholm.

(1946) 'Något om Keynes' "General Theory"' ur ekonomisk-historisk synpunkt', ('Some reflections on Keynes's "General Theory" from the standpoint of economic history'), *Ekonomisk Tidskrift*.

Others

Hansson, B. (1988) 'The immediate response in Sweden to the *General Theory*', in H. Hagemann and O. Steiger (eds), *Keynes' General Theory nach fünfzig Jahren*, Berlin.

Landgren, K.-G. (1960) *Den 'nya ekonomien' i Sverige (The 'New Economics' in Sweden)*, Uppsala.

Lewin, L. (1967) *Planhushållningsdebatten (The Planned Economy Debate)*.

Lundberg, E. (1984) *Kriserna och ekonomerna (The Crises and the Economists)*, Stockholm.

Montgomery, A. (1945) in *Tre tal hållna vid den middag som ett antal kolleger och lärljungar gav för Eli F Heckscher och hans anhöriga den 13 dec på restaurangen Tre Kronor i Stockholm (Three Speeches made at a Dinner given by a number of Colleagues and Students for Eli F. Heckscher and members of his Family at the Tre Kronor Restaurant, Stockholm, on 13 Dec)*, Stockholm.

—— (1947) 'Gustav Cassel', *Economic Journal*.

Nationalekonomiska föreningens förhandlingar (Proceedings of the Swedish Economic Society).

Nyman, O. (1947) *Svensk parlamentarism 1932–1936 (Swedish Parliamentarism 1932–1936)*, Uppsala.

Ohlin, B. (1972) *Ung man blir politiker (A Young Man turns Politician)*, Stockholm.

—— (1981) 'Stockholm and Cambridge: four papers on the monetary and employment theory of the 1930s'. By the late Bertil Ohlin. Edited with introductions and comments by Otto Steiger, *History of Political Economy*, no. 2.

Patinkin, D. (1982) *Anticipations of the General Theory? And Other Essays on Keynes*, Chicago.

Steiger, O. (1971a) *Studien zur Entstehung der Neuen Wirtschaftslehre in Schweden. Eine Anti-Kritik*, Berlin.

—— (1971b) 'Till frågan om den nya ekonomiska politikens tillkomst i Sverige' ('On the question of the genesis of the new economic policy in Sweden'), *Arkiv*, no. 1.

—— (1973) 'Bakgrunden till 1930-talets socialdemokratiska krispolitik. Ett tyvärr ganska långt svar på Karl-Gustav Landgren: genmäle' ('The background to the Social Democratic crisis policy of the 1930s. An unfortunately somewhat lengthy rejoinder to Karl-Gustav Landgren's reply'), *Arkiv*, no. 4.

—— (1976) 'Bertil Ohlin and the origins of the Keynesian revolution', *History of Political Economy*, no. 3.

Uhr, C.G. (1977) 'Economists and policymaking 1930–1936, Sweden's experience', *History of Political Economy*, no. 1.

Wigforss, E. (1954) *Minnen III 1932–1949 (Memoirs III 1932–1949)*, Stockholm.

11

THE DEVELOPMENT OF THE SWEDISH CONTRIBUTIONS TO THE INFLATIONARY GAP ANALYSIS

Claes Berg*

Economic policy problems have always been influential in the development of macro theory. Keynes's theory of aggregate demand, for example, grew out of a response to the Great Depression in the 1930s. Another strong and obvious influence on economic theory is the role played by various wars in enforcing the scientific study of inflation. A concrete example of this is given by the inflationary gap analysis which was undertaken during the Second World War. The inflationary gap is also connected with Keynes and his pamphlet *How to Pay for the War* (1940). There was, however, a very interesting discussion of the inflationary gap analysis in Sweden at the same time. This discussion was in many respects more sophisticated than the one that was developed in Britain and the US.

The roots of the Swedish contributions to the inflationary gap analysis are to be found in Wicksell's monetary work, *Geldzins und Güterpreise* (1898), and in the writings of the neo-Wicksellians of the Stockholm School. The fundamental starting-point of the gap discussion in Sweden is Erik Lundberg's dissertation *Studies in the Theory of Economic Expansion* (1937). Subsequently, it was Erik Lundberg, as director of the Swedish *Konjunkturinstitut*, who developed the inflationary gap analysis further. However, as time passed he became one of the leading critics of this type of applied economic theory. This seems to be due to the fact that these analyses became more Keynesian as they were used as tools in work on the Swedish

195

national budget. Interesting contributions to this late discussion were made by many individuals. However, the works by Bent Hansen are the most important. It was mainly due to his achievement that the Swedish discussion stands up so well by international comparison. In a short chapter, it is of course not possible to make deep inroads into the Swedish debate. Besides it has hardly ever been treated in retrospect before. Therefore, it must be stressed that all of Erik Lundberg's and Bent Hansen's contributions to the theory of inflation are not analysed here. Our ambition is to focus on the main points of the Swedish discussion and to clarify how the inflationary gap analysis in Sweden differs from the Keynesian analysis.

A COMPARISON BETWEEN THE CENTRAL WORKS OF ERIK LUNDBERG AND J.M. KEYNES

In his dissertation *Studies in the Theory of Economic Expansion*, published in January 1937, Erik Lundberg introduced a more general way of discussing the theory of aggregate demand than Keynes did in *The General Theory of Employment, Interest and Money* (1936). While Keynes analysed the causes of lasting unemployment in a rather static setting, Lundberg's model was more dynamic, as he provided an explanation of unemployment in a business-cycle perspective.

Keynes's central message was summarized by Paul Samuelson in the famous 45°-diagram. The level of output is on the horizontal axis, aggregate demand is on the vertical axis and the equilibrium is given by the intersection of the aggregate demand function with the aggregate supply function of the 45°-line. Patinkin (1982) formulated with its help the central message of *General Theory* in the following manner. The intersection of the aggregate demand function with the 45°-line determines the equilibrium real output Y_0 at a level that may be below that of full employment. If the economy is in a state of excess aggregate supply at the level of output Y_1, then the resulting decline in output, and hence income, will depress supply more than demand and thus eventually bring the economy to equilibrium at Y_0.

There is, however, no description in *General Theory* of how a change in investment brings about a change of income. Keynes does not study how the economy is moving from one equilibrium to another, e.g. the time-effect is missing in his multiplier. Lundberg,

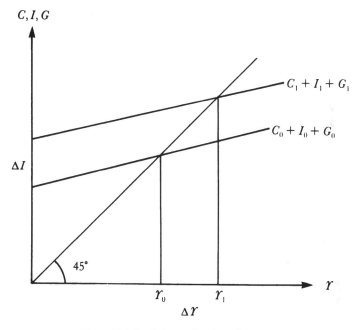

Figure 11.1 Paul Samuelson's 45°-diagram.

on the other hand, formalized five types of sequences. In the first type, with constant investment, Lundberg showed how the economy is moving towards a stable equilibrium, in which the final value of total receipts is given by the normal Keynesian multiplier. In the second sequence, the dynamic role of inventories was integrated into the analysis. Lundberg showed how a business-cycle peak precedes the attainment of equilibrium. In the third type of sequence, the accelerator was introduced into the accumulation of capital investment. Influenced by Robertson's *Banking Policy and the Price Level* (1926), where there is a consistent separation between saving and investment, Lundberg specified how a recession is unavoidable, since the rate of expansion of total receipts is decreasing and thereby causes a halt in the expansion of investment. This is due to the continuing increase of savings as total receipts rise. When the difference between gross investment and gross saving becomes negative the business-cycle downturn begins.

In the fourth type of sequence, Lundberg allowed investment to be influenced by the interest rate as well as the rate of increase of total receipts. He showed how a cumulative expansion can be interrupted by an increasing interest rate. If investment in the present period increases in comparison to saving in the following period, the rate of interest will increase. According to Siven (1985) it is difficult to understand the motive for this increase. Why did Lundberg not use Keynes's liquidity preference theory? Siven (1985) points out that Lundberg's assumptions in this case are the classical ones. The reason behind the downturn of the business cycle is not too *much* saving, but too *little*. When the supply of loans contracts and the rate of interest increases, the expansion of investment will sooner or later be broken. According to Lundberg, this is an example of how Hayek's business-cycle theory can be formulated.

In the last type of sequence Lundberg studied economic growth, anticipating the Harrod–Domar growth model. Introducing the accelerator as a determinant of investment, Lundberg, in contrast to Keynes, linked the effect of the multiplier to the level of the ratio of profits and total income. Instead of applying a 'Robertsonian' lag between income and expenditure, the outlays of consumers are directly influenced when there is a change in income. There is instead a one-period 'Lundbergian' lag between a change of sales and a change of the volume of production. The increase of receipts in one period does not affect the consumers' demand in the same period. Only the volume of production and investment in the following period is influenced. Thus, a dynamic mechanism was introduced into Keynes's system. Actually, Lundberg was the first one to formalize a model of the multiplier–accelerator: see Siven (1985) and Berg (1991).[1] As will soon be shown, there is also an early formalization of an inflationary gap in a multi-period setting in Lundberg's dissertation. Hence, in Sweden during the 1930s, there was an independent development of 'Keynesian' models of growth, the multiplier–accelerator and inflationary gap analysis. The roots were of course in the works of Wicksell, who as early as 1898 formalized a dynamic model of inflation in *Geldzins und Güterpreise*.

LUNDBERG'S FORMALIZATION OF THE INFLATIONARY GAP

In general, prices are fixed in Lundberg's models. He was mainly interested in explaining changes in real output. Studying the first type of sequence, however, Lundberg introduced the possibility of analysing price changes, and an inflationary gap is formalized and quantified. The following assumptions govern the period analysis:

each unit-period is considered as a reaction interval, measuring the average distance between the change in demand and the subsequent change in production activity. Only a part of the costs of production generates income.

On the basis of realized receipts in period t, the enterprises determine their production and induced investment in period $t + 1$. They presume that the income in period t will be the same in period $t + 1$. As prices are assumed to be constant, the costs of production in period $t + 1$ will be the same as the receipts in period t. Lundberg created a sequence leading to a stable value of expenditure on consumers' goods output after 17 periods.

The conclusion is straightforward: with a constant volume of investment and fixed prices there is a stable equilibrium. The development of the sequence shows how this equilibrium is attained. Lundberg subsequently assumed that the supply of inputs is totally inelastic and that prices are flexible. Moreover, it is assumed that the non-income-generating costs on consumers' goods production are constant. The system of equations was transformed to:

$$E_t = 0.9D_{ct} + 350$$
$$D_{ct} = C_t - 200$$
$$C_t = E_{t-1}$$

where

E_t = expenditure on consumers' goods output;
D_{ct} = disposable income derived from the output of consumption goods;
C_t = total business expenditure on the production of consumption goods;
0.9 = marginal propensity to consume;
350 = autonomous investment in consumers' goods production;
200 = production costs that do not induce income.

the solution is given by:

$$E_t = 0.9E_{t-1} + 170$$

This is a difference equation of a first order with the solution:

$$E_t = (E_0 - 170/1 - 0.9))0.9^t + 170/(1 - 0.9)$$

which implies that

$$\lim_{t \to \infty} E_t = 170/0.1 = 1700$$

Lundberg did not give the difference equation, but has correctly solved for the limit of disposable income, which means that the price level has increased by 50 per cent in comparison with the initial level. Lundberg's inflationary analysis was only a parenthesis in a dissertation in which, according to Ohlin, 'the grass is growing rampant'. But the analysis is interesting for several reasons.

First, Lundberg has formalized an inflationary gap in an aggregate economic model and introduced the possibility of quantifying its value two years before Keynes published *How to Pay for the War*. (There are some stray ideas in *General Theory*, p. 301, but the gap was not formulated there.)

Second, the price level reached during each period determines the expectations for the next period and causes a further rise in the prices of production factors up to the corresponding level. As a consequence of the subsequent increase of income and expenditure, the prices of the products are subjected to further increases, etc.

Third, Lundberg used period analysis to formalize the gap, implying certain advantages in comparison with Keynes's equilibrium approach. We will return to this question later.

Fourth, it must be possible to make a similar remark about Lundberg's other sequences as was made about Dag Hammarskjöld's dissertation: 'Hammarskjöld has constructed a system that may be applied to any causal analysis of a sequence of economic changes' (*Studies*, p. 84). The fact is that it is also possible to introduce flexible prices in the more complicated sequences in *Studies*. If, for example, flexible prices are introduced in the second type of sequence, one will get a formalization of how an income inflation transforms into a profit inflation and then gradually returns in a process of deflation to a state of equilibrium.

HOW TO PAY FOR THE WAR

During the first month of the Second World War, the cost of living in England increased by 6.5 per cent. Two and a half months after the outbreak of war, Keynes presented an analysis of how the British war economy should be organized in the situation of excess demand for goods and production factors that had replaced the excess supply of goods and factors that prevailed during the depression. Keynes now applied the macroeconomic view of *General Theory* and paved the way for a general use of national income statistics. Keynes first published three articles in *The Times* on 14, 15 and 28 November, and one article in the *Economic Journal* in December 1939; these articles were then turned into a pamphlet *How to Pay for the War* (1940). What is interesting in this pamphlet is that Keynes regarded the inflationary gap as the most important factor in explaining the inflation and also quantified the gap. But why did he not do this earlier, in *A Treatise on Money* (1930), which, contrary to *General Theory*, is a book mainly devoted to the study of price fluctuations? First, it was probably mainly due to the lack of proper national income statistics at the time when *A Treatise* was published. Keynes himself complained of 'the present deplorable state of our banking and other statistics'; see Patinkin (1982, p. 230). Second, the inflationary gap analysis in *How to Pay for the War* also needed the macroeconomic view first introduced in *General Theory* and also looked for by Bertil Ohlin in the early 1930s. This macroeconomic approach was subsequently emphasized by him in his presentation of the Stockholm School in the *Economic Journal* in 1937.

A general inflationary gap is easily illustrated in the 45°-diagram shown earlier (see Fig. 11.1). Suppose there is a situation of full employment at the equilibrium output Y_0. If the planned increase of investment is then ΔI there will be an inflationary gap amounting to ΔY, as resources are already fully utilized. This means that the national product nominally increases by ΔY, while its real value is unchanged.

THE INFLATIONARY GAP ANALYSIS AT THE SWEDISH NATIONAL INSTITUTE OF ECONOMIC RESEARCH

The originator of the National Institute of Economic Research (NIER) was Dag Hammarskjöld. The proposal to establish the institute was made in 1935 by the Committee on Unemployment, where Hammarskjöld served as secretary. The NIER then started its activities in 1937 with Erik Lundberg as its first director. He wrote the first business-cycle report of the institute by himself; many views in that 1937 report are influenced by his dissertation which had been published the same year.

The outbreak of the war interrupted the work at the NIER. It was resumed again in 1943, but not with a business-cycle report, but with an inflationary-gap estimate. The war had rendered long-run forecasting meaningless. Swedish national income statistics were at that time highly defective and Lundberg later wrote that 'a number

of quite curious calculations and approximations had to be made'
(Lundberg, 1957, p. 173).

After the war, systematic national income statistics were drawn
up by the NIER; these provided an important basis for economic
analysis. The inflationary gap was calculated for 1947, 1948 and
1949. In attempting to measure the inflationary gap, certain radical
simplifications had to be made in the framing of the problem. The
assumptions made in the approach of the NIER were conditioned
by the lack of reliable statistical information and, according to
Lundberg, the partly insoluble theoretical problems linked with this
type of analysis. The excess of purchasing power should, according
to the theory of the Stockholm School, be calculated as the difference between planned demand and planned supply. The NIER
instead used the tension between *active* demand and the *available*
quantity of goods. At the same time, the NIER was aware of this
simplification.

The calculations of the inflationary gap related only to changes
from one year to the next. It was assumed that the expected changes
deduced from the figures for the base year referred to conditions
which would hold good for the average during the next year.
Lundberg later criticized this assumption 'since the very difficult
theoretical and statistical problems of the speed of reaction of
expenditure and incomes and the consequent multiplier effects are
involved' (Lundberg, 1957, p. 181).

Another simplified assumption was the treatment of price and
wage developments as exogenous factors. The difficulties are
thereby reduced to the question: if price and income developments
are as presumed, will there then be an equilibrium between total
demand and supply?

Finally, the factor gap was disregarded; for example, the difference between the businessmen's expected demand for factors of
production and the expected supply of such factors. It was considered impossible to visualize the businessmen's production plans.
This caused the NIER to disregard the possibility of these plans
being inconsistent with one another. Thus we can establish the fact
that the inflationary gap analysis actually carried out at the NIER
had more in common with the Keynesian equilibrium approach in
How to Pay for the War than with the period analysis in Lundberg's
Studies. This was due to the defective national income statistics
rather than a lack of theoretical awareness. As will be shown soon,
Lundberg returned to this question in 1948. However, the one who

took the initiative in the revival of the criticism of the Keynesian approach was Bent Hansen.

CRITICISM OF THE INFLATIONARY GAP AND THE EQUILIBRIUM APPROACH

At the same time as the NIER made its post-war inflationary gap calculations, a discussion was held in *Ekonomisk Tidskrift* regarding the possibility of using the Keynesian equilibrium approach in the gap analysis. Important contributions were made by Bent Hansen, Erik Lundberg and Ralph Turvey in 1948 and 1949. The discussion focused on the definition of the inflationary gap, the problem of unstable consumption and investment functions and the problem of time.

Bent Hansen

The aim of Bent Hansen's (1948) paper was to specify the circumstances which made it possible to apply a Keynesian approach in the study of an inflationary gap. Hansen's article begins with an important remark. A general, implicit, precondition for a Keynesian approach (the 45°-diagram) to the gap analysis is that the income expectations of wage-earners are in correspondence with the businessmen's production plans. If the income expectations do not correspond to the planned purchases of factors, the equilibrium analysis is possible only if consumption or saving is considered as a residual.

Hansen's model takes as its starting-point the equilibrium between aggregate demand and total output in the 45°-diagram. He then studied how variable income expectations will influence consumption, saving and investment, when there are no corresponding changes in the planned purchase of factors. Hansen was inspired by Ohlin's presentation of the Stockholm School in the *Economic Journal*:

> Even if planned saving and planned investment should happen to be equal, a process of expansion is possible. The only thing then required is that expected incomes grow and that consequently consumers increase their purchases.
>
> (Ohlin, 1937, p. 66)

Assuming various wage and price increases and certain presumptions regarding expected wage and price changes, Hansen was studying a number of cases with different consumption and investment functions. It was thereby possible to analyse the conditions that make the equilibrium approach useful, for example when the aggregate-demand curve intersects with the 45°-line. On the other hand, it is of no use, for example when the aggregate-demand function does not intersect with the 45°-line, which is of course an expression of the identity between aggregate demand and total output. Let us look at some of Hansen's cases.

Let us assume that there is an economy with full employment. Then regard three different cases of expectations of future wages and prices:

1   If businessmen as well as wage-earners are expecting an unchanged rate of price and wage increases, the inclination of both the consumption graph and the investment graph will be 45°. Thus the function expressing aggregate demand will be parallel with the 45°-line and inflation will rise cumulatively and the equilibrium approach is not feasible.

2   If businessmen as well as wage-earners are expecting rising rates of price and wage increases, the inclination of the aggregate demand function will be more than 45°. Again the equilibrium approach is not practicable.

3   If both groups are expecting a diminishing rate of price and wage increases, the consumption and investment functions will both have an inclination less than 45° and inflation will be of a limited order. In this case the equilibrium approach is feasible.

Hansen gave an algebraic treatment of the general case when income expectations do not coincide with the planned purchases of factors. He also derived a condition with values for the income elasticities of consumption and production that were compatible with the equilibrium approach. The general conclusion was thus that only under specific conditions will it be possible to use the Keynesian model of inflationary gap analysis. Hansen also reckoned that an *ex-ante* approach coupled to the equilibrium approach would be unfeasible. It would be more advantageous to use period analysis when determining the inflationary gap and the short-run development.

Erik Lundberg

Erik Lundberg's paper 'Inflationary analysis and economic theory',

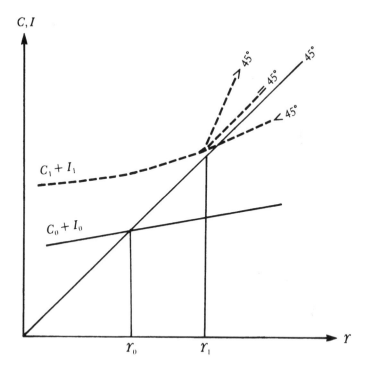

Figure 11.2 Bent Hansen's use of the 45°-diagram.

published in *Ekonomisk Tidskrift* in 1948, is to a great extent a comment on Hansen's above-treated essay. Lundberg discussed the relations between the Keynesian theory and the statistical measurement of the inflationary gap and also focused on the limitations of this approach. Considering the Swedish aggregate supply-and-demand account, Lundberg criticized the statistical deficiencies, particularly regarding corporate profits.

Lundberg then took Keynes's fundamental equations in *A Treatise on Money*, supplemented with some Stockholm School vocabulary, as a starting-point for the discussion. National income is divided into two parts from the point of view of income formation. The first part corresponds to normal costs of production including normal profits defined in such a way that, at the normal level of profits, there is no reason for businessmen to alter the total volume of production; the second part designates abnormal ('unexpected') profits or losses. In this system, the profits actually realized become the criterion of disequilibrium.

An inflationary gap is characterized by the fact that total demand, determined by the sum of the consumption and investment expenditures, is greater than the value of the total supply of goods and services at given prices, which in the position of equilibrium correspond to current costs and normal ('expected') profits. The difference – the windfall profits – provides the measure of the inflationary pressure; it arises from the fact that investments exceed the savings derived from these normal incomes.

According to Lundberg, Keynes's fundamental equations can be given a causal interpretation, in which unexpected profits become symptoms of general economic disequilibrium:

> This equilibrium then refers to the division of total production between investment and consumption which does not agree with the division of current incomes between savings and consumption expenditure.
>
> (Lundberg, 1948, p. 154)

Lundberg then derived a generalized view of the inflationary gap; disequilibrium can be deduced from deviations, from positions of equilibrium of every single point of the system: between actual and planned expenditure on consumption, between actual and planned investment expenditure, between actual and planned public expenditure, between actual and planned exports and between actual and planned imports. Lundberg's analysis was broadened. The additions to aggregate demand from consumption, investment, exports, etc., cannot easily be aggregated, since they are not independent of one another. According to Lundberg, one cannot accept an exogenously determined total level of income. He was thus stepping from the analysis in *A Treatise* (with its assumption of an unaltered volume of total output) to the approach of *General Theory*, focusing on the determination of the level of aggregate demand and output. Clearly, Lundberg was influenced by Hansen's inflationary analysis. He considered the identity of aggregate demand in the 45°-diagram and said that according to one possible way of describing an inflationary process:

> the addition to aggregate demand during each unit period (the length of which is determined accordingly) will be placed against the supply of goods and services of the preceding period. The excess of demand, in this way, creates a tension, which will cause prices to rise above 'normal' costs and the

'abnormal' profits (windfall profits) give rise to business saving that adjusts the tension between increased investment and saving. Inflation reaches a maximum in the first period and is then decreasing successively to the ordinary level at the new position of equilibrium.

(ibid., p. 158)

Analysing an inflationary economy with full employment and an inelastic supply of goods and services, Lundberg thought it might be possible to apply the approach of the 45°-diagram. But at the same time it was pointed out that:

One should for excellent reasons question the validity, during full employment, of the assumed or experienced relations between income, consumption, investment and saving, visualized as straight lines in the diagram.

(ibid., p. 159)

According to Lundberg, during a process of inflation it is plausible to assume that businessmen will maintain a given volume of investment and wage-earners will keep up the real value of their consumption; for example, the graphs of both investment and consumption functions are changing in the same way as in Hansen's model:

This means that the rise in prices will not even cause a tendency towards a position of equilibrium, but create new additions to aggregate demand, which implies a constant relative pressure of inflation.

(ibid., p. 160)

Finally, Lundberg offers some general reflections:

The general equilibrium approach is rejected as unnecessary and a diversion as it leads astray (and furthermore tempts analytical and geometrical orgies and a waste of highly qualified mental exertion). One restricts oneself to try to determine if established tendencies, manifesting the actual development, might cause the tension (inflationary gap) to increase or decrease. Fixed relations, elasticity coefficients and other functions are not accepted without a thorough test, which will normally lead to a disaggregation and an introduction of more explanatory variables than in the simpler systems. In most cases (regarding profits, foreign trade, investment, public consumption expenditure, the relation between the wage level and national income and other variables), we completely lack the historical and statistical experience needed to construct useful relations.

(ibid., p. 165)

Obviously, there was little in the Keynesian approach that Lundberg found attractive. However, he moderated his statement by adding:

This of course does not restrain the theory of the inflationary gap in its simplest Keynesian formulation from being useful when clarifying the problem and bringing some semblance of order to our train of thought.

(ibid., p. 169)

What is needed as a complement, rather than as a substitute, for the Keynesian type of analysis, is a study of the details of economic mechanism.

(ibid., p. 170)

Ralph Turvey

Ralph Turvey published 'A further note on the inflationary gap' in *Ekonomisk Tidskrift* in 1949. Studying the timing problem of the inflationary gap, Turvey divided the year into four quarters. To calculate the gap of the whole year, it was necessary to compute the gap of each quarter. It is also important to calculate them in a consistent way and not mix *ex-ante* with *ex-post* variables. If only the total gap is known, this does not imply that it corresponds to one of the four quarterly gaps multiplied by four, as each quarterly gap can be of a different magnitude. This means that the concept of a total gap is irrelevant, except for very special conditions. Turvey showed this by assuming that the gaps of the third and fourth quarters are very small. If economic policy now aims to reduce aggregate demand each quarter by one quarter of the total gap, then a rise in prices will occur during the first six months, as the first two gaps were so large. As soon as inflation begins, it will not be restrained by the tight aggregate demand policies. The point is that although aggregate demand was reduced by the same magnitude as the total inflationary gap, the erroneous timing made it impossible to prevent an inflationary development.

A STUDY IN THE THEORY OF INFLATION

Bent Hansen's dissertation, *A Study in the Theory of Inflation*, was published in 1951 and attracted international attention. Hansen started out from Erik Lindahl's terminology and presentation of the Stockholm School, but was also influenced by Keynes and Hicks:

> This study is likewise Wicksellian in its analysis of inflation, but goes further than the post-Wicksellians in that spontaneous price increases are taken into account, and further than the post-Keynesians in that monetary excess demand in the factor-markets is also taken into account. Furthermore, repressed inflation, hitherto much neglected in purely theoretical analysis, is also considered.
>
> (Hansen 1951, p. 21)

The first three chapters of the dissertation ingeniously treat the concepts of open and repressed inflation, the approach of the Stockholm School and the inflationary gap analysis of the NIER. Then Hansen developed models of two inflationary gaps, one in the commodity market and one in the factor market, using various assumptions regarding repressed and open inflation, perfect competition and monopoly and also considering changes in productivity.

Hansen developed a general quasi-equilibrium system in which the rise in price and the rise in the wage-rate will both follow a persistent upward trend; the real-wage is thus constant and the inflationary gap in the commodity market and the inflationary gap in the factor market will not be eliminated.

Hansen's comparison between the Swedish *ex-ante/ex-post* approach and the inflationary gap analysis was very instructive. He showed, as will soon be seen, that the Stockholm School model gives a more general inflationary analysis than the one developed in England and the US. The factor gap was not analysed at the *Konjunkturinstitut* either. But naturally the investigators at the NIER were in various respects influenced by the Stockholm School approach.

When it comes to *supply*, for example, the NIER (and likewise British and American investigators) used only the actually available quantity of goods. As a starting-point for that calculation, it was the actual production rather than planned production which was used. But at the NIER, one was aware of the significance of the distinction between planned production and production actually carried out. Hansen cites a report of the NIER, written by Ingvar Ohlsson:

> Excess demand is to be taken as the difference between planned demand and planned supply.... The private production plans are not to be taken into account, for statistical reasons among others.... All the enterprises could of course plan to increase production by taking labour-power from another. A high national product could in that way be obtained, *ex ante*. It is here that a 'clearance' [in the statistical sense – B.H.] enters into the matter.... It is the probable supply of production factors which is transformed to end-products and entered as gross national product in the balance of goods and services. 'Full employment' is thus a fundamental working hypothesis. It can also be said, more strictly, that the planned supply of labour-power is taken into consideration, and this serves to determine the limit of actual production in the calculation of the excess demand.... On the other hand, calculations of a balance of labour-power could, with advantage, make use of information about the planned demand for labour made by enterprises.
>
> (Hansen 1951, p. 67; Report B:10 of the NIER 1949, pp. 121–2)

Turning to the question of taking stocks into account, there is a fairly good agreement between the NIER and Hansen. If the actual stocks are less than normal, then this difference is to be deducted from the production actually carried out, before calculating aggregate supply. This differs from Keynes's view. According to Hansen:

> Keynes, in *How to Pay for the War* (and with Keynes many American investigators, too), seems inclined to take the existence of stocks as something which of itself always diminishes the inflationary gap in the commodity-markets, because the existing stocks can be added to the actual production to arrive at the quantity of commodities actually available for sale.
>
> (Hansen 1951, p. 68)

In the case of demand, the calculations of the NIER were also in agreement with Hansen's view. Instead of using the cumbersome concept 'planned demand', a clearance is made so that the active demand is used. Hansen cited the following sentence:

> The plans concerning demand are thus introduced into the calculation of the excess demand in that form in which they may be considered to exercise *active* demand in the open market.
>
> (Hansen 1951, p. 69; Report B:10 of the NIER 1949, pp. 122–3)

Hansen gave an elegant formalization of *ex-ante/ex-post* gaps and compared them with inflationary gaps and showed how the inflationary-gap analysis deprives the investment-saving relation (in the *ex-ante* sense) of its significance as an indicator of the state of the commodity and factor markets, especially as an indicator of whether a monetary pressure of inflation exists. The following symbols are used:

A = sales (at market price)
B = purchases for productive purposes (at market price)
C = purchases for purposes of consumption (at market price)

Subscripts: 0 = *ex ante*, 1 = *ex post*, g = finished goods, l = labour.

In a simplified model of a closed economy, Hansen formalized the 'fundamental equation' of the Stockholm School:

$$I_0 - S_0 = {}^g B_0 + C_0 - {}^g A_0 + {}^l B_0 - {}^l A_0 \qquad (1)$$

$$\underbrace{\phantom{{}^g B_0 + C_0 - {}^g A_0}}_{\substack{\textit{ex-ante} \\ \text{commodity gap}}} \quad \underbrace{\phantom{{}^l B_0 - {}^l A_0}}_{\substack{\textit{ex-ante} \\ \text{factor gap}}}$$

An inflationary pressure implies that planned investment exceeds planned saving, but the reverse is not true; for example, if planned investment exceeds planned saving, this cannot be taken as a necessary condition for the existence of the monetary pressure of inflation.

Suppose we are substituting the available quantity of factors for the expected sales of factors. If ${}^g A_1 = {}^g B_1 + C_1$ is added to equation (1), then

$$I_0 - S_0 = {}^g A_1 - {}^g A_0 + {}^g B_0 + C_0 - {}^g B_1 - C_1 + {}^l B_0 - {}^l B_1 \qquad (2)$$

$$\underbrace{\phantom{{}^g A_1 - {}^g A_0}}_{\substack{\text{unexpected} \\ \text{sales of} \\ \text{commodities}}} \quad \underbrace{\phantom{{}^g B_0 + C_0 - {}^g B_1 - C_1}}_{\substack{\text{unrealizable} \\ \text{purchases of} \\ \text{commodities}}} \quad \underbrace{\phantom{{}^l B_0 - {}^l B_1}}_{\substack{\text{unrealizable} \\ \text{purchases of} \\ \text{factors}}}$$

Assuming that *ex-ante* relations cause outcomes *ex-post*, it is possible to say that if planned investment exceeds planned saving, this will result in unexpected sales of commodities – for example, inventory disinvestment – and at the same time planned purchases of commodities and factors turn out to be unrealized.

If planned purchases are now replaced by active attempts to purchase commodities and factors and if planned increases in stocks are included as an added item in the planned purchases of commodities then actual production equals ${}^{g}A_1$.

The inflationary gap in the commodity markets $- {}^{g}B_0 + C_0 - {}^{g}B_1 - C_1$ can be inserted in equation (2):

$$I_0 - S_0 = {}^{g}B_0 + C_0 - {}^{g}B_1 - C_1 + {}^{l}B_0 + {}^{l}B_1 + {}^{g}A_1 - {}^{g}A_0 \qquad (3)$$

| inflationary gap in the commodity markets | factor gap | unexpected sales of commodities |

Hansen pointed out that this equation differs from the fundamental equation of the Stockholm School. First, the difference between planned investment and planned saving tells us nothing about the size of the inflationary gap in the commodity markets or of the factor gap. Second, it is possible for the difference between planned investment and planned saving to be negative at the same time as there exists a positive inflationary gap in the commodity markets and a positive factor gap. This is the case if unexpected sales of commodities exceed the sum of the inflationary gap in the commodity markets and the factor gap.

It is important to emphasize that all of the quantities in the fundamental equation of the Stockholm School are given *ex ante*. This means that full knowledge of the expectations of all the participants in the commodity markets and the factor markets is needed to explain the difference between planned investment and planned saving. Hansen's equation, on the other hand, includes both *ex-ante* and *ex-post* quantities and thus illustrates the main difficulties in the equilibrium approach treated in the preceding passage: the time problem, the missing factor gap and the problem with unstable functions of investment and consumption in a situation of inflationary pressure.

ERIK LUNDBERG'S REVIEW OF THE
DEVELOPMENT

In the Swedish edition of *Business Cycles and Economic Policy* (1953) two chapters on the inflationary-gap analysis were included; one theoretical and one more practical on the calculations actually worked out at the NIER. Both chapters are on much the same lines as the article in *Ekonomisk Tidskrift*, 1948. But Lundberg could now build on the works by Hansen and Turvey, and his criticism of the Keynesian equilibrium approach is more pronounced.

In the British edition of *Business Cycles and Economic Policy* (1957) some of this criticism was excluded. We will return to this question. The object of the first chapter is to test the significance and reliability of the theories and statistics involved. The defective Swedish statistics and the simplifying assumptions were once again criticized. Discussing income formation, Lundberg criticized the fact that prices and income are exogenously introduced in the analysis. It thus becomes merely a question of estimating the primary inflationary gap, while the complication of secondary price and income changes is ignored. Treating the estimation of the development of the inflationary gap, Lundberg discussed the difficulty of producing quantitative estimates, due to the fact that it is difficult to know whether the base year was in a position of equilibrium or not. Hence, an insoluble difficulty in interpreting an inflationary-gap calculation is that of timing. The calculations in practice therefore include the assumption that the expected changes deduced from the figures for the base year refer to conditions which will hold good on the average during the next year.

Among the theoretical difficulties discussed by Lundberg was the problem of clearly defining and determining the items on the supply side. The lack of relevant statistics forces the factor gap, named by Hansen, to be left out of account. According to Lundberg the businessmen's plans for production and purchases are almost impossible to catch. Hansen's analysis is commented on in two footnotes. On the one hand, Lundberg said:

In pure theory at rarefied Alpine heights, one can 'solve' the difficulty by, for example, presupposing a marginal cost curve for the community as a whole, deducing from this the demand for manpower and other productive resources at different relative prices. This is Bent Hansen's method. But, as far as I can see, the method provides no guidance at all for practical statistical calculations.

(Lundberg 1953, p. 337)

On the other hand he added:

There is no doubt that Bent Hansen's analysis of the factor gap directed attention to an important problem. The analysis of the factor gap should form a link in the analysis of inflation, a link which has yet for various, especially statistical, reasons been neglected in current gap calculations. In earlier discussions, however, the double problem of equilibrium was fully appreciated; equilibrium between the supply of and demand for finished goods for consumption and investment and equilibrium between the supply of and demand for the factors of production, especially manpower.

(ibid., p. 371)

One interesting part of the Swedish edition, regarding the possibility of the use of the 45°-diagram to analyse an inflationary gap, was left out of the British version of the book.

Assuming a situation of full employment at Y, a planned increase of investment, ΔI, will result in an inflationary gap equal to ΔY. The advantage of this model, according to Lundberg, is that not only the primary gap (ΔI), but also the total inflationary gap (ΔY), will be observed through the multiplier process. Nevertheless, Lundberg was sceptical of this method.

One major problem still remains: how are purchases influenced by the inflationary position? Neither the intercepts nor the slopes of the functions of investment and consumption will remain the same and they cannot be assumed to take exogenously given values. The purchasing plans will, according to Lundberg, be influenced by the altered distribution of income. He said:

If the primary inflationary gap is assumed to cause a rise in the prices of the goods sold by the businessmen during the first period, this will result in increased company profits. Such a redistribution of income will then cause a new position of the functions of investment and consumption during the period after the base period. Hence, the analysis becomes a prognosis with the use of *period analysis*. Instead of working with a total multiplier effect, determined according to a given process, one has to consider a development, where income and expenses are calculated successively according to changes in the distribution of income. This conclusion implies that the estimation of a 'total' inflationary gap in the sense given in diagram 17 [the 45°-diagram – C.B.] can generally be of little help in business-cycles analysis or when implementing economic policy.

(Lundberg 1953, p. 370; original emphasis)

Thus, we have returned to fundamental thoughts in Lundberg's dissertation. Naturally, one should ask why Lundberg deleted the paragraph above, where he gives preference to the period analysis, in the British edition of *Business Cycles and Economic Policy*.

Was it because the Keynesian equilibrium approach had been so successful internationally in comparison with the casuistic models of the Stockholm School? Or was it Lundberg who changed his opinion regarding the feasibility of a period-analysis approach? It is hard to tell. What we do know is that Lundberg remained sceptical of the inflationary-gap analysis actually worked out at the NIER, with its more Keynesian than Stockholm School flavour. This is evident in the following paragraph, which is the same in the Swedish and British editions of *Business Cycles and Economic Policy*:

The final conclusion must be one of strong scepticism towards the possibility, through the preparation of a national budget, either of explaining economic disequilibrium by means of inflationary-gap analysis or of gaining a clear indication of the line of policy to be pursued in order to achieve equilibrium. This scepticism applies not only to the results hitherto achieved but also to the possibility of making decisive improvements in method in the future. The theoretical problems in the concepts and methods involved are in part at least insoluble. I have drawn attention also to the inadequacy of some of the statistical data available and to the strong and largely unpredictable variability in the inter-relationships between the many elements. The results so far achieved in these calculations have been so uncertain on crucial points that one has had to be thankful if these methods have at least indicated the correct direction of the trends of development.

One conclusion from the foregoing discussion is that an inflationary gap calculation is likely to be more valuable in the planning of a rigidly controlled economy than of an economy which is in the main free.

(Lundberg 1953, p. 355; Lundberg 1957, p. 201)

CONCLUSIONS

Concluding this discussion of the development of the Swedish gap analysis there are two points to be made. First, it is obvious that the Swedish debate on the inflationary gap was very thorough. As a matter of fact, we have established that the inflationary gap was first formalized by Erik Lundberg in his dissertation (1937) and not by Keynes in *How to Pay for the War* (1939–40) as is generally asserted. The Swedish discussion at an early stage was able to benefit from the terminology introduced by the Stockholm School, which draws attention to the difference between planned (*ex-ante*) and actual (*ex-post*) quantities on the demand side and the supply side. These concepts were used by Bent Hansen, Erik Lundberg and Ralph Turvey to show the limitations of the Keynesian equilibrium approach to the inflationary gap analysis, which also dominated the national budget work in Sweden. Among the difficulties that attracted attention were the problem of timing the inflationary gap, the measurement of the factor gap, and the instability of the functions of consumption, saving and investment in an inflationary position.

Naturally, one interesting question regards the prospective advantages of the Swedish discussion in an international comparison. As we have seen, the Swedish analysis was characterized partly by Lundberg's emphasis of the dynamic period analysis at the expense of the equilibrium approach, partly by Hansen's introduction of the factor gap as a complement to the commodity gap. The period analysis as well as the factor gap is lacking in the contemporary international discussion. Actually, Milton Friedman, when criticizing the inflationary-gap analysis, was appealing for a dynamic analysis in much the same way as Lundberg did.

This was already done in 1942 and was repeated in 1953 in *Essays in Positive Economics* (p. 262). But there was no further development of the dynamic analysis. Instead, the equilibrium approach was revitalized by Patinkin's important contribution *Money, Interest and Prices* (1956). Patinkin's domination during the rest of the 1950s and his criticism[2] of Hansen's model probably explains why Hansen's work was not followed up for many years.

Second, we must argue that Lundberg's as well as Hansen's contributions were important developments of a late Stockholm School. Today, it is perhaps possible to consider the inflationary analysis of the Stockholm School to be of more importance than its

theory of employment. It is also possible to claim that this inflationary analysis shows that the Stockholm School was still alive
during the 1940s and the 1950s and that its approach to both
substance and methodology have not to this day attracted enough
attention by economists.[3]

However, a renewed interest in pre-Keynesian monetary analysis
has arisen lately. This is primarily due to the difficulties of introducing money in an essential way in a general equilibrium model
and shows itself in a growing interest in models with a cash-in-
advance approach and what is today called equilibrium business-
cycle theories. In an excellent survey, *Monetary Analysis, the Equilibrium
Method and Keynes's General Theory*, Meir Kohn wrote:

> This modern revival of monetary analysis could proceed more
> smoothly if those involved would realize that it is indeed a
> revival. Much of value could be learned from Robertson,
> Hayek, Lundberg, and others, and much wasteful delay and
> duplication avoided.

> (Kohn 1986, p. 1221)

It is significant that the long-neglected achievement of Erik Lundberg, in this field, at last attracts the attention it deserves.

NOTES

*I am grateful to Rolk Henriksson and Claes-Henric Siven for their
constructive advice. I have also benefited from comments by Alf Carling,
Gustav Cederwall, Bengt Metelius, Bengt Pettersson and Irma Rosenberg. I
am grateful to Set-Arne Berglund for improving my English.

1   Ohlin (1934) presented an unformalized version of this mechanism; see
     Blomqvist and Siven (1989).
2   In Hansen's model of open inflation, there is no explicit account of the
     role of the real-balance effect in eliminating the inflationary gap; see
     Patinkin (1965, p. 637).
3   But, the introduction of Muth's famous article on rational expectations
     reads:

> That expectations of economic variables may be subject to error has
> for some time, been recognized as an important part of most
> explanations of changes in the level of business activity. The '*ex
> ante*' analysis of the Stockholm School – although it has created
> its fair share of confusion – is a highly suggestive approach to
> short-run problems. It has undoubtedly been a major motivation
> for studies of business expectations and intentions data.

> (Muth, 1961, p. 315)

REFERENCES

Berg, C. (1991) 'Lundberg, Keynes, and the riddles of a general theory', chapter 8, in L. Jonung (ed.) *The Stockholm School of Economics Revisited*, Cambridge University Press, Cambridge.

Bernstein, E.M. (1950) 'Latent inflation: problems and policies', *IMF Staff Papers*, I, pp. 1–16.

Blomquist, S. and Siven, C-H. (1989) 'Bertil Ohlin', in B.S. Kastz (ed.), *Nobel Laureates in Economic Sciences*, Garland Publishing, New York.

Friedman, M. (1942) 'Discussion on the inflationary gap', *American Economic Review*, vol. 32, pp. 314–20.

——— (1953) 'Discussion on the inflationary gap', in *Essays in Positive Economics*, University of Chicago Press, Chicago.

Hammarskjöld, D. (1933) *Konjunkturspridningen: en teoretisk och historisk undersökning*, SOU 1933:29, Stockholm.

Hansen, B. (1948) 'En note om inflationsgab och ligevaegtskonstruktioner, *Ekonomisk Tidskrift*, pp. 81–98, Uppsala.

——— (1951) *A Study in the Theory of Inflation*, Allen & Unwin, London.

Johansson, A. (1934) *Löneutvecklingen och arbetslösheten*, SOU 1934:2, Stockholm.

Keynes, J.M. (1930) *A Treatise on Money*, Macmillan, London.

——— (1936) *The General Theory of Employment, Interest and Money*, Macmillan, London.

——— (1940) *How to Pay for the War*, Collected Writings, vol. XII, Macmillan, 1973, London.

Kohn, M. (1986) 'Monetary analysis, the equilibrium method and Keynes's "General Theory"', *Journal of Political Economy*, vol. 94, no. 6, pp. 1191–1224.

Konjunkturinstitutet: Meddelanden från Konjunkturinstitutet, Serie A och Serie B, Isaac Marcus Boktryckeriaktiebolag:
A:15 *Konjunkturläget hösten 1947*, 1948, Stockholm;
B:2 *Inkomstutveckling och köpkraftsöverskott under krigsåren*, 1943, Stockholm;
B:10 *Ekonomiska utredningar våren 1949*, 1949, Stockholm.
B:13 *Nationalbokföring 1946–1950*, 1951, Stockholm.

Lindahl, E. (1939) *Studies in the Theory of Money and Capital*, Allen & Unwin, London.

Lundberg, E. (1937) *Studies in the Theory of Economic Expansion*, P.S. King & Son, Stockholm.

——— (1948) 'Inflationsanalys och ekonomisk teori', *Ekonomisk Tidskrift*, pp. 143–70.

——— (1953) *Konjunkturer och ekonomisk politik*, Konjunkturinstitutet och Studieförbundet Näringsliv och Samhälle, Stockholm.

——— (1957) *Business Cycles and Economic Policy*, Allen & Unwin, London.

Muth, J.F. (1961) 'Rational expectations and the theory of price movements', *Econometrica*, 29, pp. 315–35.

Ohlin, B. (1934) *Penningpolitik, offentliga arbeten, subventioner och tullar som medel mot arbetslösheten*, SOU 1934:12, Stockholm.

Patinkin, D. (1965) *Money, Interest and Prices*, Harper & Row, New York.

———— (1982) *Anticipations of the General Theory*, University of Chicago Press, Chicago.

Robertson, D.H. (1926) *Banking Policy and the Price Level*, P.S. King & Son, London.

Siven, C-H. (1985) 'The End of the Stockholm School', *Scandinavian Journal of Economics*, 87, pp. 577–93.

Turvey, R. (1949) 'A further note on the inflationary gap', *Ekonomisk Tidskrift*, pp. 92–7.

Wicksell, K. (1898) *Geldzins and Güterpreise*, Jena.

———— (1936) *Interest and Prices*, Macmillan, London.

12

ECONOMICS AND MATHEMATICS IN FOREST ECONOMICS: SOME SWEDISH CONTRIBUTIONS

Karl-Gustaf Löfgren *

Forest economics is, today, at best a speciality within the fast expanding field of natural resource economics. Once upon a time – more precisely in the 1850s – German foresters were among the leading researchers in capital theory. Spearheaded by Martin Faustmann and Max Robert Pressler, they made fundamental contributions to capital theory, and to the classical normative problem of when to cut an evenly aged forest stand.[1] The solution to this problem is identical with the solution to what is now sometimes referred to, within the applied techniques of operations research, as 'the chain of replacements problem'.

Within economics, the famous German location theorist, von Thünen, had addressed the rotation problem a few years earlier[2] than Faustmann and had solved it incorrectly. A lot of prominent economists, among them Irving Fisher the founder of present-value calculations in economics, were later to suggest 'incorrect' formulae.[3]

THE PROFITABILITY WAR

The correct solution, introduced by Faustmann and Pressler, was already 'known' to Swedish foresters in 1876 through Holmerz's book *Studier i skogstaxation* (*Studies in Forest Surveying*), (Stockholm 1876), but it is probably fair to say that few people had any fundamental insights. The obstacles were at least twofold: in the first place there was not, at that time, any theoretical explanation of why and when the maximization of present value would constitute a correct investment criterion, in the sense that an investment with the

220

present value is preferred independently of the intertemporal preferences of the investor. Second, the derivation of the cutting rule,
given the correct goal function, required either extremely good
economic intuition or knowledge of differential calculus.

The human properties, implied by these two obstacles, were
clearly scarce goods at the time. This became even more apparent
during 'the Swedish profitability war'.[4] One of the battles took place
on 23 March 1911[5] when the Master of Forestry, Ernst Andersson
held a speech at the annual meeting of 'The Swedish Society for
Silviculture' on the topic 'According to which Economics Principles
should Rational Forestry be Conducted? Among those in the audience who subsequently participated in the discussion were people
such as Eli F. Heckscher, the famous professor of economics at the
Stockholm School of Economics, and the Master of Forestry Uno
Wallmo, a well-known advocate of the selection system for final fell-
ings which has threatened to cause a drop in the timber balance in
Sweden around the year 2000. In his talk, Andersson proposed[6] the
same solution to the rotation problem, which had earlier been
suggested by von Thünen, and which was later to be suggested by
Eli F. Heckscher. The idea is the following: if we look upon standing
timber as capital in a bank account, it can never be profitable to
keep the capital as standing timber as long as the interest rate, here
represented by the rate of increase in the value of the stand, is lower
than the market interest rate. An analogous argument would
suggest that it is profitable to keep the capital as standing timber as
long as its rate of increase in value and the ruling market interest
rate are the same. More formally let:

$$V = V(T) \qquad (1)$$

be the value of the stand as a function of time and let r be the interest
rate. The present value of the stand can, hence, be written:

$$\pi = V(T)\,e^{-rT} \qquad (2)$$

The first-order condition for an interior maximum is obviously:

$$\frac{V'(T^*)}{V(T^*)} = r \qquad (3)$$

which seems to confirm our intuition. A year later, Heckscher
provided an exact verbal statement of formula (3) in a paper on the
profitability of forestry.[7] He might have been inspired by Jevon's or

Wicksell's solution to the wine ageing problem.[8] He could also have based his results on his extremely good economic intuition. He knew very little mathematics, and this bothered him sometimes according to one of his pupils, the well-known Swedish industrialist, Ruben Rausing.[9]

The discussion on the economic principles of forestry continued at the annual meetings of the Society for Silviculture. Many of the leading foresters proposed a solution to the rotation problem in terms of the maximization of the annual volume over the rotation period, i.e. they advocated what, in natural resource economics, would be called a maximum sustainable yield solution. More formally let:

$$v = f(T) \tag{4}$$

be the volume of a stand which is T years old. The goal function can now be written:

$$\max_{T} f(T)T^{-1} \tag{5}$$

The first-order condition for an interior maximum is:

$$f'(T^0) = f(T^0)(T^0)^{-1} \tag{6}$$

i.e. the optimal rotation period, T^0, according to the goal function (5) is implicitly defined by the equality between the current annual increment and the mean annual increment. The principle implied by formula (6) is sometimes called 'the theory of forest rent' or in German *Waldreinertragswirtschaft*.[10]

Some of the participants in the Swedish discussion were, of course, vaguely aware of the Faustmann–Pressler solution, but lacked deeper insight into what really constituted the difference between the reasoning behind the wine ageing solution in equation (3) and the Faustmann–Pressler solution.

A young man who understood the difference between wine ageing and forestry was the future Nobel Prize laureate Bertil Ohlin. The fact that a forest stand must be cut down before the land can be used again for a new stand, creates a difference in 'harvesting policy', between wine ageing and forest management.

The solution to the rotation problem is well-defined provided that the following conditions are met:

(i) the capital market is perfect in the sense that one can lend and borrow any amount at the prevailing interest rate, and the future interest rates are known;

(ii) the future price of timber is known;

(iii) forest land can be bought and sold in a perfect market;

(iv) the future technical lumber yields are known.

Following Ohlin, let

$V(T) = pf(T) =$ the value of the forest stand at time (T);

$f(T)$ = the stock of timber at time (T);

p = the price of timber;

r = the discount rate;

The rotation problem can now be formulated as the maximization of the present value (PV) of the infinite income stream with respect to T:

$$\max_{T} PV = pf(T)\, e^{-rT}(1 + e^{-rT} + e^{-2rT} \ldots) = \max \frac{pf(T)}{e^{rT}-1} \qquad (7)$$

This formula, which shows the present value of the forest land as a function of the rotation age, T, is known to foresters as Faustmann's formula.

The first-order conditions for an interior solution to (7), derived by the young Ohlin, can be written in the following manner:

$$pf'(T^1) = rpf(T^1) + \frac{rpf(T^1)}{e^{rT1}-1} \qquad (8)$$

Interpreting (8), I arrive at:

Theorem (Faustmann–Pressler–Ohlin): a forest stand shall be cut down, when the time rate of change of its value is equal to the interest on the value of the stand plus the interest on the value of the forest land.

A point worth mentioning is that Ohlin derived this result when he was only 18 years of age. He had, at the time, asked Heckscher for permission to participate in his seminar. Heckscher felt that Ohlin was too young, but decided to give him a chance. Ohlin was then asked to act as a discussant for a paper written by a forester on the rotation period of a forest.[11] Needless to say, he became a permanent member of Heckscher's seminar after this, his 'inaugural lecture'.

Ruben Rausing, who was present at the seminar, cannot recall whether Ohlin made use of mathematics during the seminar. As Rausing indicates in a letter to Mrs Ohlin, Heckscher would have neither liked nor understood a mathematical argument. Rausing writes:[12] 'Whether he [Heckscher] later studied enough mathematics to be able to understand Bertil's formulae,[13] I do not know. To us who had studied natural sciences [*reallinjen*] in high school, they did not constitute a problem.'

The formulae and their explicit derivations were presented in a paper in *Ekonomisk Tidskrift* (1921).[14] The rotation period implied by (8) corresponds to what the Germans called *Bodenreinertragswirtschaft* (the theory of soil rent). The theoretical foundations of formula (8) are that conditions (i)–(iv) make the present value of land, under the given circumstances, equal to (7).

Until recently, it has been believed that the wine ageing solution is the closest Knut Wicksell came to forest economics. However, from a recently unpublished manuscript on capital theory, see Wicksell (1987), the paper by Hedlund-Nyström *et al.* in this volume, and the text below, it is crystal clear that he understood the difference between the logical structure of the rotation problem and the wine ageing problem. Given his approach to the maximization of the internal rate of return (the 'yield energy'), under a constraint of a given land rent (the same general approach is also used when he solves the wine ageing problem), he comes up with the correct first-order condition for the optimal rotation period.

The problem encountered by foresters in accepting the rotation period implied by (8) was that they felt it meant, given the ruling market interest rates at the time, a 'too-short rotation' period. This problem was, for the moment, concealed by inventing a special forest discount rate.[15] The reasoning was, roughly speaking, the following: assume that we have a price increment for timber governed by the differential equation:

$$\dot{p} = ap \qquad p(0) = p_0 \qquad (9)$$
$$a > 0$$

$$\dot{p} = \frac{dp}{dt}$$

The solution of (9) is:[16]

$$p(T) = p(0)\, e^{aT} \qquad (10)$$

If this information is used in equation (7), the formula for present value (land value) is modified to read:

$$PV = \frac{p(0)f(T)}{e^{(r-a)T}-1} \tag{11}$$

and $(r - a) < r$ implies a longer rotation period, since the FPO-rotation period is a decreasing function of the discount rate. Given that both a and r are measured in real or in nominal terms, formula (11) is correct.

The relationship between the rotation periods implied by equations (6) and (8), T^0 and T^1, respectively, are consequently:

$$T^1 \leq T^0 \tag{12}$$

Conditions of equality prevail when $r = 0$. *Waldreinertragswirtschaft* (sustained yield forestry) is, consequently, consistent with a perfect capital market investment criterion, provided that the ruling interest rate is zero. To be able to solve the optimal rotation problem in the latter case, the method must be able to handle the fact that present value is unbounded (the infinite series (7) does not converge).

To understand how this can be done, let me remind the reader that, according to the conditions introduced in connection with the derivation of the FPO-theorem, forest land can be rented in a perfect market. Instead of demanding the maximum land value, one could instead demand the maximum annual rent that a perfect market would generate for the privilege of being allowed to use the land for forestry. When properly defined, these concepts are, in a perfect market setting, equivalent as devices for determining the rotation period. Formally, the rent emerges as the solution of the problem:

$$\max_{T} R(T) \tag{13}$$

subject to

$$pf(T)\,e^{-rT} - R \int_0^T e^{-rt}\,\mathrm{dt} = 0 \tag{14}$$

where $R =$ the constant land rent in the open interval dt. Solving (14) for R when $r > 0$ yields:

$$R = \frac{rpf(T)}{e^{rT}-1} = rPV(T) \tag{15}$$

225

where R is the interest on the capital, and it is maximized at the same T which maximizes the value of the capital. For $r = 0$ one obtains:

$$R = pf(T)T^{-1} \tag{15a}$$

which, if maximized with respect to T, gives the first-order condition (6) above.[17]

Wicksell solved a 'dual problem' to the one formulated in equations (13)–(14) by asking for the maximum annual interest rate (yield energy), given the annual cost to rent the land. He solved:

$$\max_{r,\ T} r \tag{16}$$

subject to

$$R - \frac{rpf(T)}{e^{rT-1}} = 0 \tag{17}$$

which, if R equals the value emerging from the Faustmann problem, yields the market interest rate as the optimal solution of the FPO-optimal rotation period.

THE BIG SLEEP

By the time Thorsten Streyffert wrote his influential book in 1938, *Den skogsekonomiska teorin* (*The Theory of Forest Economics*), it was quite generally agreed that the FPO-rotation period was the 'correct' rotation concept, even if most people were not aware of the many qualifications. Streyffert wrote his book without using any elaborated mathematical methods. He mentions how to derive the optimal rotation period using differential calculus. However, when he writes down an explicit derivative, the differentiation is often carried out with respect to the wrong variable (x instead of $t =$ time). It could, of course, be a slip of the pen, but it happens so often that one suspects more fundamental defects. Parenthetically, it is interesting to note how much Gunnar Myrdal's dissertation *Prisbildningsproblemet och föränderligheten* (*Price Formation and Change*), (Stockholm 1927) must have impressed Streyffert. Streyffert's frequent use of the term 'inoptimality losses' is, for example, a loan from Myrdal. The term is still used by elderly Swedish foresters.

During the 1920s, mathematics became a tool in the everyday

226

toolkit of positive economics. John Hicks and Paul Samuelson developed the comparative static method rigorously.[18] Abraham Wald and John von Neman, both members of Karl Menger's seminar in Vienna, proved the existence of general equilibrium. The latter made use of his own more general version of Brouwer's fixed point theorem.[19]

Swedish forest economists were surprisingly unaffected and probably also very unaware of the development of mathematical methods useful for economic analysis. Strangely enough, nothing essential, in addition to the concepts and methods already presented by Petrini (1937) and Streyffert (1938), was added to the toolkit between 1938 and the end of the 1950s.

Just to give the reader a feeling for the conservatism in the field: in 1956 a dissertation entitled *Prisförändringarnas inverkan på omloppstiden*, (*The Effects of Price Changes on the Rotation Period*), (Stockholm 1956) written by Einar Stridsberg was published at the Royal College of Forestry. It contains a very tedious, but, as far as I can see, almost correct analysis of how the rotation period is affected by changes in the timber price, the interest rate and planting costs.

No explicit planting costs were introduced when the FPO-rotation period was discussed above, but in a more general formulation of the problem it holds that:

$$T^1 = T^1(p, w, r)$$
$$- \ + \ -$$

(18)

where w denotes planting costs, and the signs under the arguments denote the signs of the partial derivatives. The necessary calculations to sign the derivatives can be carried out in a couple of pages using the Hicks–Samuelson comparative static method.[20]

It is also fair to say that the methods of positive economics have been used parsimoniously, even after 1956. Before 1973, when Karl G. Jungenfelt published his *Goals and Means in Forest Policy*,[21] there is, for example, no explicit derivation of the timber supply function. There are, however, a few outstanding contributions. As early as 1948, Erik Ruist and Ingvar Svennilson estimated a timber supply function using price and quantity data generated by the timber trade during the 1950s in the northern parts of Sweden. This must be one of the first applications (not to say *the* first) of econometric methods to forestry.

A quasi-supply function of timber, i.e. a relationship between the prices of saw timber and pulp wood, and the number of cubic metres that can be profitably harvested, was constructed by Gustaf von Segebaden, in the early 1960s.[22] He used engineering data on 'the best-practice' cutting technology and ruling factor prices. His quasi-supply function is one of the first of its kind.[23] He was also aware that it was indeed a quasi-supply function, which is not made equally clear by people who have later used his results. This does not apply to Lars Wohlin who, in his impressive thesis,[24] forecasts the composition of the Swedish forest industry ten years ahead using a vintage approach. In retrospect, it is fair to say that he was successful.

None of them was ever professionally a forest economist. Sven-nilson (a member of the Stockholm School of Economics), Jungen-felt and Wohlin are pure economists, while Ruist is an econo-metrician, and von Segebaden is a professor of forest surveying.

THE OR-DECENNIUM

Given the inertia among forest economists in using positive econ-omics, it is interesting to note how relatively quickly the normative methods of operations research (OR) were assimilated by foresters who were carrying out applied work on problems that had important economic dimensions. OR – as a science – was developed during and shortly after the Second World War. The irony of fate saw to it that Einar Stridsberg, whose dissertation I have just criti-cized for obsolete methods, wrote one of the first papers on linear programming at the College of Forestry back in 1959.[25] As early as 1963, there were a series of articles in *Svenska Skogsvårdsföreningens Tidskrift* dealing with how methods within classical OR-fields such as allocation processes (simplex and transportation algorithms), waiting-line processes (queuing theory), competitive processes (game theory), and inventory processes (the square-root formula) can be applied to forestry.[26] Interestingly enough, most articles were not written by pure forest economists, but by people in the Depart-ment of Operational Efficiency at the Royal College of Forestry.[27]

One of the first pure forest economists to use OR-methods was Bertil Näslund (educated in business administration and nowadays professor of finance), who in 1965 published a paper which contained a discussion of the potential gains from the use of OR-methods in forestry. He subsequently wrote a textbook together with Jan-Eric Lindgren entitled *Planeringinom skogsburket med använ-dande av matematisk programmering* (*The Planning of Forestry using*

Mathematical Programming), (Stockholm 1968). The book contains a chapter written by Näslund on the simultaneous determination of the rotation period and the thinning policy. This chapter, which a year later appeared in *Forest Science*, contains, even in terms of an international comparison, an early application of optimal control theory to forestry (probably the first); see also Näslund (1966).

During the 1960s and early 1970s, a number of dissertations were written in which OR-methods – most of the time LP – were used to solve applied planning problems in forestry. To mention a few: Göran von Malmborg applied LP to optimize the activities on a farm where forestry is combined with agriculture (farm forestry); Göran Lönner developed a system for the short-term planning of logging, storing and transportation of wood, where LP was one of the techniques used; Stig Andersson developed long-term forest management plans using LP; and Alve Hägg used LP for short-term planning of saw-log acquisition,[28] sawmill production and sales. Finally, Jan-Eric Lindgren surveyed mathematical planning models for logging and final felling in his dissertation.[29] In this context, it is also worth mentioning that in the early 1970s the former managing director of MoDo (a big Swedish forest company), Björn Sprängare, used simulation techniques in forestry[30] for the first time in Sweden.

MATHEMATICS OR FORESTMANSHIP

'The profitability wars' have taught us that economic theory and mathematics are useful techniques for forest management. The rotation problem, for example, has proved to be one of those problems where forestmanship or even good economic intuition can lead one astray.

It is also interesting to note that many prominent Swedish economists active during the first quarter or this century have contributed to the development of forest economics. Wicksell's, Heckscher's, Ohlin's and Myrdal's (indirect) contributions have already been mentioned. However, Gustaf Cassel, invited by the Swedish Society for Silviculture, also contributed an early lecture on forest taxation.[31] He discussed whether an annual constant imputed income from forestry should constitute the tax base, or whether a special excise tax should be levied on realized forest income. He preferred the latter, and the decision seems to be implicitly based on the presence of an imperfect capital market, since the annual lump sum alternative is said to shorten rotations.

It is not particularly surprising to find that the normative models and methods of operations research are more firmly integrated in forest economics than the methods of positive economics. Forestry is to a large extent an 'applied science'. The surprising thing is that the methods of modern positive economics are hardly used at all during the period under consideration.[32] After all, to conduct forest policy – and we have frequently tried hard in Sweden – it is necessary to have a positive theory of how agents in the forest sector react to stimuli such as prices, taxes and subsidies.

Karl G. Jungenfelt made a serious effort to convince the professional foresters of the need to base forest policy on both positive and normative economic methods back in 1973, when the report from the official commission *Mål och medel i skogspolitiken* (*Goals and Means in Forest Policy*), (Stockholm 1973) was published. The attempt resulted in the immediate appointment of a new commission, the staff of which was loaded with foresters, but completely free from people even remotely connected with economic science. *Ex post*, it can be argued that Jungenfelt was almost clairvoyant when he suggested means to avoid a decline in timber supply. If he had been taken seriously, some of the recent timber-supply problems might have been avoided.[33]

In my survey of mathematical methods in forest economics, I have only found one piece of applied (or theoretical) econometrics written during the period under consideration. However, this is a masterpiece!

Turning to more applied methods, linear programming is by far the most popular mathematical method in applied work in forest economics. One probable reason is that the solution algorithms of non-linear programming models have been too complicated and unreliable. On the other hand, the assumptions implying the so-called basic theorem of linear programming, i.e. that an optimal solution can be found by considering only basic solutions (corners) are unattractive features when applied to forestry. Most foresters would agree that today's cutting and logging technology exhibits non-linearities such as increasing returns to scale, because among other things it pays to merge cuttings.

The practice of analysing cuttings at the stand level, rather than in a more complete forest with stands of different age classes, which was introduced by Faustmann and his followers, is, loosely speaking, valid only in a 'linear forest'. In other words, if you believe that linear programming can be realistically applied to pick the particular stands that should be cut, you can just as well forget about LP and solve the management problem, stand by stand.[34] This does not mean that I feel that LP is a superfluous analytical tool within the forest sector. On the contrary, in our computerized world LP and other OR-methods save enormous amounts of resources within both forestry and the forest industry. What I am trying to say has been said before: naïve users of LP should learn more about why it suffices to search the corners of the feasible set to find an optimal solution. In the meantime, we can hope for a take-over by non-linear models through further research in applied mathematics and a more elaborated use of existing computer capacity and software.

NOTES

*The author acknowledges comments from Runar Brännlund, Department of Economics, University of Umeå, and Claes Berg, Department of Economics, University of Stockholm. A slightly different version of this chapter was published in the *Scandinavian Journal of Forest Research*, 5, 1990.

1 Faustmann's first article on the problem was published in 1849 (see Faustmann 1849). In this article, he defined land value correctly – as a sum of an infinite series – and there are indications that he knew how to solve the optimization problem. This can also be seen from a later article by Faustmann (1853), where he points out flaws in solutions suggested by other foresters. The first clearcut solution was presented in Pressler (1860), where Pressler introduces the concept '*das Weiserprozent*'. See also Stridsberg (1956).

2 von Thünen (1826).

3 For more details on the classical mistakes, see Samuelson (1976). The latest example is Hal Varian in his textbook *Intermediate Microeconomics* (1986, pp. 206–7).

4 The same kind of war had already been fought in Germany. It started in 1813 when König introduced an incorrect formula for the land value.

5 Some people would say that the war started in 1907, when Uno Wallmo gave the annual talk on *Sustained Yield Forestry* (*Uthålligt skogsbruk*).

6 Andersson is not very easily interpreted, but Heckscher makes the same interpretation as the author of this paper in the discussion following the presentation of Andersson's paper. The German name for this principle is *Geldreinertragswirtschaft*.

7 Heckscher (1912).

8 See Jevons (1888) and Wicksell (1911).

9 Letter from Ruben Rausing to Mrs Evy Ohlin.

10 A variation of the rule implied by formula (6) is obtained if planting costs are deducted from the volume function, i.e., if the goal function is written $v = (f(T) - w)T^{-1}$, where w is planting cost. The resulting rotation period – the maximization of net sustainable yield – will be longer

than the rotation period according to (6).

11 See also Löfgren (1983).

12 Letter to Mrs Evy Ohlin in 1979. The quotation is translated into English by the author.

13 This paper is one of the few where Ohlin makes explicit use of mathematics. His dissertation *Handelns teori* (1924) is another example, but the celebrated Heckscher–Ohlin Theorem – that a country will export the goods that are intensive in its abundant production factor – is presented in essentially verbal terms by its inventors. See also Flam's chapter in this volume (Chapter 9).

14 The special issue of *Ekonomisk Tidskrift* was dedicated to Knut Wicksell on his 70th birthday.

15 Before the Swedish discussion faded away, Tor Jonson (see Jonson 1913) – to add to the confusion – introduced a cutting criterion, which strictly interpreted implied an infinite rotation period (provided that $f'(T) > 0$ all T). See also Streyffert (1938, p. 16).

16 The constant a is often referred to as *dyrtidstillväxt* (*Teuerungszuwachs* in German).

17 This condition can also be derived directly by taking the limit of the first-order condition (8) when $r \to 0$. to see this, (8) can be rewritten.

$$\frac{f'(T)}{f(T)} - \frac{r}{1-e^{-rT}} - \frac{r}{rT - (rT)^2 H(rT)}$$

where $(rT)^2 H(rT) \to 0$ when $r \to 0$. The method is, however, imprecise, since we do not know what the objective function looks like. The rent, but not the value of land, is defined for $r = 0$.

18 See Hicks (1937) and Samuelson (1947). The latter book is a collection of essays written between 1936 and 1945.

19 See Wald (1935) and von Neuman (1937). John von Neuman also develops game theory during the century; see von Neuman (1928). He would not have liked to be mentioned together with Hicks and Samuelson. In a letter to Morgenstern at the end of the 1930s he writes: 'You know, Oskar, if those books [Hicks' and others's] are unearthed sometime a few hundred years hence, people will not believe they were written in our time. Rather they will think that they are about contemporary with Newton, so primitive are their mathematics.' See Morgenstern (1976).

20 For a recent reference, see Johansson and Löfgren (1985, pp. 80–3).

21 *Mål och medel i Skogspolitiken*, SOU 1973:14.

22 See von Segebaden (1969).

23 The first study of this kind is Vaux (1954).

24 See Wohlin (1970).

25 See Stridsberg (1959).

26 The earliest 'application of OR' in Sweden is an attempt by Gösta Luthman to model the cutting technology from a work scientific point of view. He ran into problems due to a lack of computers and 'nasty' elliptic integrals! See Luthman (1943). I owe this information to Kjell Kilander.

27 See Andersson and Lönner (1963), Lönner (1963), Rönnbo (1963), Lönner (1964, 1965) and Näslund (1965).
28 See von Malmborg (1967), Lönner (1968), Andersson (1971) and Hägg (1973).
29 Lindgren (1973).
30 Sprängare (1975). The manuscript was first published in 1973. The method, Monte Carlo-simulation, was already introduced in 1964. See Andersson (1964).
31 See Cassel (1909).
32 One can hope that a similar flaw has not hampered the more biological parts of forestry.
33 This claim probably induces foresters to exclaim: certainly not!
34 I am of course exaggerating a little as different kinds of restrictions, not directly related to the biotechnology of the forest and the market for timber, may invalidate the stand-by-stand strategy.

REFERENCES

Andersson, E. (1911) 'Enligt vilka principer bör en rationell skogshushållning bedrivas?' *Svenska Skogsvårdsföreningens Tidskrift* (Allmän del), 285–331.

Andersson, S. (1964) 'Monte Carlo-metoden som hjälpmedel vid drivnings planläggning', *Svenska Skogsvårdsföreningens Tidskrift*, 359–63.

—— (1971) *Modeller för lasngsiktiga driftsplaner i skogsbruket*, Stockholm: Forskningsstiftelsen Skogsarbeten.

Andersson, S. and Lönner, G. (1963) 'Transportproblemet – drivning året om', *Svenska Skogsvårdsföreningens Tidskrift*, 261–8.

Cassel, G. (1909) 'Skogsbeskattningsfrågan', *Svenska Skogsvårdsföreningens Tidskrift* (Allmän del), 349–76.

Faustmann, M. (1849) 'Berechnung des Werthes, welchen Waldboden, sowie noch nicht haubare Holzbeständen für die Waldwirtschaft besitzen', *Allgemeine Forst- und Jagdzeitung*.

—— (1853) 'Uber Bemessung der Einträglichkeit der verschiedenen Bestnades – Betriebs- und Kulturarten, in *Neue Jahrbücher der Forstkunde*, edited by von Wedekind.

Hägg, A. (1973) *En modell för kortsiktig planering av sågverkens råvaruanskaffning, produktion och försäljning*, Stockholm: Institutionen för virkeslära.

Heckscher, E.F. (1912) 'Skogsbrukets räntabilitet', *Ekonomisk Tidskrift*, 139ff, 253ff.

Hicks, J.R. (1937) *Value and Capital*, Oxford: Oxford University Press.

Holmerz, C.G. (1876) *Studier i skogstaxation* (del 1), Stockholm: Norstedts.

Jevons, W.S. (1888) *The Theory of Political Economy*, London: Macmillan.

Johansson, P.O. and Löfgren, K.G. (1985) *The Economics of Forestry and Natural Resources*, Oxford: Blackwell.

Jonson, T. (1913) 'Omloppstidens inverkan på skogsbrukets ekonomi', *Svenska Skogsvårdsföreningens tidskrift* (Allmän del), 275–331.

Jungenfelt, K.G. (1973) *Mål och medel i skogspolitiken*, SOU 1973:14.

Lindgren, J.E. (1973) *En studie av planeringsmodeller för drivning och avverkning*,

Stockholm: Institutionen för skogsekonomi, research notes, no. 15.

Lindgren, J.E. and Näslund, B. (1968) *Planering inom skogsbruket med användande av matematisk programmering*, Stockholm: Norstedts.

Löfgren, K.G. (1983) 'The Faustmann–Ohlin Theorem: A Historical Note', *History of Political Economy*, 261–4.

Lönner, G. (1963) 'Linjär programmering – simplexmetoden: Sortimentsplanläggning', *Svenska Skogsvårdsföreningens Tidskrift*, 375–82.

—— (1964) 'Ett köproblem – servicebussar som reparerar traktorer', *Svenska Skogsvårdsföreningens Tidskrift*, 15–21.

—— (1965) 'Spelteori – försäljning av skogsfastigheter', *Svenska Skogsvårdsföreningens Tidskrift*, 215–20.

—— (1968) *Ett system för kortsiktig planläggning av drivning, lagring och vidaretransport av rundvirke*, Stockholm: forskningsstiftelsen Skogsarbeten.

Luthman, G. (1943) *Studier i Skogsbrukets Arbetslära*, Stockholm: Industriens Utredningsinstitut.

von Malmborg, G. (1967) *Ekonomisk planering av lantbruksföretaget*, Stockholm: Jordbrukets Utredningsinstitut.

Morgenstern, O. (1976) *Selected Economic Writings of Oskar Morgenstern*, edited by Andrew Schotter. New York: New York University Press.

Myrdal, G. (1927) *Prisbildningsproblemet och föränderligheten*, Uppsala.

von Neuman, J. (1928) 'Zur theorie der Gesellschaftsspiele', *Mathematische Annalen*, 295–320.

—— (1937) 'Uber ein ökonomisches Gleichungssystem und eine Verallgemeinerung des Brouwerschen Fixpunktsatzes', *Ergebnisse eines Mathematischen Kolloquiumes*, 1935–1936, Heft 8. Edited by Karl Menger, Wien.

Näslund, B. (1965) 'Företagsekonomiska forskningsmetoder med synpunkter på deras tillämpbarhet inom skogsbruket', *Svenska Skogsvårdsföreningens Tidskrift*, 55–61.

—— (1966) 'Simultaneous Determination of Optimal Repair Policy and Service Life', *Swedish Journal of Economics*.

—— (1969) 'Optimal Rotation and Thinning', *Forest Science*, 446–51.

Ohlin, B. (1921) 'Till frågen om skogarnas omloppstic', *Ekonomisk Tidskrift*, 89–113.

—— (1924) *Handelns teori*, AB Nordiska Bokhandeln. Translated as 'The Theory of Trade', in Eli F. Heckscher and Bertil Ohlin (eds), *Heckscher–Ohlin Trade Theory*, MIT Press, Cambridge, 1991.

Petrini, S. (1937) *Skogsuppskattning och skogsekonomi*, Stockholm: Lars Hökerbergs bokförlag.

Pressler, M.R. (1860) 'Aus der Holzzuwachslehre', *Allgemeine Forst- und Jagdzeitung*.

Rausing, R. (1979) Letter from Ruben Rausing to Mrs E. Ohlin. (Copy available on request from the author of this chapter.)

Rönnbo, C.A. (1963) 'Vägplanering – operationsanalytisk lagerbestämning?' *Svenska Skogsvårdsföreningens Tidskrift*, 383–9.

Ruist, E. and Svennilson, I. (1948) *Den norrländska skogsnäringens konjunkturkänslighet under mellankrigsperioden*, Stockholm: Industriens untredningsinstitut.

Samuelson, P.A. (1947) *Foundations of Economic Analysis,* Cambridge: Harvard University Press.

—— (1976) 'Economics of Forestry in an Evolving Society', *Economic Inquiry,* 466–92.

von Segebaden, G. (1969) 'Studies on the Accessibility of Forest and Forest Land in Sweden', *Studia Forestalia Suecia,* no. 76.

Sprängare, B. (1975) *En metodik för analys av långsiktsplaneringens känslighet för fel i fältdata,* Stockholm: Institutionen för skogsteknik, research notes, no. 87.

Streyffert, Th. (1938) *Den skogsekonomiska teorin,* Stockholm: Svenska Skogsvårdsföreningens förlag.

Stridsberg, E. (1956) *Prisförändringarnas inverkan på omloppstiden,* Stockholm: Institutionen för skogsekonomi, research notes, no. 1.

—— (1959) 'Linjär programmering som hjälpmedel vid planläggning av ett skogsbruksprogram', *Institutionen för skogsekonomi,* mimeographed.

von Thünen, J.H. (1826) *Der Isolierte Staat, Vol. 3.* Published posthumously in 1863 by H. Schumacher.

Varian, H. (1986) *Intermediate Microeconomics,* New York: Norton.

Vaux, H.J. (1954) 'The Economics of Young Growth Sugar Pine Resources', *Berkeley, University of California, Div. of Agricultural Sciences Bull. no. 78.*

Wald, A. (1935) 'Uber die eindeutige positive Lösbarkeit der neuen Produktionsgleicherung (I)', in K. Menger (ed.), *Ergebnisse eines mathematischen Kolloquiums 1933–34,* Heft 6, Wien.

Wallmo, U. (1907) 'Uthålligt skogsbruk', *Svenska Skogsvårdsföreningens Tidskrift* (Allman del), 305–38.

Wicksell, K. (1911) *Föreläsningar i nationalekonomi,* (del 1), Lund.

—— (1987) 'Ett opublicerat manuskript av Knut Wicksell med en kapitalteoretisk model', *Ekonomiska Samfundets Tidskrift,* 123–34. Published in this volume as Chapter 4.

Wohlin, L. (1970) *Skogsindustrins strukturomvandling och expansionsmöjligheter,* Stockholm: Industriens utredningsinstitut.

INDEX

Printed in the United States
by Baker & Taylor Publisher Services